FINANCIAL REFORM IN CENTRAL AND EASTERN EUROPE

Financial Reform in Central and Eastern Europe

Edited by

Stephany Griffith-Jones
Fellow
Institute of Development Studies
Sussex University

and

Zdeněk Drábek
Czech National Bank
Prague

St. Martin's Press

First published in Great Britain 1995 by
THE MACMILLAN PRESS LTD
Houndmills, Basingstoke, Hampshire RG21 2XS
and London
Companies and representatives
throughout the world

A catalogue record for this book is available
from the British Library.

ISBN 0–333–62298–7

10   9   8   7   6   5   4   3   2   1
04   03   02   01   00   99   98   97   96   95

Printed in Great Britain by
Ipswich Book Co Ltd
Ipswich, Suffolk

First published in the United States of America 1995 by
Scholarly and Reference Division,
ST. MARTIN'S PRESS, INC.,
175 Fifth Avenue,
New York, N.Y. 10010

ISBN 0–312–12364–7

Library of Congress Cataloging-in-Publication Data
Financial reform in Central and Eastern Europe / edited by Stephany
Griffith-Jones and Zdeněk Drábek.
p. cm.
ISBN 0–312–12364–7
1. Finance—Europe, Eastern—Case studies.   2. Europe, Eastern–
–Economic policy—1989–   3. Finance—Central Europe—Case studies.
4. Central Europe—Economic policy.   I. Griffith-Jones, Stephany.
II. Drábek, Zdeněk.
HG186.E82F568   1995
332. 1'0947—dc20   94–24885
                                                    CIP

Contents

Part IV   Conclusions and Policy Implications

Acknowledgements

This book was made financially possible due to a grant from the EU-PHARE-ACE programme and due to financial support from the United Kingdom Overseas Development Administration. We very gratefully acknowledge both these contributions, particularly because we believe the project, the workshops and this resulting book are making an important contribution to financial reform in Central and Eastern Europe, as well as helping to show the value of collaborative research between West and East European colleagues and institutions.

Many people have made valuable contributions to our project and we wish to thank them all. We are firstly grateful to our colleagues, the authors of the papers for their commitment to the project. Secondly, we warmly thank the many people who contributed to the high standard of our workshops by their comments and/or presentations. In particular, we would like to thank Karel Dyba, Czech Minister of Economy, for his support and participation at the Prague workshop, Mr J. Kunert, President, Czech Zivnostenska Banka, Mr H. Kierzkowski, then Deputy Chief Economist at the EBRD, Mr Wiessels from the European Commission, Ms K. Mortimer, from the UK Know-How Fund and Mr C. Morgan then from Coopers and Lybrand for their valuable comments at the Prague workshop. We are equally grateful to Mr T. Rybczynski, Visiting Professor at City University, Dr J. Rostowski, Senior Lecturer at the School of Slavonic Studies, University of London, Mr David Begg, Professor at Birkbeck College, as well as, again, Ms Mortimer and Mr Kierzkowski, for their valuable comments at the Sussex workshop. We are also grateful to the Czech National Bank and the EBRD for inviting part of our team to present the main results of our project, and to Mary Walker, for organising our presentation at the House of Commons.

Last, but certainly not least, we wish to thank Olda Dĕdek and his colleagues for superb organisation of the Prague workshop and Angela Dowman for excellent organisation of the Sussex Workshop and London meetings.

STEPHANY GRIFFITH-JONES
ZDENĚK DRÁBEK

Notes on the Contributors

Oldřich Dědek is the Deputy Director of the Institute of Economics at the Czech National Bank. After graduating from the Prague School of Economics, he was Visiting Fellow at the London School of Economics and at the Economics Department of Warwick University. He is a member of the executive board of the Czech journals *Political Economy* and *Prague Economic Papers*, and former adviser to the Deputy Minister of Economics. He has published extensively on various aspects of economic policy including *Voucher Privatisation and the Development of the Capital Market in Czechoslovakia*. He has translated the Macmillan *Dictionary of Modern Economics*.

Zdeněk Drábek is Principal Adviser to the Governer of the Czech National Bank. He has been a chief negotiator for his country in dealing with the European Community and GATT. Previously he was a Senior Economist with the World Bank and Chairman of the Department of Economics at the University of Buckingham.

Stephany Griffith-Jones is a Fellow of the Institute of Development Studies, at Sussex University. She has acted as senior consultant to many international organisations, including the European Community, the World Bank, the Inter-American Development Bank, UNICEF and others. She has also acted as consultant to the UK Know-How Fund. Her research and consultancy cover the fields of macroeconomic policy, financial sector development, and international finance. She has published widely. Her most recent book was *Loan Guarantees for Large Infrastructure Projects*.

E.V.K. FitzGerald is Director of the Finance and Trade Policy Research Centre at the University of Oxford and a professorial fellow of St Antony's College, Oxford. Trained at Oxford and Cambridge, he was Assistant Director of Development Studies at Cambridge and Professor of Development Economics at The Hague from 1981 until 1992. His current research interests include international capital flows to, and private investment behaviour in, semi-industrial economies.

Miroslav Kerouš is a banking consultant, chairman of the board of a large investment fund, a member of the board of a Czech bank and an investment fund representative on the board of a large brewery. He studied at the Prague School of Economics. He was awarded the fellowship at the Georgetown University School for Foreign Service. In 1990 he was appointed Deputy Chairman of the Central Bank of former Czechoslovakia. From 1990 to 1993 he was responsible for the implementation of monetary policy and for the supervision and management of the Central Bank's branches. He was also a member of the board of the National Property Fund of the Czech Republic.

Jan Klacek is Head of the Research Unit of the Czech National Bank. He graduated from the Prague School of Economics in 1966. He was affiliated to the Institute of Econ-omics at the Czechoslovak Academy of Sciences as Research Fellow and in 1985 he was appointed Head of the Department of Economic Growth. In 1990 he was promoted to the post of Director of the Institute. From 1990 until 1992 Dr Klacek was adviser to the Minister of Economics.

Tadeusz Lamacz is adviser to the Polish Government in the fields of foreign direct investments and the reform of the financial system in Poland, and is a member of the Advisory Team on Economic Policy attached to the Prime Minister's Office. Lamacz undertook research in the Institute of Developing Countries at Warsaw University in the field of intra-regional trade in the Third World in the 1970s.

Gabriella Rosta Lutz graduated at the Budapest University of Economics in 1980 and since then has worked for the National Bank of Hungary, specialising in the development of the banking sector, concentrating on the main problems of the transition of the Hungarian economy.

Rezsö Nyers is Managing Director, a member of the board and Head of the Economic Research Department at the National Bank of Hungary. He graduated from the University of Economic Sciences in Budapest in 1969 and continued there as assistant lecturer. From 1974 until 1986 he was Economic Adviser to the Hungarian government. In 1986 he was appointed Managing Director of the Hungarian Credit Bank and in 1989 he moved to his present position at the National Bank of Hungary. He has published studies on the Hungarian banking system, monetary policy in Hungary during the transitional period, the process of foreign debt and debt management policy in Hungary, currency convertibility, the Hungarian capital market and the reorganisation of the Hungarian banking system.

Rob Vos is Senior Lecturer of Development Economics and International Finance at the Institute of Social Studies, in The Hague. He has worked as a consultant and adviser to international agencies (including the United Nations, the Inter-American Development Bank and the World Bank) and to developing country governments in various Asian and Latin America countries. Recent publications include *Debt and Adjustment in the World Economy* (1994), and *Finance and Development: A Structural Approach to Monetary Policy* (with E.V.K. FitzGerald, 1989).

Part I

Introduction and Non-Banking Financial Flows

1 Introductory Framework
Stephany Griffith-Jones*

I INTRODUCTION: FUNCTIONS OF THE FINANCIAL SECTOR IN THE TRANSITION TO THE MARKET

The financial sector has several particularly important roles to play in the transition to the market of Central and East European countries. These roles are especially difficult to play properly given the long-term tradition of passivity which characterised banks' functions and behaviour during the period of central planning, and the non-existence of other financial institutions common in market economies, such as stock exchanges. Indeed, the monetary system, which consisted broadly of the mono-bank and its specialised branches, was a tool of the plan. The mono-bank had little autonomy; it guaranteed enterprises the loans needed to carry out planned transactions, in observance with the central plan. Therefore, risk considerations did not affect lending decisions. As a result, there was no tradition of risk evaluation in these banking systems. Furthermore, when the mono-bank lent money to enterprises with losses, which they would be unlikely to pay back, it was performing not just a banking function, but essentially a fiscal function. Therefore, it was – and to some extent still is – difficult to separate fiscal from monetary policy.[1]

At a basic level, the functions of a banking and financial sector in economies in transition to the market are similar to those in a market economy. As G. Corrigan,[2] the President of the Federal Reserve Bank of New York, clearly states, 'a particularly important function of a banking and financial system in a market economy is to (a) *help mobilise a society's savings* and (b) *to channel those savings rigorously and impartially into the most efficient and effective uses and investments*' (my italics).

The mobilisation of domestic savings is particularly crucial in these economies (as well as insufficiently stressed in the literature and discussions in these countries), because capital will, and will have to, come in large part from domestic sources.[3] This would also parallel the central role of domestic savings in the history of economic development both in industrial and developing countries.

*I am grateful to David Begg, Jenny Corbett, Zdeněk Drábek, Jan Klacek, Jiri Kunert, Millard Long, Nemat Shafik and Andres Solimano for useful suggestions in relation to this chapter.

However, the financial sector needs, in a market economy, also to play an important role to help attract important categories of foreign sources of capital.[4] Again here the experience of developing countries is interesting; *one* of the reasons explaining a rapid increase in private capital flows to the Latin American region in recent years is the previous development of capital markets.[5]

At a very simple level, the financial and especially the banking sector has to perform the crucial function of having an efficient payment system.[6] This is normally performed rather well even in simple market economies; however, unlike market economies, centrally planned ones did not rely on liquidity management, as there was no concept of the opportunity cost of money, and current systems are still operating very slowly and inefficiently.

An efficient payment system is the basis for the development of a well-functioning financial system in a market economy, as it allows liquidity management and generates trust among banks and bank users. First it enables bank users to dispose immediately of their resources and avoids the use of cash in settling their claims (which is costly and may lead to abuses). Second, an efficient payments system encourages bank intermediation and increases the volume of deposits in the banking system. Third, the payment system also reduces bank intermediation costs.

Another fairly traditional function that the banking sector should provide is that of allocating credit. First, banks influence the total level of credit in the economy. Even though acting in the context of monetary policy, banks may for example lend less than allowed by existing credit ceilings, having an undesired deflationary effect on output. This was reportedly the case, for example, in CSFR in the first part of 1991. Second, as we will discuss more below, the form in which banks allocate credits contributes to determine the economy's supply response. Thus if banks respond in similar ways as enterprises to economic policy changes, then enterprises favoured by the economic policies will also have access to more bank credit and will be able to increase output. If banks misallocate credit, for example due to institutional problems such as non-performing loans and unskilled person-nel, then the credit can flow in a different direction to that anticipated by policy-makers and prevent the desired supply response. Third, in deciding who is creditworthy and thus eligible for bank credit, banks provide important information to other economic actors, such as non-bank insti-tutions granting trade credit. In developed countries, such information is provided also by specialised credit agencies, which on the whole do not yet exist in Central and Eastern Europe (CEE). These indirect effects make accurate credit risk assessment by banks in countries in transition to the market even more important than elsewhere.

Last, but certainly not least, the financial system – and banks in particular – need to play an important role in enterprise restructuring, privatisation and control. This is a subject on which there has been much debate recently.[7]

Though the discussion has several strands, it seems to focus fundamentally on two issues. First, there is a debate on how to restructure (including dealing with debt overhangs) and privatise enterprises in a manner that avoids large-scale liquidation of enterprises, avoids – if possible – formal bankruptcy procedures and provides incentives to maintain potentially viable firms as a going concern, or at least maintain potentially successful sub-divisions as going concerns. Bankruptcy reform throughout the Western world has tried to remove the liquidation bias from such proceedings. This is even more crucial in countries in transition to the market. As Roland[8] points out, in market economies there is a continuous flow of bankruptcies, *but there is also a continuous flow of entry of new enterprises, allowing not only the absorption of the human and material resources left idle, but also a better use of those resources.* In the absence of capital markets, well-functioning banking systems and a developed private sector in the countries of CEE, bankruptcies hurt more and pressures to bail out insolvent enterprises become much stronger. This would seem to point both to the need to accelerate support (including that by the financial system) of the new private sector and design restructuring mechanisms that reduce unnecessary costs of losses of output and employment.[9] We will return to this issue below, particularly while the private sector is not yet offering alternative sufficient opportunities to absorb resources.

Second, there is the related but separate issue of the role which banks should play in controlling enterprises in the restructuring period and after. In particular, Corbett and Mayer (see note 7) have for example argued that banks (and especially those involved in funding industry) in Central and Eastern Europe should play a central role in controlling enterprises. This conclusion is partly based on recent developments in financial economics,[10] that seem to show the importance of debt contracts to the monitoring and control of enterprises, and that the most efficient mechanisms for monitoring and controlling enterprises will involve the participation of debt rather than equity issuing financial institutions. The other reason why advocates of this position pursue such a line is that such systems where banks play a key control role (mainly by owning equity) in the non-financial corporate sector and by having representatives on boards of firms) characterise the relatively more successful economies of Japan and Germany. However, the strength of this argument needs to be qualified by the relative lack of monitoring skills in the new banks in Central and Eastern Europe, the need and difficulty in these countries to develop particularly strong bank regulation and supervision, which is especially necessary if there were to develop a close relation between banks and enterprises, and the need to encourage competition, where possible, and the use of anti-trust agencies to avoid collusive behaviour and monopoly abuse. Indeed, in both Japan and Germany the authorities place great emphasis on strong bank regulation and supervision, as well as banks' compliance of it; in particular, such regulation takes account of the nature of investments made by banks; especially where these take the form of very risky equity participations, higher capital requirements and more active supervision is required.

The implication therefore is that if a system of greater bank control is to be pursued in countries of Central and Eastern Europe, then both suitable institutional arrangement of a regulatory type have to be made and training requirements have to be met. It is interesting that certain recent trends in Central and Eastern Europe may lead implicitly to greater control of privatised enterprises by banks; reportedly, in CSFR, 70 per cent of privatisation vouchers have been acquired by ten investment funds, half of which are owned by banks. Therefore, *de facto*, banks will be playing a controlling and monitoring role over enterprises.[11]

II   KEY ISSUES FOR RESEARCH

Progress in financial sector reform in Czechoslovakia, Hungary and Poland has been quite significant. As can be seen in Table 1.1, Hungary was the first country to break up the mono-bank and start two-tier banking (January 1987). In general, Hungary seems rather unique in that reforms started early and followed a very gradual process. In January 1989, the Polish authorities broke up the mono-bank into nine state-owned commercial banks and established a two-tier banking system where commercial banks were separated from the Central Bank. In the CSFR, a similar break-up of the mono-bank and the establishment of the two-tier banking system *coincided* with the abolishment of the central plan target and the greater role for enterprise managers, and *followed* the political opening, taking place in January 1990. As a result, in CSFR, both enterprise reform and banking reform started simultaneously, while in Poland and Hungary enterprises' management had been granted greater freedom before bank reform started.

In the second stage of reform, permission has been granted for the entry of new banks (three-tier banking), mainly taking the form of cooperative or joint-stock companies. The process of bank privatisation has also started, for example, on a fairly large scale in CSFR in 1992.

Table 1.1   Banking system reform in CSFR, Hungary and Poland

	CSFR	Hungary	Poland
Date of political opening	Nov. 1989	1989	April 1989
Date of break-up of the mono-bank and start of two-tier banking system	Jan. 1990	Jan. 1987	Jan. 1989
Number of:			
Large commercial banks	2	5	9
Other banks (inc. co-ops)	30	15	100

Sources: Thorne (see note 6), based on World Bank data and Corbett and Mayer (note 7).

Efforts are being made to encourage greater autonomy of lending and to introduce commercial credit evaluation. Prudential supervision has also begun to be developed. A number of important tasks need to be tackled in the near future, which are crucial for the financial sector to support the process of economic reform, to help avoid unnecessary output declines and to support expansion of the emerging private sector.

In this project, we will tackle some of these issues. In the country studies, we will focus more on the development of banking, as historically the commercial banking system has been far more important in allocating resources to enterprises than the stock market in the majority of industrial countries.[12] Furthermore, as Tanzi (see note 1) correctly argues, commercial banks can to a certain extent perform some of the functions of a stock market, while the latter cannot perform the functions of the commercial banks. However, because the non-banking financial sector is beginning to develop rapidly in the three countries studied, and has also important functions in the reform process, a separate paper will be devoted to that sector's development and its link with foreign flows.

The Issue of 'Bad Debts'

An important issue which needs further study and probably greater policy action is that of 'bad debts', for if sufficient and timely action is not taken, *important distortions can take place in the reform process.*

The problem relates to the widespread failure of enterprise debtors to make scheduled payments of principal and interest to creditors, whether to bank or other enterprises. These 'bad debts' have two separate origins: (a) the 'old bad debts', coming from the central planning period, when there were unclear distinctions between fiscal and monetary policies, and many so-called debts were *de facto* grants or quasi-grants;[13] (b) the 'new bad debts', which have arisen since the market reform started. These have occurred as a result of the trade shock resulting from the collapse of CMEA (the magnitude of this shock is illustrated by the fact that between 1987 and 1991, the volume of Hungary's exports to the former CMEA countries fell to about a *quarter* of its previous volume), the declines in output resulting from the macro-economic adjustments and the short-term effect on enterprises of the operation of market forces. Furthermore, the fine-tuning of regulations also, reportedly, implied that the range of loans qualified as non-performing also expanded.[14] Many state-owned enterprises found themselves producing, at least in part, not for sale, but for unsold inventories; as a result, their response was to suspend payment of amortisation and request new credit both to roll over their existing loans and capitalise interest. Thus, reportedly, in Poland the capitalisation of interest accounted for 100 per cent of the bank credit expansion in 1991.[15]

Precise data on bad bank debts are difficult to define and obtain. (See also data in Chapter 9 of this book, especially Table 9.1). As can be seen in Table 1.2, for CSFR total non-performing loans were estimated by the World Bank to have reached Kc205 billion by the end of 1991, which was 29 per cent of total bank loans.

Table 1.2   Estimates for bad bank loans, Dec. 1991 (Kcs billion)

Total loans	Bad loans	%
555	205	29

Source: World Bank, CSFR *Financial Sector Review,* Memo, 31 March 1991.

Table 1.3 shows the fairly rapid increase in bank credit to CSFR state-owned enterprise, as well as the far more dramatic increase in inter-enterprise credit, from Kc7 billion in December 1989 to Kc155 billion in December 1991.

In Hungary, bad debts are estimated, based on balance sheets of commercial banks, to have increased very significantly from 2.8 billion Hungarian Florints in late 1987 to 43.3 billion Hungarian Florints in late 1990 (see Table 1.4).

If inadequate credit control were only a legacy of the past, for example due to surviving relationships between those running banks and those man-

Table 1.3   Credit to enterprises and households, CSFR (Kcs billion)

End period Bank credit to	1989	II	1990 IV	II	1991	IV
SOEs	531	532	530	587		611
Private firms			3	25		67
Households	47	47	50	52		54
Inter-enterprise	7	14	54	123		155

Note: Bank credit to SOEs excludes a government-funded 38b. Crown write-off of enterprise bad debt.
Source: K. Dyba and J. Švejnar, 'Stabilisation and Transition in Czechoslovakia', presented at NBER Conference on Transition in Eastern Europe, Cambridge, Mass., February 1992.

Table 1.4   Total banks' bad debts, Hungary
(Fl. billion)

1987	1988	1989	1990
2.8	6.5	21.2	38.8

Source: Nyers and Rosta Lutz (see note 14).

aging state enterprises, then such limitations of corporate control would be overcome by bank privatisation and development of a market in corporate control. However, this, as Begg and Portes (see note 9) argue, may not be sufficient. Indeed, the OECD 1991 Report on the Polish economy reports that for Poland 'the deterioration in the portfolio quality has been as rapid, if not more so, in private banks as in state banks, i.e. ownership *per se* has had little impact on the quality of loan assessment, although banks with foreign capital have tended to do better'. (Thorne – see note 6 – however, reports a different trend, showing that both in CSFR and Poland, private banks have increased their credit to the private sector faster than state-owned banks have.)

Continued lending to old loss-making clients may be due to 'creditor passivity', possibly shared by private banks in these transitional situations.[16] Such passivity could be because banks may not wish to initiate bankruptcy when the expected value of the debtor's assets are less than the costs of enforcing bankruptcy, or because there may be a value in waiting; secondly, if action is taken against debtors, this may show the extent of the bank's non-performing loans, both to depositors and regulators. Finally, there may be free-rider problems when there are multiple creditors. Similar arguments of creditor passivity seem to explain the rapid growth of inter-enterprise credit, though to a certain extent growth of such credit is an 'adjustment' by economies in transition to levels that are 'normal' in a market economy.[17]

Van Wijnbergen (see note 7) and others have argued for the need for *bank re-capitalisation up front*, on an ex ante basis, as part of an overall banking reform and enterprise restructuring plan. If this is not done, it is argued that incentives for commercial banks to collect claims are destroyed; if re-capitalisation ex post is expected, every dollar written off will be expected to be replaced by the government with an interest-earning asset, implying that banks have no incentive to try to collect debts or take equity stakes. The issue of incentives for banks to collect as much debt as is feasible seems a central one for policy-makers to tackle.

One of the most serious problems reportedly arising out of the issue of 'bad debts' is the distortion it creates for credit policy. The widely presented argument is as follows. When banks are pushed to re-finance (and/or increase credit) to loss-making state-owned enterprises, especially in a situation of credit rationing (that is, in the context of a tight monetary policy), the new private enterprises may become *crowded out of sufficient access to volumes of credit and/or may obtain it at higher costs*. This would be a perverse result, as the reform process precisely aims to support and strengthen the emerging private sector enterprises, and access to sufficient credit is an important precondition for their development. A somewhat less important negative effect would be crowding out of households (see Table 1.3 for CSFR), which would deprive them of pursuing inter-temporal consumption smoothing through domestic borrowing. At the same time, resources seem to be misallocated because clearly non-viable state enterprises survive, but also because state enterprises that could become viable, via efficiency improve-ments, do not due to a lack of incentives linked to easy access to debt.

The argument can be taken one step further. Thus, it can be argued that the type of microeconomic distortions described above in the banking sys-tems of Central and Eastern Europe considerably increase the real costs of monetary austerity in economic transitions, as there is a risk that the credit rationing initiated by monetary tightening would affect the more profitable enterprises in the economy, and not – as usually occurs in market econ-omies – only the more marginal producers. This is given both as an argument against excessively constrained monetary policy, which would in any case not be sustainable, and as an argument for early and sufficient financial restructuring.

Returning to the issue of sufficiency of credit to the emerging private enterprise sector, there is some preliminary evidence. Thus a survey, conducted amongst a fairly large sample of private enterprises, concludes that credit limits to the private sector vary to an important extent across individual countries, even though it is a problem in all three countries studied. According to this survey, in CSFR the private sector (albeit a very small one) had quite good access to the banking system, with 80 per cent of respondents having a short-term bank loan; in Poland, 65 per cent of firms surveyed had a short-term bank loan; however, 28 per cent of firms had not applied for credit *because interest rates were too high*. Hungary emerged as the country having a far smaller percentage (around 30 per cent) of surveyed private firms having bank loans; many more problems in obtaining bank credit were reported, even for cases of private firms which show considerable success. This has led to second-best options, such as leasing capital goods instead of their sale. However, it should be stressed that the Hungarian private sector is fairly large.

Given the importance of these problems, it would therefore be desirable for each case study to examine the following questions:

(a) To what extent in each country does the problem of bad debt exist, and what is its scale, distribution and evolution?

(b) To what extent in each country is there empirical evidence that the above-described distortions in credit policy effectively occur and to what extent can they be attributed to 'bad debt overhangs'? Is there evidence of 'excessive' lending to loss-making state enterprises; how much new credit is going to enterprises with non-performing loans; is there evidence of 'insufficient' lending to the private sector? How has this evolved over time? What are the reasons for this? Are there other reasons which limit lending to the private sector? Survey evidence and interviews would be valuable here.

This seems important as little empirical evidence has been presented to substantiate the above analysis. It would provide a more solid basis for appropriate policy action.

(c) What measures have been taken to deal with the problem of banks' bad debts in each country? What was the logic behind them? How were they funded? Were the measures *ad hoc* or did they imply institutional changes? Are they sufficient? If not, why not? What is the link with the process of enterprise privatisation, and what is the likely effect of such privatisations (e.g. in CSFR) on the level of bad loans, on enterprises' and banks' viability? What further measures should be taken? Should a greater share or the totality of certain debts be

erased? How should this be financed? How can fiscal/monetary
impact be minimised? How will moral hazard problems be avoided?

(d) What should the links be between debt write-offs and privatisation of
     banks? Is there not a case for doing both simultaneously? If this was
     not done, what are second-best solutions?

(e) To what extent should debt restructuring contain a debt–equity con-
     version, which would potentially have several advantages, such as
     avoiding large-scale liquidation, accelerate privatisation, reduce use
     of formal bankruptcy procedures, allow non-cash bids and reserve a
     large role for commercial banks in the process? Reportedly, in Poland,
     enterprise restructuring and privatisation will involve debt relief for
     enterprises, including debt–equity swaps.

     One such proposal[18] would aim simultaneously to achieve fast clar-
     ification of ownership and control through privatisation, provide a
     mechanism for resolving creditor conflicts and do this as part of debt
     restructuring. The restructuring of debt would imply complete write-
     off of debts, creation of equity, all of which would go to the senior
     creditor, while the junior creditors would receive a call option on
     shares; managers and workers would also receive call options on
     shares. Simultaneously, the administrator of the scheme would
     request reorganisation proposals, either from the creditors, workers,
     management or from outside investors. The main creditor bank would
     play a major role at this stage.

(f) Does such a scheme seem attractive? Would such a scheme be institu-
     tionally practical in each country? Would banks have sufficient skills
     to carry out such a task? Would it have any undesirable effects? What
     other schemes have been implemented or seem preferable? Would it
     be simpler just to cancel *some part* of the debts?

(g) What other measures, such as bank re-capitalisation, need to be car-
     ried out simultaneously or previously?

     It is important in this context that bank re-capitalisation should be a
     once-for-all event, and not a government pledge to underwrite banks
     continuously. Both simultaneous bank privatisation *and* an efficient
     system of bank supervision would be very helpful; indeed, once the
     financial system was cleaned up, supervision should be facilitated.

(h) What parallel measures need to be carried out simultaneously to
     strengthen supervisory and regulatory control of banks? To what
     extent have such changes been introduced? What progress has been
     made, for example, in introducing standards for loan classification
     and provisioning; what tax incentives, if any, are provided for banks
     to make sufficient provisions? Are banks with large 'bad debts'

allowed to distribute dividends? What are the main bottlenecks (e.g. lack of trained personnel, lack of information) faced?

The importance of adequate regulation and supervision at a time when the banking system is being liberalised (and particularly when large macroeconomic changes and external shocks are occurring) is particularly well illustrated, for example by the Chilean experience.[19] In Chile, as in several other Latin American countries, banking and the financial sector were rapidly liberalised with very weak and inappropriate efforts made to develop supervision, particularly of the overall risks affecting the operations of each bank. This was a major factor contributing to the large banking crisis that occurred in the early 1980s, a crisis which was costly both in terms of its immediate effects on output reduction, and in terms of its immediate and long-term costs on the fiscal and quasi-fiscal deficit.[20]

(i) As regards both availability and appropriate distribution of credit to the emerging private sector, and particularly to small and medium enterprises (SMEs), a number of important issues arise (besides those outlined above).

To what extent is lack of financing for the private sector a major constraint to its development, in each country? Is this particularly the case for small and medium enterprises?

(j) If so, is it mainly linked to tight monetary policy and too much credit still going to the old clients of the banks, or are other factors more important in constraining credit to the private sector?

What are the other main factors limiting willingness to grant credit to SMEs? Is it the fact that the emerging private enterprises have no history of entrepreneurship? Is it that the new private entrepreneurs have little or no assets to provide as guarantees, as there is lack of private wealth? What special problems are being created by lack of clarity on property rights?

(k) What measures could be taken to help overcome such constraints? Should special institutions/mechanisms be created, for example to provide *guarantees* on bank lending to small and medium private enterprises (mechanisms used both in advanced and developing market economies)? Should special facilities be given to private SMEs, via training, help in project preparation and/or should credit be subsidised? If the latter, how should this be funded and how should potential distortions in resource allocation be avoided? What is the experience of special institutions set up for these purposes, such as the Czech-Moravian Bank of Guarantee and Development; is the scale meaningful; what lessons can be learned from institutions such as this one and from institutions in market economies set up for this purpose? For example, experience in market economies seems to indicate that guarantee schemes tend to work best when guarantees are given for creditworthy clients with good projects, unable to obtain loans, because they have no or insufficient collateral.[21]

(l)   Should further measures be taken to support the private sector. For example, reportedly in Poland it has been established that a minimum share of bank lending should be allocated to private firms. Is this desirable, on a temporary basis? Or should other, more indirect, measures be used to encourage lending to the private sector?

(m) Given the special features of the private sector in CEE and the scale of transformation taking place in these economies, *should* conventional credit risk evaluation used in market economies be adapted? How? More generally, have banks got appropriate procedures, and sufficiently trained staff to evaluate credit risk appropriately, in general and in the special circumstances of the transition? What distinctions, if any, should be made between evaluating credit risk to privatised former state enterprises and new private enterprises? Do difficult issues/problems emerge? What special unmet training needs exist? What specific role should be played in satisfying those yet unmet needs, in this and other aspects, by foreign specialists?

(n)   Last, but certainly not least, this project will address in two separate papers two important issues: (i) non-bank financial sector development and its link to foreign capital flows, and (ii) mobilisation of financial resources and the role of policy in increasing the level of savings. As these themes will be addressed in separate papers (and not examined explicitly in the country studies), the key issues will not be outlined here.

Notes

1.   For a good discussion, see V. Tanzi, 'Financial Markets and Public Finance in the Transformation Process', in CEPR, *The Economic Consequences of the East*, London, CEPR, April 1992.

2.   E.G. Corrigan, 'The Role of Central Banks and the Financial System in Emerging Market Economies', *FRBNY Quarterly Review* (Summer 1990).

3.   For a useful overview of the limitations of external sources of capital and the crucial role of domestic mobilisation in Central and Eastern Europe, see P. Aghion and R. Burgess, *Financing and Development in Eastern Europe and the Former Soviet Union*, mimeo, EBRD, March 1992.

4.   See Z. Drábek, 'Central and Eastern Europe – Emerging Capital Markets', paper prepared for AS II Bali Conference, 2–5 August 1992.

5. See S. Griffith-Jones with A. Marr and A. Rodriguez, *The Return of Private Capital Flows to Latin America*, FONDAD, October 1992, Holland.

6. I thank Barbara Insel for stressing the importance of this point. For a good discussion, see A. Thorne, *The Role of Banks in the Transition: Lessons from Eastern European Countries' Experience*, World Bank ECA/MENA, Washington, D.C., mimeo, June 1992.

7. See, for example, S. van Wijnbergen, *Economic Aspects of Enterprise Reform in Eastern Europe*, mimeo, World Bank, Washington, D.C., May 1992; J. Corbett and C. Mayer, 'Financial Reform in Eastern Europe: Progress with the Wrong Model', *Oxford Review of Economic Policy*, vol. 7, no. 4; Aghion and Burgess, *Financing and Development*.

8. G. Roland, 'Issues in the Political Economy of Transition', in CEPR, *The Economic Consequences*.

9. See D. Begg and R. Portes, 'Enterprise Debt and Economic Transformation: Financial Restructuring in Central and Eastern Europe', CEPR, mimeo, May 1992; S. van Wijnbergen, *Economic Aspects*; and P. Aghion, O. Hart and J. Moore, 'The Economics of Bankruptcy Reform', paper presented at NBER Conference on Transition in Eastern Europe, 26–29 February 1992.

10. See, for example, M. Hellwig, 'Banking, Financial Intermediation and Corporate Finance', in A. Giovannini and C. Mayer (eds), *European Financial Integration*, Cambridge University Press, 1990.

11. I thank Jan Klacek for this point.

12. See Corbett and Mayer, 'Financial Reform'.

13. An example of these are the CSFR 'permanent inventory loans' (TOZ), which were in effect perpetual loans with *no amortisation schedules*, and were spread across all state-owned industrial and commercial enterprises. An important proportion of these loans were transferred to a 'consolidation bank' in the spring of 1991.

14. For Hungary, see R. Nyers and G. Lutz, 'The Structural Reform of the Banking System in Hungary, and the Solution to the Problem of Bad Debts in the Hungarian Banking System', OECD, 1992.

15. See Thorne, *The Role of Banks*.

16. See J. Mitchell, 'Creditor Passivity and Bankruptcy: Implications for Economic Reform', presented at CEPR-Fundacion BBV Conference on Financial Intermediation in the Construction of Europe, San Sebastian, March 1992.

17. See Begg and Portes, 'Enterprise Debt'.

18. For details of such a scheme, see van Wijnbergen, *Economic Aspects*.

19. See, for example, M. Larraín, 'How the 1981–83 Chilean Banking Crisis Was Handled', *World Bank Working Paper*, WPS 300.

20. A separate paper on Latin America experiences will be prepared as part of this project.

21. For this and other lessons, as well as an extensive review of country experiences, see J. Levitsky and R. Prasad, *Credit Guarantee Schemes for Small and Medium Enterprises*, World Bank Technical Paper No. 58, Industry and Finance Series.

2 Non-Banking Financial Sector and the Link to Foreign Investment
Zdeněk Drábek*

I INTRODUCTION

The development of the non-banking financial sector in the former centrally planned economies has received considerable attention among policy-makers in these countries and among financial experts in the West. The reason is very simple. The financial sector of these countries was extremely poorly developed under central planning and it was confirmed, almost exclusively, to the banking sector. Capital markets were non-existent after the abolition of stock markets in the early stages of central planning and the non-banking financial institutions thus included only property, trade, travel and car insurance. It became very clear to the reformers in Central and Eastern Europe that in the transformation from central planning to market economy the introduction of capital markets had to occupy a central place.

The development of capital markets is vitally important for the emerging market economies for several reasons. With the abolition of central planning the mobilisation of domestic savings has become dependent on the effectiveness of market instruments and institutions. Central planners had an advantage: they could mobilise domestic savings through price controls, indiscriminate taxation and effective elimination of choice for both households and enterprises. Since capital markets play an important role in attracting savings in market economies, their absence is a considerable handicap for Central and Eastern European countries. In addition, these countries are in a great need of long-term capital. Supply of capital currently comes primarily from banks but these are extremely risk-averse. As a result, most of the current lending takes the form of short-term or

* In preparing this paper, I have greatly benefited from my discussions with top officials of the Ministry of Finance, Central Banks, the Stock Exchanges, regulatory bodies, journalists and businessmen in Prague, Budapest and Warsaw. I am also very grateful to comments of my friend and colleague Dr Griffith-Jones and to Charles Harman of Credit Suisse First Boston, Kate Mortimer of the UK Know-How Fund, Tad Rybczynski of Hambros and the participants of the Sussex Seminar. The usual disclaimer, of course, holds.

medium-term credits. Once again, stock markets are a possible answer to this problem.

The purpose of this chapter is to review the development of the non-banking financial sector in Central Europe and to identify the major outstanding issues in the link between the capital markets and foreign investments. We see the link between capital markets and foreign investments primarily in four areas. The first area concerns the institutional features of capital markets and the extent to which they affect the entry of foreign investors (for example, the role of investment funds and banks, regulations of stock exchange, organisation of capital markets). The second area concerns liquidity of capital markets. For capital markets to be active and thus interesting for foreign investors not only must the demand for stocks and securities be high but so also must be the extent to which it will be possible to sell these stocks and securities. This means that our study should identify specific barriers for entry of foreign investors as reflected in the legislative framework, institutional imperfections or government policies towards capital markets. The third area concerns privatisation. Even though the private sector is a *sine qua non* of capital markets, the effect of the development of capital markets on privatisation is far less obvious. Last but not least, the fourth important factor affecting the activities of capital markets is macroeconomic performance. The extent to which governments are successful in bringing down the rate of inflation plays an important role in attracting investors into capital markets. Fast growth of output will typically be also beneficial in this respect. Declining interest rates, too, will be conducive, *ceteris paribus,* to the growth of demand for equities and for fixed income securities.

We shall cover four countries – the Czech Republic, Slovakia, Hungary and Poland – but the bulk of the report covers only the Czech Republic. It became obvious during the preparation of this report that a full coverage of all four countries would exceed its scope. Details of each country's legislation, policies and institutions vary so much that it would be impossible to carry a full analysis of each in the limited space of this chapter. However, the present analysis will include, as far as possible, a comparison of the Czech capital markets with those of Hungary and Poland. The omission of specific treatment of Slovakia is not considered to be serious. The Czech and Slovak legislations, policies and institutions were identical until the end of 1992 when both countries were part of the federation but the subsequent introduction of national legislation and policies was insignificant in terms of the objectives of this chapter.

The study will cover only a certain period. The evolution of capital markets in these countries is, not surprisingly, a 'living mechanism' which is in the process of evolution. This process will undoubtedly continue to change for some time until it is stabilised in a more or less firm structure. The description and analysis of the reform had to refer, therefore, to a particular cut-off period. For the purpose of this study the period is the end of April 1993. This effectively means that the report excludes those changes which might have taken place subsequently.

The final comment concerns the depth of our analysis. Most of the issues covered in this chapter are highly technical and cover a wide range of sub-issues. Due to limitations of time and space, the present analysis often touches only the surface of the issues in point. It is clear that better understanding of specific issues may require further analysis and work. Exluded from the following discussion also will be questions concerning macroeconomic policy. In particular, monetary policy is well known to be a major factor in influencing the performance of capital markets – it affects nominal economic aggregates and it directly influences the level of interest rates and hence the attractiveness of money markets as an alternative source of investment. It can also affect the liquidity of banks which are major actors in emerging capital markets.

The rest of this chapter is divided into two main parts. Section II reviews the two major institutions of the non-banking financial sector – investment funds and the stock market respectively – and then identifies the main issues of the stock market and the operations of investment funds regarding regulations, supervision and other institutional features. Section III reviews the factors leading to pressures for establishing capital markets in the region, and continues with a discussion of impediments due to privatisation. The chapter concludes with policy recommendations.

II THE STRUCTURE AND THE MAJOR ISSUES OF THE NON-BANKING FINANCIAL SECTOR

In order to better understand the role of the non-banking financial sector in the region it is useful to begin with a brief review of the privatisation process. Privatisation is one of the key elements of the transformation process in the whole region. It is fully recognised that the introduction of a market economy cannot be successful without a transfer of ownership from the state to the private sector. Even though the scope of privatisation and the speed with which assets are or will be privatised vary from country to country, all countries of the region adopted privatisation as one of the most important goals of their economic policies.

Nevertheless, the methods of privatisation vary considerably in the region. They range from a highly centralised approach in the former East Germany, where all privatised assets are sold through a huge bureaucracy known as 'Treuhandanstalt', to a highly decentralised and market-based approach pursued in the former Czechoslovakia. These two countries are also most advanced in this area, while others are still discussing their options in choosing among different methods of 'mass' privatisation.

The Czechoslovak Experiment in Privatisation

The Czechoslovak experiment has been divided into the so-called 'small' privatisation and 'large' privatisation. The former typically covers smaller assets – restaurants, shops, etc. – which are sold in auctions. In the course of 1991, the 'government' privatised in this way more than 24 000 units. Large privatisation covers other assets in all sectors of the economy with the aim of privatising the majority of public enterprises. The additional important objective of the 'large' privatisation was to privatise public assets rapidly so that more than 1500 enterprises changed ownership by the end of 1992. It is hoped that an additional 2000 enterprises will be privatised in 1993–4. All above figures refer to the former Czechoslovakia.

Clearly, the unusual speed of privatisation requires unusual methods. The Czechoslovak experiment focuses on the so-called 'voucher' scheme which is based on the distribution of vouchers to all adult Czechoslovak citizens for a small nominal fee. These vouchers are exchanged for shares in publc companies in the same manner as investors buy shares in standard stock markets. Each citizen receives a limited number of vouchers (or rather, points) which he/she can 'bid' for shares. The 'purchase' can be done either directly (in the absence of stock markets in Czechoslovakia this is done through post offices against the published list of 'offers', i.e. public enterprises offered for 'sale'). Alternatively, individual citizens can invest their 'vouchers' through investment funds, which have been spontaneously established on a large scale. In sum, privatisation by voucher method means that assets are virtually given away free of charge to the population, that private ownership will be initially highly dispersed and consequently will have limited influence on management of acquired companies, and that the relative values of shares will be established – a highly desirable feature given the current difficulties in ascertaining the values of public companies.[1] There are currently no restrictions on the resale of actual shares by Czechoslovak citizens once acquired against vouchers. It is anticipated that many will be sold and that these sales will take place through stock markets which are currently being established in the country, as we shall see further below.

The voucher method is not the exclusive method of privatisation. Standard methods are also used – such as direct sales to domestic or foreign investors. In the first round of privatisation in which about 1500 public enterprises were privatised as noted above, direct sales to foreigners amounted to just over 200 deals. These deals are typically combined with the voucher method, i.e. a percentage of shares is reserved for Czechoslovak citizens against vouchers, but – exceptionally – some deals have been allowed without any 'voucher reserve'.

Investment Funds

Financial sector reforms in the region foresee the establishment of stock markets, investment funds and other financial institutions. As noted above, we shall use the example of the Czech Republic to provide some specifics and more detailed description of the process of establishing these important institutions, and we shall start with a review of investment funds and proceed with a discussion of stock markets.

Investment funds have already played an important role in the Czech and Slovak Republics, in contrast to Hungary and Poland, where operations of investment funds have been delayed by legislative and administrative difficulties. By 21 January 1992, 296 investment funds had been approved in the Czech Republic; about 170 investment funds had been approved in Slovakia. According to the then Federal Minister of Finance, V. Klaus, 437 investment funds were actually functioning in 1992, in both republics. The 'voucher' privatisation has led to the investment of 8.53 billion of the so-called privatisation points. Out of these 8.53 billion points, the investment funds will have at their investment disposal 6.13 billion points, or 72 per cent. These are points which have been invested through investment funds by their true owners – individual citizens. Together, the ten largest investment funds control about 40 per cent of all investment points and about 56 per cent of all points that were allocated to investment funds.[2]

In contrast, the role of investment funds in Hungary and Poland remains limited. Due to the delays in passing the privatisation law by the parliament, the establishment of investment funds in Poland has been formally prepared but delayed in practice. The activities of investment funds are currently regulated by the Securities Act and they cover only 'open-ended' funds. 'Closed-end' funds are not included. The absence of a legislative framework together with discriminatory taxation of investment funds meant that Poland had in the middle of 1993 only one operating investment fund – 'Pioneer Investment Fund' (Boston).

In Hungary the limited number of investment funds reflects primarily the extreme illiquidity of the Hungarian stock market and the absence of a 'mass privatisation' plan. The Hungarian sector currently has only four investment funds. They represent closed-end funds (3–5 years), they must be registered on the Stock Exchange, and they are Hungarian-owned even though foreigners get access to the fund shares. They own and trade primarily government securities. Distortion in the tax system is the explanation given by the authorities for the small liquidity of investment funds in the Stock Exchange – the holders of investment units are reluctant to lose their tax benefits associated with the listing.

Types of Investment Companies   The Czech law on investment funds opens the door for the establishment of both investment funds *per se* and mutual funds. The latter mobilise resources from sales of shares of funds which they create while the former do so by issuing their own shares which constitute their own equity. Investment funds can issue shares in name only but must not issue employee or priority shares.

Establishment of Mutual and Investment Funds   Permission is required for the establishment of mutual and investment funds. The permission is typically given if certain conditions are satisfied, such as conditions on subscription capital, internal organisation, professional standing, staff and physical arrangements, and on notifications about the bank in which financial resources of the funds will be deposited. Authorities must be also notified about any changes in the management.

Types of Mutual Funds   Mutual funds can be 'open-ended funds' or 'closed-end funds'. The former has no restriction on the number of shares of the fund and repurchase agreements are also allowed. 'Closed-share-funds' are more limited in the sense that the number of shares of a given fund and the period during which the shares are issued are both limited. Repurchase agreements are not possible.

Capital   Capital of mutual and investment funds can be in the form of securities traded either in the domestic stock market or abroad. However, the choice of foreign stock market must be approved by the authorities. The authorities also determine the proportion of capital in the form of securities. Capital can also be in the form of real estate and other tangible assets. The total amount of capital required to set up an investment or mutual fund is small – 1 million crowns (about US$34 000) for funds established after 1991. For funds established before the end of 1991, the requirement was even smaller – 100 000 crowns (about US$3400).

Distribution of Benefits Principles for distribution of benefits are the same for both mutual and investment funds. Benefits are either distributed among shareholders or used to increase capital.

Spread of Risk The government has also decided to regulate the risk spread by imposing restrictions on capital and investment holdings:

(1) *Capital* – The total equity of any joint-stock company must not exceed 10 per cent of the capital of investment and mutual funds.
(2) *Investments of Mutual and Investment Funds* cannot exceed 20 per cent of total volume of shares of any given company.
(3) *Exclusions* – Investment and mutual funds cannot buy shares of other investment and mutual funds.
(4) *Fees* are set at maximum, 2 per cent of the total annual amount of capital.

Conflict of Interest There are also regulations concerning representations on the Board of Directors. For example, bank representatives cannot represent more than one-third of all members of the Board. Members of parliament, ministers and other public officials are excluded. There are also some restrictions on purchases by board members (e.g. own stock of shares).

Bank Control Banks which manage financial resources of investment and mutual funds are obligated to verify the values of shares, which are traded by these funds. Banks cannot own investment funds.

Stock Exchange

There seems to be a general agreement that administrative hurdles are the main constraints on the growth of foreign investment in the region[3] The actual process of establishing stock markets in the region is arguably the least advanced component of institutional reform in the financial sector. The reform is well under way but the establishment of stock markets will be a formidable task. Due to their complete absence in the past, stock markets had to be created from scratch and this includes adopting of legislative measures, finding suitable physical locations, training staff, establishing organisational rules, etc. So far, relevant legislation has been passed in all four countries and the first stock markets are already open – in Budapest (Hungary), Warsaw (Poland), Prague (Czech Republic) and Bratislava (Slovakia).

The Prague Stock Exchange was established in April 1993. Neither its membership nor investments in the stock market have any nationality restrictions. Foreigners receive 'national treatment'. The Stock Exchange has 53 members, including several domestic and foreign banks (see Appendix 2.B). The trading will take place in three sections: for companies with equity capital more than 500 million crowns (section 1); for companies with equity capital 100–500 millions crowns (section 2); and the rest in section 3 (over-the-counter). Currently the market is extremely thin – only seven securities were traded in 1993 but the representatives of the stock exchange hope that shares of about 20–30 companies will be traded by the end of 1994. The stock exchange hopes to list in Prague about 300 firms with over 500 million crowns in total equity and 20–30 companies of that size in Bratislava by the end of 1994.

The Budapest Stock Exchange was reopened in June 1990 and is the most developed in the region, with 25 shares traded in the market, 4 shares of investment funds and one so-called 'compensation note' (see Appendix 2.C). The Exchange has currently 45 members; banks are no longer members (since 1992) but they can have their own brokerage firms.

The Warsaw Stock Exchange was established in April 1991 and opened in July 1991. By mid-1993 it was trading in 20 equities and 7 government securities. The market has been extremely active since the end of February – early March 1993. The stock market index has increased about seven times between February and mid-September 1993; the brokers were receiving on average about 3000 orders from investors per day in mid-1993, only marginally less than the daily average in the London Stock Exchange (3200). The total market capitalisation was about US$ 1.5 billion at that time.

Major Issues

Investors' Protection

One of the vital conditions for efficient stock market operations is to ensure that investors have adequate protection against improper activities in the market. The most serious dangers constitute misleading claims of companies which float their shares in the market, improper activities leading to predatory and speculative merges and acquisitions and, arguably, insider-trading.[4] Similarly, the supervisors of investment funds and/or competition must ensure that the interests of investors are protected and that fraud and other improper activities of investment funds are avoided. Regulators of the stock exchange must aim at protecting buyers and sellers of stocks and securities and avoiding fraud. In many well-established stock markets, these issues are typically addressed with more or less detailed rules about company disclosures, about mergers and acquisitions and about insider-trading.

The formulation of the rules noted above is, in the Czech and Slovak Republics, currently less advanced in comparison with the other two countries. Neither the Czech Republic nor Slovakia has so far established a detailed administrative system of regulations to address these issues. The regulations have so far been formulated only in general terms in the Law on Securities (see Appendix 2.A). On the other hand, the process is quite advanced in Hungary and Poland even though the regulations of security issues in Poland are considered by Polish officials to be out of date and inadequate. In all countries under consideration the regulations on public equity listings cover the following areas: supervision and state control, disclosure rules and insider information. These topics will now be discussed together with other relevant issues.

Supervisory Control

The supervisory control in the Czech Republic covers all publicly traded securities and their actual trading, stock exchange as well as markets for unquoted shares, brokers, traders and the printers of securities. The responsibility for supervisory control is with the Ministry of Finance. The supervisory control of investment funds in the Czech republic is also in the hands of the Ministry of Finance. As far as the activities of stock exchange traders are concerned, the Ministry is entitled by law to award a licence to deal with stocks and securities, but this is only one of the necessary conditions to obtain a licence to trade in the stock exchange. Other conditions have to be fulfilled and the conditions are set by the stock exchange itself.[5]

The scope of supervisory control is rather rudimentary and it covers only limited activities. The current regulations require only that the authorities ensure public access to approved prospectuses, to information about financial performance of the issuers of shares, about the list of printing companies which are permitted to print securities and information about the list of security traders. The underlying assumption of the law – not stated explicitly – is that the question of propriety is also the responsibility of the supervisory authorities. This suggests that the responsibility lies with the licensing authorities.

The Hungarian supervisory system is one step ahead of the Czech one. The government has created the State Securities Supervision (SSS) which is a state body to supervise the public issue of, and trading in, securities. The SSS itself operates under the supervision of the Ministry of Finance and its head is appointed by the Council of Ministers. The SSS approves and/or amends propectuses prepared for the flotation of securities, and gives licence to traders to engage in the trading of securities. For the public issues of securities in Hungary denominated in foreign currency or the marketing abroad of securities issued in Hungary permission is also required from the National Bank of Hungary. The SSS also supervises the Stock Exchange, where only banks could originally become members. Its effectiveness in early stages has been questioned by some domestic and foreign experts. The supervisory control in Poland is also organised along the lines of the Hungarian SSS through the Security Exchange Commission (SEC). The SEC is a government agency that reports directly to the Prime Minister. It regulates the listing requirements, the disclosure rules, capital requirements for brokers and other activities. It is also responsible for the supervision of investment funds, but no formal rules exist. The top regulatory body of SEC includes the chairman and it has two deputies, and representatives from the Ministry of Finance, central bank and anti-monopoly office and ministry of privatisation. At present, the SEC proposes to include also representatives of brokers and the Stock Exchange for consultations. In general, good supervision and good share listing are considered in Poland to be the main reasons for the activity of the Warsaw Stock Exchange.

Disclosure Rules

The disclosure rules about companies in the Czech Republic include a number of highly specific regulations. They seem adequate for the purpose at hand even though there may be other areas of activities which may still be addressed in the future. Under current regulations the companies whose shares are publicly traded are required to publish once a year the results of their financial performance. They also have to report to the Ministry all changes in their financial performance which could affect the price of shares in point. These changes should include in particular the start of bankruptcy proceedings or the termination of activities of the company through official decision, merger or division of the company, or any reduction of capital in excess of 10 per cent, legal disputes about the company's assets greater than 5 per cent, or any changes in the supervisory, statutory or management bodies of the company.

In Hungary, the disclosure rules include also the requirement for companies to publish once a year a detailed annual report. In addition, companies are required to publish once a quarter shorter reports about their financial performance. The companies must also notify, within 24 hours, the Stock Exchange about special events such as changes in management, newly contracted loans, plans for mergers or acquisitions, and issues of new shares. The disclosure rules appear to be sufficiently detailed to provoke criticism in the country among experts, who consider the regulations to be excessive.

Disclosure rules about investment funds seem to be more problematic. A recent independent report found that 'usually a full prospectus of an investment fund with full disclosure of its capital stock, personal history of members of the board of directors, and a description of operational charges, is not widely available'.[6]

Securitisation

Another issue related to disclosure rules concerns the securitisation of assets. Investors will require a proper security on their investments to minimise other than commercial risks. The present arrangements for their security are, however, considered by some experts as not completely adequate in all four countries. For example, in Hungary the ability of any single creditor to veto a restructuring plan of the debtor company may force some salvageable companies into premature liquidation.[7] The current Czech situation seems even more problematic where investors' security is typically protected by real (fixed) assets. However, those assets are not always reliably priced, increasing therefore the investors' risk as well as the costs of lending.

Insider Information

Once again, the Czech law on securities addresses only the major issues in general terms. The law specifies the circumstances which are subject to regulations about insider information in terms of access to confidential information. The important element of the ruling is that only information which could influence the share price is relevant. Further, the ruling restricts the activities of persons who have access to confidential information. These persons are not allowed to make transactions with shares about which they have confidential information. Similar regulations exist also in Hungary, Poland and Slovakia.

Clearing and Settlement

There was a major discussion in the Czech and Slovak republics about the most suitable way of clearing and settling accounts of clients in the stock market. The discussion reflected to some extent the unresolved issues resulting from the attempted introduction of the fully computerised system 'Taurus' in the London Stock Exchange. In the end, the decision has been taken to introduce a system of payments which is fully computerised. The system has been installed and adapted from French technology and with considerable technical assistance from French experts.

While there seems to be a general satisfaction with the decision to go with the highly computerised system, there have been nevertheless some voices of criticism. One of them pointed to the fact that the actual transaction settlement consists of two independent circuits – physical settlement and the actual cash payment, which are not tightly integrated. In fact, the cash settlement should take place within three days. This could lead to some delays in the final settlement of transactions. In addition, the brokers' risks might unduly increase, which in turn may lead to higher brokers' fees and hence higher transaction costs to investors. Recent reports already suggest amendment to the securities law to modify the role of the Central Register.[8]

In Hungary, the argument has been taken one step further. The Stock Exchange authorities argue that the clearing and settlement system should be separated from the Stock Exchange itself in order to shift the risk from non-payment elsewhere. They are proposing to establish a separate company to handle the clearing and settlement operations. The company would have its own capitalisation and it should provide other services such as financial services and registration of shares.

In Poland, the settlement system is on the delivery-versus-payment basis. The settlement with the Deposit and Clearing Bank must be settled within T+3 days, as in Prague. Each investor must hold a securities account and a money account with a broker. The transfer of ownership takes place in dematerialised form. Even though this is considered to be an impediment to over-the-counter trading, the clearing and settlement system seems to work reasonably well. In general, the Polish officials are satisfied with their clearing and settlement system – they are able to satisfy eight out of nine recommendations on clearing and settlement made by the Group of Thirty.[9] Nevertheless, settlement and custody issues are allegedly the two most important factors which have discouraged institutional investors from investing on the Polish and on the other Central European stock markets so far. True incorporation into the major Western European settlement systems (Euroclear and Cedel) would be useful.

Role of Banks

The role of banks in capital markets has been surrounded by considerable controversy in many countries. The controversy has not been resolved in a uniform manner and the result is that the permissible range of activities of banks varies from country to country. The German universal system of banks is at one extreme while the prohibition to underwrite shares by commercial banks looms at the other extreme such as in the United States. The main concerns of regulators are essentially two potential problems – lack of competition and dangers of serious conflict of interest. The separation of the banking sector into investment and commercial banks is intended to address both issues.

These issues are addressed in more detail in Chapter 3 of this volume. It may suffice here to summarise the main relevant points with regard to the banking sector of the Czech and Slovak republics. While the original thoughts might have favoured the separation of investment and commercial banks, the actual process has led to the creation of a system which makes the banks' operations universal. There is no doubt that the role of banks is already beginning to be very substantial in different areas. First, virtually all banks are involved not only in commercial lending and in taking deposits but also in the type of lending which have been traditionally considered in these countries as lending for investment purposes. In addition, some have already started activities which are typical of investment banks such as issuing investment certificates. Nevertheless, it will take some time before the commercial banks will be in the position to get seriously involved in underwriting and in other such activities. In this respect, the situation in the Czech and Slovak banking sectors is similar to that in Poland where banks are also searching for their best role and where their investment exposures (purchase of equities) is limited by the level of 25 per cent.

Second, there are extremely close ties between the major domestic banks and the non-financial sector. It explains the high level of debt of non-financial enterprises to banks. The total outstanding debts of industrial enterprises to the banking sector (the so-called 'primary debt') amounted to about 11.4 billion Czech crowns at the end of 1992 in the Czech Republic alone, or about US$ 393 million. These debts are in addition to the total of 50 billion Czech crowns worth of debts which had been originally on the books of banks but were removed from the balance sheets in the course of 1991. All these debts have been classified by the banking sector as 'non-performing', or highly doubtful.[10] Again, a similar situation exists in Hungary and Poland. In Poland, for example, where bad loans have been recognised as a problem later than in the Czech Republic, high officials at the Ministry of Finance estimate that bad and doubtful loans constitute about 20–30 trillion zlotys, or about 20–30 per cent of bank assets.

Third, all major banks have established through intermediaries their own investment funds. This is an extremely important feature of the financial sector in the Czech and Slovak republics since investment funds have concentrated in their hands a majority of shares privatised through the 'voucher' method, as noted above. Whether banks will participate – directly or indirectly – in the capital market more actively than at present will also depend on the liquidity of capital markets. At present, they are less liquid than money markets.

Fourth, major banks have applied for and received licences to operate as brokers in the stock market. This corresponds to the pattern that has developed in Poland and Hungary. In fact, the Hungarian authorities have at first relied exclusively on banks as brokers, as noted above. It can therefore be assumed that banks are going to be active in all segments of the financial sector.

Thus, the emerging trends in the Czech and Slovak banking sectors are for relatively powerful banks. At the same time, we shall probably also see the emergence of banks whose impact on the development of the non-financial sector in general and on the development of the stock market in particular remains unknown and may be rather worrisome. Strong banks often mean that the development of non-banking financial institutions is to some extent crippled. The example of this phenomenon is Germany, where capital markets have developed slowly and continue to be relatively thin. The fact that the banks' activities will be closely intertwined with the activities of investment funds and those of the stock market increases the dangers of restricted competition and will need to be closely monitored.

Competing Markets for Shares

The peculiar feature of capital markets in the Czech and Slovak republics is the emergence of two markets for shares – the regular stock market and the so-called RM-S market. The former refers to a typical stock market complete with regulations about stock market membership, organisation of stock exchange listing of companies and other typical activities of these markets (see also further discussion below). In addition, members of the formal stock market have also agreed to undertake trading with unlisted shares in view of the anticipated offers of shares by households and investment funds. In other words, the representatives of the formal stock market intend to create a secondary market for shares.

Parallel to the formal stock market has then developed a competing market for secondary trading of shares – the RM-S market. The main function of this market is, again, to enable trading with shares obtained through the 'voucher' privatisation. This alternative market has been developed from the computer system, which was originally used to distribute shares against 'points' in the 'voucher' privatisation. The main feature of this market is to enable the trading of unlisted shares – like the secondary trading in the stock market. It relies on hundreds of the so-called 'collecting locations' which collect information about intentions to sell and about shares on offer. The actual market clearing – without any prior 'means test' of companies – takes place on computers in the RM-S headquarters.

How the two systems will coexist next to each other remains a big unknown. Initially, at least, they enter as competitors. The 'push' for the RM-S market was originally justified on the grounds of a big network of offices capable of handling offers of shareholders scattered around in a geographically large area, and on the grounds of considerable experience with the 'voucher' privatisation. In contrast, the establishment of secondary trading in the formal stock exchange was justified on the basis of low transaction costs, but this argument has been recently put in doubt.[11]

High transaction costs would, of course, be a major concern since they could represent a serious disincentive to invest in the capital markets. Some foreign experts have also argued that foreign investors will be put off by this 'over-the-counter' method of trading. Their argument seems to assume that such a trading does not provide any protection to investors.

Other Transaction Costs Issues

In addition to the transaction costs issues discussed above other relevant matters should be raised. Among those, arguably the most important question is the issue of costs of different instruments. These questions will have to be addressed by the authorities soon since there does not seem to be much logic in the pricing of different services. For example, each new issue of securities is subject to a fee of 1 per cent of the nominal value of the issue. Thus, securities are currently not competitive with discounted bills[12] and the high fee has been subject to serious criticism.

Other Stock Exchange Rules and Regulations

Other stock exchange rules and regulations appear to have been worked out reasonably well in all four countries. Nevertheless, some, albeit probably minor, issues still remain and will most likely be addressed in due course of time. In addition, the stock markets in all four countries will suffer from other 'teething' problems which are and will be typical of all emerging market economies. These are problems related not so much to the actual rules and regulations but rather to their implementation. The problem of 'policing' seems to be a general difficulty of all four countries.

One rule which has been widely discussed in the Czech republic and which has been rather controversial concerns the minimum size of companies to make them eligible for listing in the stock market. The current requirement has been set at 100 million Kc (about US$3.5 million) which is considered by some experts as low. Another example is the requirement concerning the age of the company. The rules now state that companies older than two years can qualify for being considered for listing. Once again, this rule has been criticised as extremely generous although understandable in the circumstances in view of the ongoing transformation of these countries into market economies. Profit forecasts are also going to be initially of dubious value partly due to the short history of firms noted above and partly due to the lack of experienced staff. This is likely to contribute to volatility of profits and hence volatility of share values, which in turn will put off foreign investors since they will be unlikely to offset the volatility of profits by a large volume of traded shares (see discussion in section III). Some experts have also criticised the rules concerning the presentation of the company prospectus, which they found vague. As a result, the liability arising from information provided in the company prospectus remains questionable.

Highly problematic still remains the question of investors' protection. As noted above, neither the government nor the stock exchange have so far come up with detailed and firm rules about disclosures and rules concerning mergers and acquisitions. This is in contrast to the rules valid in Poland and Hungary which are generally considered to be comprehensive, sufficiently detailed and strict. The lack of rules could be detrimental to the interests of small and individual investors and it could also lead to predatory and highly inefficient acquisitions.[13] Also, no rules have been set up for the maximum percentage of shares which can be acquired in the market and which must be reported either internally or in the form of a public announcement. Furthermore, there is no requirement of capital adequacy for securities traders, which could considerably increase the vulnerability of those traders trading with large volumes.

Taxation

A major policy issue affecting the future development of capital markets could be government taxation of capital gains and income. The heavier the tax burden the stronger will be the disincentives to investors to invest in the capital markets. In addition, heavy taxation of capital gains and other investment income will provide a strong disincentive to save. For these reasons, the rational government policy is to minimise the taxation of capital income except in cases of highly speculative capital movements in order to reduce the instability of capital markets.

The taxation level in the Czech Republic is currently higher than in most other Central and East European countries.[14] In addition, there are signs that taxation of investment income could become a major issue both on equity and efficiency grounds. While the present level of taxation is roughly comparable to many other countries for the taxation of dividends and interest from securities the government intends to raise the tax burden of investors. Interest income is currently taxed at a rate of 15 per cent for the so-called 'physical' persons (i.e. households) as well as for the 'legal' persons (i.e. primarily for incorporated entities). However, interest taxation is currently under review and may be increased up to 25 per cent. Income from deposit certificates is currently taxed at a rate of 15 per cent but the rate may be also increased to 25 per cent. Dividends are taxed at a rate of 25 per cent. Thus, the tax incentive structure is currently tilted towards deposits rather than towards equities and securities.

Exactly the opposite situation exists currently in Poland. The government policy favours savings rather than consumption and investments into equities rather than bank deposits. Interest income is tax exempt but so are any capital gains (the latter have currently a 3-year time limitation). The tax on dividends is 25 per cent but zero if all dividends are reinvested.

The Czech law makes two further exceptions on the treatment of taxes from dividends. The tax rate on dividends paid by investment funds is 25 per cent but only on that portion of their income which is not subject to a different tax regime. For example, income (dividends) of investment funds from shares and other securities which they own, is taxed differently. The taxable income of investment funds which is subject to a 25 per cent level of tax is obtained only after the deduction from total income of the dividends from these shares and other securities. The second exception is the tax rate applied on dividends paid out to banks which is the corporate tax rate, currently 45 per cent.

An even more serious problem appears to be the taxation of capital gains. One aspect of the problem is the complexity of the capital gains taxation. Another is inefficiency and, with one exception, extremely high tax rates. At present, the government is following on its commitment not to levy a separate tax on capital gains. Nevertheless, capital gains are taxable at rates which depend on circumstances. The taxation of capital gains of physical persons depends on whether the shares have been obtained from resources dedicated for business activities or not. If shares were acquired from resources which were not obtained from business activities of the person, the capital gain is free of tax if the share was owned for more than one year. (This seems to have been a political concession made on behalf of individual citizens who obtained shares through the 'voucher' privatisation.) If the share was owned for less than one year, the appropriate tax schedule is the tax on the person's income less costs of acquisition of the share. If the share is acquired from resources obtained from the business activity of the person concerned the appropriate tax schedule is the tax on incomes from business activities. Capital gains of legal persons are taxed according to the corporate tax schedule.

It can be seen that capital taxation is heavy. In particular, the taxation of capital gains is likely to be highly detrimental as a government policy instrument to attract domestic savings and investments. For example, since top marginal income tax rates were at that time as high as 47 per cent, the application of the income tax schedule would make investments in capital markets almost prohibitive. This issue should certainly be reviewed by the government without delay.

In contrast, the Hungarian taxation of dividends and capital gains is normally 10 per cent – the same tax rates as are applied on the interest from deposits. Investments in shares are also encouraged by 30 per cent tax deductions from taxable income and no tax is applied on dividends by institutional investors. As noted above, trading of investment funds is encouraged through tax concessions given to the holders of investment units (the tax concession does not apply in the case of government securities).

The tax policy includes other distortions. For example, while interest on bank loans is tax deductible, the same rule does not apply in the case of interest on bonds. The current system discriminates, therefore, between two types of corporate borrowing strategies, favouring borrowing from banks. In addressing all these issues it must be borne in mind that tax compliance in the stock exchange is likely to be higher than that in the private sector of self-employed businessmen. The latter will provide even stronger incentive for small investors to avoid stock exchange, as evidenced in Hungary.

Foreign Exchange Regulations

The Czech foreign exchange regulations are given primarily by the Foreign Exchange Law. The law determines the relevant conditions under which it is possible to dispose of foreign currency and make foreign currency transfers abroad. These conditions are fairly liberal for foreign investors in both the Czech and Slovak republics. The only restriction of note is the requirement of licence (permission) from the central bank to obtain credits from abroad and to transfer investment funds within 12 months from the date of investment. In contrast to these short-term investments, long-term investments into securities (i.e. more than 12 months) have no transfer restrictions. The restrictions noted above were motivated by the governments' concerns to minimise instability of capital markets. However, since portfolio investment are typically very fluid and are made by investors with short-term horizons the restriction could be a strong disincentive for foreign investments.

The Hungarian and Polish regulations of foreign exchange regimes are not much different. In Hungary, there are virtually no foreign exchange restrictions which would affect stock market operations. There are no restrictions on capital repatriations or income transfers. There are also no restrictions on transactions involving foreigners in terms of maturity of securities or sectoral allocations. However, the first issue of government bonds and some other special issues have been reserved solely for foreigners while other special issues have been reserved for nationals only. The local issues for the nationals have carried more favourable interest rates. In Poland, the foreign exchange regulations include the requirement to report export of currency more than US\$ 2000, the approval of credits from abroad in excess of US\$ 1 million, some restrictions on purchases of treasury bills (most likely to be removed from July 1993) and on purchases of banks.

III PRIVATISATION AND CAPITAL MARKETS

Introduction

There is no doubt that the recent growth of foreign investment in Central Europe reflects mainly the opening of these economies and, very importantly, the governments' decision to privatise public enterprises. In this sense, privatisation has enabled foreign companies to wholly or partially acquire assets offered for sale or it has, at least, opened considerable opportunities for joint ventures. But the decision to sell public enterprises – as remarkable as it is – is only the first in the series of steps that have to be taken in order to marry privatisation and foreign investment. Privatisation is closely linked to influences emerging outside the privatisation process[15] and to factors endemic to the administration of privatisation. The latter included, for example, delays in legislation, and the lack of rules and transparency on tenders, on hiring foreign consultants, on financing privatisation transactions, etc. Delays have been encountered also in deciding the most fundamental questions – which enterprises should be privatised and which should be left in the public sector, or how to privatise those enterprises which the governments identified for sale. It is clear that if any of these issues are not successfully addressed the barriers to foreign investments will remain immense.

The purpose of this section is to identify the main factors which originate in the privatisation process and which can slow down the expansion of capital markets. This could be a serious weakness in the transformation of these countries and could stall the overall market reforms. The presence of strong and dynamic capital markets is vital for the inflow of foreign capital and will help domestic companies seeking additional resources in the form of new equity. It is no coincidence that the best performing economies in the world in recent years include the emerging economies in South East Asia where we have witnessed an impressive emergence of capital markets. Clearly, the expansion of the manufacturing sector in these countries has been highly conducive to the establishment of capital markets. *Pari passu*, the existence of capital markets has played an extremely important role in augmenting domestic savings to finance a high rate of domestic investments and in strengthening the foreign exchange reserves of the countries.

In this section we first describe the economic factors which are conducive to the creation of capital markets. Indeed, these factors constitute in many instances real economic pressures to establish capital markets in the region. Next we identify the main issues which will inhibit the expansion of capital markets. Finally, we specify the main conditions for a more effective functioning of capital markets and offer some policy conclusions.

Pressures for Establishing Capital Markets

Pressures for establishing capital markets in Central Europe are very strong. The financial sector reforms started in all countries with fundamental reforms of the banking sector. The countries are now entering the second phase that will emphasise the need for a greater role of the non-banking financial sector. As we saw in section II, the role of the non-banking financial sector will be very important. The importance of the sector emerges from the need of companies to mobilise resources for growth and restructing and to intermediate the links between domestic and foreign investors and the corporate sector. Thus, the pressures for establishing capital markets have their origins both on the demand and supply side. These are now discussed in turn.

Demand for Long-Term Capital

Arguably the most important reason for establishing capital markets in the region is the strong demand of the corporate sector for long-term capital. Financial needs of companies are great and they originate from the need to modernise their technologies, to finance the expansion of the private sector and to restructure existing companies. The needs are currently met primarily from bank borrowing which has been increasingly tilted towards short-term and medium-term credits. This adversely affects corporate investments, which typically have longer gestation periods and which require adequate 'recoupment' periods to repay bank credits. It also encourages more speculative investments which have shorter time horizons. (See Table 2.1.)

Related to this problem is the current leveraging of companies, which in many instances appears to be too high. Over-leveraged companies may require a change in the structure of financing which may be met through greater equity financing. As indicated by gross debt data for the Czech Republic, for example, the debt problem appears to be indeed quite serious. As noted above, the total outstanding debt of the corporate sector amounted

Table 2.1   Time structure of credits in the Czech Republic[a]

	12/91	03/92	06/92	09/92	12/92	03/93
			Billion Kc			
Short-term	195.6	198.2	210.4	214.1	216.6	240.7
Medium-term	90.1	96.7	109.3	139.2	154.2	161.8
Long-term	209.7	204.9	202.4	198.0	207.8	202.6
Total	495.4	499.8	522.1	551.3	578.6	605.1
			Percentages			
Short-term	39.5	39.8	40.3	38.8	37.4	39.8
Medium-term	18.2	19.3	20.9	25.2	26.7	26.7
Long-term	42.3	41.0	38.8	35.9	35.9	33.5
Total	100.0	100.0	100.0	100.0	100.0	100.0

[a] Excluding foreign exchange loans.
Source: Czech National Bank.

to 94.2 billion Czechoslovak crowns at the end of the third quarter 1992. This compares to the total amount of profits in the non-private sector of 18 billion crowns in the same period. In other words, the total debt exceeded total profit 5.3 times. The situation has been even more serious in Slovakia where the total outstanding debt amounted to 60.2 billion Czechoslovak crowns, or about 15 times higher than the total profits of Slovak enterprises in the non-private sector in the same period.

Nevertheless, how important the current debt problem is remains still uncertain. This is partly because, as noted above, a large part of companies' indebtedness is due to secondary debt, i.e. inter-enterprise debt. The latter has in turn emerged partly because of the difficulties of companies to survive in a new market environment, which is a genuine market reason. The debt is quite sizeable in all four countries. In Poland, for example, the size is estimated to be about 300–400 trillion zlotys (about the same amount as the total outstanding credit to the private sector) and in the Czech Republic the size is relatively smaller (about 50 per cent of total outstanding credit) but still absolutely quite significant (more than 100 billion Kc). However, another reason has been the lack of financial discipline of companies which refused to pay their own suppliers in response to the failure to receive payments from their clients. In the latter case, the total debt of a company should be adjusted for all receivables which have a real chance of being paid in order to ascertain the true debt service of these companies.

On the other hand, the current debt problem is not the only issue. In addition to current liabilities, many companies in the Czech Republic have future liabilities which arise from the privatisation of these companies. The financing of privatisation of many companies has been provided by the government in the form of a liability to be serviced from the future profits of the privatised company. Furthermore, many companies are facing additional liabilities, as we shall see further below. In sum, it appears therefore that there are companies which will be in serious financial situations due to extremely heavy debt burden arising from current and future financial liabilities. How many and in which sectors these companies can be found remains a big unknown.

Another important factor affecting demand for capital is the method of 'voucher' privatisation in the Czech Republic. Privatisation has led to a significant dispersion of shareholding among individual investors and investment funds (see Table 2.2). As discussed above, the latter have been restricted by law on how they should spread their own risk and how much control they can get in each company. As a result, it is expected that many investment funds will seek to obtain more effective control of companies by consolidating the shareholdings in their portfolio. This will lead to a

Table 2.2   Key dimensions of Czechoslovak voucher privatisation

	Before reorganisation	*After reorganisation*
Total number of companies privatised	1491	1491
– Czech Republic	943	988
– Slovak Republic	487	503
– Federation	61	0
	Billion Kčs	*Billion $*
Book value of property:	299.4	10.3
– Czech Republic	206.4	7.1
– Slovak Republic	90.1	3.1
– Federation	2.9	0.1
Number of shares offered for sale:	299 393 282	with a face value of Kčs 1000, or $34.50
– Czech Republic	212 490 000	
– Slovak Republic	86 900 000	
	Million	
Number of participating investors:	8.54	
– Czech Republic	5.95	
– Slovak Republic	2.59	
	Million shares	*% of total*
Unsold shares	21.55	7.2%
– Czech Republic	14.46	6.8%
– Slovak Republic	7.09	8.2%

Source: Planecon, Report of 31 December 1992, Washington, D.C.

shift in portfolio holdings of investment funds through transactions in capital markets.

Neither Hungary nor Poland has yet started their 'mass' privatisation programme and the establishment of a market for secondary trading is therefore much less pressing.[16] The slow process of privatisation is particularly serious in Poland, where there have been delays in passing legislation on the Mass Privatisation Plan and lack of consensus on the selection of 600 companies that would be privatised as part of the Plan. This has greatly restricted the total number of shares available in the market and, together with booming demand for equities, it has resulted in the explosion of equity prices and of traded volumes as noted above. It is evident that the major issue of stock trading in Poland is currently not the lack of liquidity as in the Czech Republic but the shortage of shares. The recently approved law on Mass Privatisation should therefore go a long way in widening the stock market but the actual selection of companies still remains unresolved.[17]

The Liquidity of Capital Markets

On the supply side, there are principally two factors which are pushing for the establishment of capital markets. The first factor is the availability of long-term domestic resources which are not currently translated into long-term investments. The main reason is the absence of intermediation between the institutions which manage the resources and those which demand them and the high level of interest rates which encourage the growth of bank deposits. The long-term resources available in these countries are the pension funds, medical and other insurance funds and social security funds. It appears that these funds are currently partly deposited with the banking sector and partly managed by the funds themselves. In either case, these long-term resources are not sufficiently translated into long-term lending of the banking sector as noted above nor are they reflected in long-term investments of the funds due to the absence of appropriate market instruments. Moreover, even in those situations in which some of these funds have been allowed by regulators to provide credit, such as in the case of the Czech Insurance Company, the result has been the same as in the case of the banking sector – the lending has been almost exclusively concentrated on short- and medium-term credits.

The highly limited amount of long-term investments is not only due to lack of market instruments but also due to the limited availability of long-term resources. The lack of long-term resources reflects in turn the saving habits of economic agents, availability of credit and the effect of taxation. This can be quite well documented in the Polish example. The explosion in demand for equities in Poland in early 1993 was due to the fall in interest rates, the increased availability of credit for purchases of shares (about 50 billion zlotys), and the abolition of capital taxation. In contrast, the liquidity of the Czech stock market has remained relatively limited partly because Czech savers have not moved their savings out of bank deposits into the purchases of shares.

The second factor on the supply side is the availability of foreign capital. As is well known, a large and ever growing proportion of foreign investments in world markets takes the form of portfolio and indirect investments. This type of investment seeks liquid markets which enable the possibility of trading and 'exit' and which do not require direct involvement in the management of those companies whose shares are acquired by these investors. Moreover, there is plenty of evidence to suggest that some, and, needless to say, not an insignificant proportion of this type of capital seeks opportunities in Central and Eastern Europe for which the establishment of capital markets is, therefore, vital. In Poland, for example, the share of foreign investors in stock market trading is estimated to be currently in the range of 25–30 per cent.

The impediments to foreign investments are still numerous and they vary from country to country. In general, the impediments have institutional and policy origins. The major institutional matters include unresolved ownership rights (Czech Republic) and liability issues (all countries), which will be discussed further in the text as will be other impediments due to privatisation. In addition, the countries also impose other restrictions on foreign investors. For example, Poland requires permission for foreigners to engage in (i) management of ports (sea, air), (ii) real estate agency or sale of property, (iii) defence industry, (iv) wholesaling of imported consumer goods, (v) giving legal assistance, (vi) banking, (vii) stockbroking, (viii) production of alcohol, cigarettes and medicines[18]. The current Czech regulations restrict foreigners to the purchase of securities with maturity longer than one year. Similar restrictions exist in the other countries. The countries still suffer from some policy distortions such as pricing of land or energy or from unresolved problems of restitution. Once again, the specific policy issues may vary country to country and a detailed review of these issues would go beyond the scope of this study.[19]

The importance of foreign capital for domestic capital markets is increased by the additional fact that none of the countries in question has sufficient domestic savings to finance all the privatisation deals, the restructuring needs and the expansion of the private sector. For example, the total domestic savings in the Czech Republic – a country with a traditionally high propensity to save – amounted to 551 billion Czech crowns at the end of April 1993.

In contrast, the financial requirements of privatisation alone greatly exceeded this amount. The total book value of assets privatised through the 'voucher method' was in the Czech Republic about 206 billion Czech crowns in the first wave alone (see Table 2.2). This figures excludes assets to be privatised in the second wave of 'voucher' privatisation, the book value of which is estimated to be almost as high as the book value of assets privatised in the first wave. Excluded also are assets privatised through more standard methods and assets privatised in the so-called 'small privatisation'. If we further allow for the fact that the book value of assets is typically greatly underestimated perhaps by a factor of 2-4, then we can see that domestic assets could not possibly be privatised through domestic capital alone.

Furthermore, domestic resources may have to be 'matched up' with foreign capital which acts as a 'catalyst' to activate these resources. For example, the highly cautious behaviour of domestic banks is partly due to the absence of proper instruments which would reduce foreign exchange risks (e.g. exchange rates hedging) and partly to their inexperience in evaluating the credit risk. Clearly, as much as foreign investors can benefit from joining the domestic banks and other financial institutions, the latter can and to some extent will benefit from partnership with foreign capital.

Impediments Due to Privatisation: Main Issues

Strictly speaking, privatisation *per se* cannot be an impediment to the development of capital markets. Capital markets require profit oriented and commercially driven entrepreneurs, who flourish best in the private sector environment. Even in countries which are not strictly capitalist economics but in which capital markets are developed, entrepreneurs' behaviour is very close to what one would expect in an economy dominated by the private sector. Nevertheless, under certain conditions privatisation may become a burden or, at least, no longer conducive to the development of capital markets. In general, privatisation becomes a hindrance if it is implemented poorly or slowly. Based on the most recent experience in the Czech and Slovak Republics, Hungary and Poland, it is possible to think of several specific aspects of privatisation which can become such impediments. These are now identified in the following discussion. It should be noted that the issues include only some, albeit perhaps the most important and relevant, aspects of privatisation.

Sequencing of Restructuring

It is widely accepted that many companies in all three countries will find it difficult to survive in a new competitive environment and will have to be restructured to assure their long-term viability. In the Czech Republic, for example, the number of enterprises with serious financial difficulties dramatically increased between 1989 and 1993, as discussed above. The question that has been on the cards for some time therefore is whether the companies should be restructured before they are sold or not. This issue has been resolved quite unequivocally in the Czech Republic where the decision has been taken to privatise all assets before they are restructured. A company is therefore sold 'as is' and restructuring may take place only after the companies have been sold to their new owners. This reflects the policy of 'getting the government out of business'. In Hungary, the decision has been taken after long discussions to restructure several companies before they were privatised. In Poland, the restructuring of essentially profitable companies is planned to be carried out at the same time as companies are transferred into the hands of specialised investment funds. Restructuring of unprofitable companies, however, has been delayed and different proposals continue to be discussed. Thus, the countries have embarked on paths which involve all possible options of sequencing, but each approach has adverse implications for the growth of capital markets. The Czech approach has simply meant that companies' restructuring programmes and financial decisions including their access to capital markets has been delayed. In Hungary, the restructuring process is slow since it is highly centralised. In Poland, it was the decision about the general privatisation and restructuring strategy which was delayed.

Pricing of Shares

The experience with these schemes is limited but, on *a priori* grounds, it is possible to identify two distinct cases of sales of companies before their restructuring which will have clear implications for the operations of capital markets – sales of strong and weak companies. The attempts to sell financially stronger companies through public issues are more likely to succeed than attempts to sell companies which are nearly bankrupt. On the other hand, sales of weak companies are going to be highly improbable. Moreover, even if such sales were to be possible through public issues, these shares could be sold only at appropriately discounted prices in order to offer prospects for their appreciation in the future – a crucial condition to attract venture capitalists. In both cases however, the trading of shares in the stock market is likely to be slow, at least in the early stages of capital markets, as we shall now demonstrate.

The importance of the first group of transactions (sale of strong companies) for the evolution of capital markets is an empirical problem. There are reasons to believe that the number of 'strong' companies will vary from country to country. The Czech Republic will probably be at the more attractive end of the spectrum with Hungary and Poland lagging slightly behind. In general, however, the number of 'strong' companies is likely to be relatively small – even in the Czech Republic. The main reason is the revenue-generating capability of most companies which remains largely untested.

Most companies in the former socialist countries have not been exposed to the pressure of domestic and, mainly, Western competition, and their ability to survive in the new market environment will have – at best – a limited historical record. Exceptions will be companies with foreign – Western – participation or 'blue chips' companies with long industrial tradition, e.g. Pilsner Urquell, Budweiser, Škoda, Becher, Moser, Petrof, etc. Other companies which are likely to become attractive for investors are companies producing primarily for the domestic market and which are not threatened by foreign competition. These are companies in the so-called 'non-traded' sector, e.g. construction, transport, telecommunications and others.

Trading of shares of other companies will be much more difficult – if not impossible. Some companies can be considered to be 'weak' companies for several reasons. Part of the problem lies in the perception of managers and government officials who see the value of companies as unrealistically high. This has led to situations in which negotiations with foreign partners were protracted and excessively cumbersome. In some instances, the negotiations have been abruptly stopped and the company withdrawn from the market and treated as non-saleable to foreigners on 'national security grounds'. All these examples suggest that the introduction of public offerings is likely to be slow in the beginning.

The alternative could be a market absorption of unrealistically priced shares with the consequence of price collapse in the subsequent periods. The example is the performance of shares in the Budapest Stock Exchange. After the initial excitement of the first equity issues in the market, investors reacted by purchasing shares at unrealistically high prices. The pricing of shares was evidently so problematic that the share prices collapsed by more than 30 per cent within one year. Investors are today more cautious and 'overpricing' of shares will become more and more difficult and, it is to be hoped, less and less frequent. The Polish experience in this respect is very interesting, because the stock market performance has been exactly the opposite.

The main reason for the difficulties in trading shares of the second – i.e. 'weak' – group of companies is that the companies will often have to be restructured – if they are to have any solid base for survival. The restructuring process may have to involve different aspects of company activities – restructuring of balance sheets, improvement of technology or management, requalification of the labour force, change in the product-mix, choice of markets, etc.

This does not necessarily mean that governments will have to intervene and/or carry out the restructuring of companies. What it does mean, however, is that whatever restructuring is to be made by the new owners must not be blocked by unresolved institutional or policy issues. Needless to say that there are still many left. These issues can be resolved only by government action or through legal proceedings which, too, may require a prior government intervention. Some of these major issues are discussed in the following text.

Unresolved Ownership Rights Issues

All four countries have resolved the longstanding problem of unclear ownership rights by transforming in the first instance public enterprises into commercial entities such as joint-stock companies in which the state was the only (or the majority) owner. Still completely unresolved, however, are the ownership rights related to restitution in the Czech Republic. For example, several legal subjects have claimed ownership rights for the same asset. New claims for restitution are also being pushed for by different political parties such as in the case of church property. These matters are considerably simpler in Poland and Hungary where restitution of assets to their previous owners has not been allowed.

Another but similar problem is the case of assets of certain enterprises, whose value is highly doubtful. Such 'assets' include claims on foreign partners in the former Soviet Union which arose as a result of special trading arrangements in the past or in the absence of proper government or bank guarantees. In addition, there are also outstanding claims in several developing countries including, *inter alia,* Syria, Iraq, Libya. In total, the outstanding claims of the Czech Republic abroad amounted to US$ 7.9 billion at the end of 1992. The implication of these unresolved questions for trading in capital markets is quite evident. The valuation of companies with unresolved outstanding claims abroad will be difficult and highly controversial, and the shares of these companies will not be traded until the matter is ultimately resolved.

Unresolved Liability Issues

Together with the unresolved ownership issues the privatisation process has been hampered by unresolved issues on the liability side of the balance sheets of non-financial enterprises. The lack of resolution on these issues means that many enterprises are burdened today with excessive liabilities which are putting them in the position of insolvency. The problem with some of these liabilities is, however, that some of them have been contracted on dubious terms and are contested by the enterprises. The liabilities can be characterised under two headings: (i) liabilities which arise from environmental damages; (ii) liabilities which arise from contracts made on behalf of the communist governments, such as the development of nuclear power technology in the Škoda works in Plzeň, etc. As in the case of unresolved ownership rights, unresolved liability issues will result in difficulties in establishing the values of companies and, consequently, in pricing shares for flotation in the market.

Shareholders' Names

Shareholding may often be highly dispersed. This is particularly the case in countries in which privatisation takes place by means of the so-called 'vouchers', which have enabled a distribution of shares across a wide spectrum of the population. The original 'voucher' privatisation was introduced first in the former Czechoslovakia and it is also the scheme which has led to the most dispersed form of shareholding. Dispersed ownership may have the disadvantage of producing an ownership structure in which no single owner has the dominating control; it may require a consolidation of ownership rights through trading of shares.

The need to consolidate shares in order to increase the concentration of shareholding raises a question regarding the publishing of the names of the (principal) shareholders. The practice of publishing names has been widely used in the Czech Republic, primarily in the context of sales to foreigners since all foreign investment deals have to be approved by the government. While understandable, the practice has meant that all foreign investment deals have automatically tended to attract much greater attention on the part of small investors who had an *a priori* greater trust for such deals than for deals which did not involve foreign investors. As a result the prices of shares have increased. There may be nothing fundamentally wrong with this system, particularly at this stage of the privatisation process, since financial and other information about companies has been rather limited. Nevertheless, there is no doubt that the publication of shareholders' names has resulted in the above-mentioned biases.

The dispersion of shares is a major issue, primarily in the Czech Republic. The reason is the greater role played by the 'voucher' privatisation in comparison with other forms of privatisation in Poland and Hungary. According to the CERGE's 'Privatisation Newsletter', the total number of companies privatised by the 'voucher' method in 1992 – outside public tenders and auctions or direct sales – was 943, which constituted 29 per cent of the total privatised business units in that year, and represented 59 per cent of the total number of privatisation projects. The numbers are much smaller in Poland and Hungary.

Trading of Unlisted Shares

The big question is also how to trade shares which are unlisted. Under present circumstances virtually all shares in the four countries remain unlisted but the issue is particularly important in countries in which shares have been acquired through the scheme, because the scheme has enabled the distribution of a large quantity of shares among a considerable number of investors and this has increased the importance as well as the scope for the trading of these shares.

As noted above, the channel through which the currently unlisted shares could be traded is, of course, the newly emerging stock exchanges in these countries. It is well known that representatives of these stock exchanges are ambitious of becoming the major markets for those shares. In practice, however, this is going to be surrounded by considerable problems, one of which is, and will be, the continuing difficulty of ascertaining the values of companies because of unresolved issues on their balance sheets, the short 'track record' of managers and of most companies, and the presence of a new competitive environment, as noted above. All this does not allow for a reliable and trustworthy credit assessment.

The alternative 'solution', which has been recently proposed in the Czech Republic, is the RM-System which has had the mandate of trading shares obtained under the 'voucher' scheme. As we have seen in section II, this involved a market-simulating approach to clear the market for shares on the basis of a computer-designed iterative process of market clearing. A similar procedure is proposed for the trading of shares acquired by individual and collective investors. However, the problem with this scheme is that it would be based only on 'bids' and 'offers' collected by the computer centre which would then find a mathematical solution without a proper and a prior assessment of the company's true credit risk. In other words, the scheme assumes that investors would have already done their background analysis on the companies – an analysis comparable to that which is required under the standard rules for the permission to float shares in established stock exchanges. It is unlikely that this analysis would be done by the computer centre itself which does not have the capacity to do so, and under the existing rules, the responsibility for the analysis and the company check has been given to the stock exchange. Moreover, in the absence of an agreement between these two institutions there is likely to be another delay in creating an efficient market place for these stocks.

Thus, what is likely to be traded on stock exchange are companies with foreign partners or wholly foreign-owned companies or companies for which there is an established 'track record'. This will greatly restrict the number of companies able to claim a sufficiently long company history to convince investors – especially foreign investors – that these are companies which are inherently 'tradeable'. As noted above, these typically will be companies with established markets abroad, in particular in the highly competitive markets in the West or companies which will have a captive market domestically. It should be also added that the number of companies is likely to vary with the maturity of each country as an industrial economy. This is the main reason for finding more of these companies in countries like the Czech Republic.

Bankruptcy

The fundamental issue – one which is related to all of the problems noted above – is the question of bankruptcy laws. The bankruptcy laws are crucially important for a normal functioning of inter-enterprise relationships in order to ensure a timely and efficient enforceability of outstanding claims. The existence of bankruptcy laws is equally important for the privatisation of public enterprises which is under way in the four countries of the region. It is clear that an effective transfer of ownership from the state to the private sector cannot be completed until all the unresolved issues of enterprises balance sheets discussed above are clarified. Until then, it will be impossible to convince any serious investor that shares offered for sale have a real positive value and/or notify them of the extent to which they must be discounted in the market. It is, therefore, not surprising that enterprise debt has increased considerably in all four countries. It is perhaps even less surprising that most of the debt has been the result of rising inter-enterprise debt as noted above. The resolution of the bankruptcy problem is extremely complex, and its related issues discussed further below are common to all four countries.

The enforcement of bankruptcy laws remains, however, a big unknown. According to independent estimates in the West, bankrupt companies could account in the Czech Republic for as much as 30 per cent of the total number of industrial enterprises. It is possible that the percentage is even higher in the other three countries. In Hungary, the total number of applications for lawsuits was about 12 000 from 1 January 1992, when bankruptcy law came into effect, until mid-1993. These figures are quite clearly extremely high, suggesting that the potential unemployment problem in these countries is equally serious. Since the political implications of the unemployment problem are also highly sensitive it is very doubtful that the bankruptcy laws will be enforced in full and without any modifications to shift the burden of debt settlement from creditors to debtors. The first indication of this process is the bankruptcy law in the Czech Republic where the original version of the law has been amended after domestic discussions lasting for more than one year.

Here are the main modifications to the original bankruptcy law: (i) a protection period of 3 months has been introduced; (ii) privatised companies cannot be taken to court for bankruptcy; (iii) agricultural farms cannot be taken to court for bankruptcy during the 'vegetation' period; (iv) in contrast to the previous draft, the law allows the sale of the whole entity of the enterprise which is under bankruptcy proceedings; (v) the amendment restricts the powers of management of companies under bankruptcy proceedings; (vi) the powers of creditors are increased (e.g. the approval of all creditors is not required in all cases).

Settlement of bankruptcies also remains unresolved. The main issue is the question of how the outstanding claims should be financed. The government is currently considering the following methods of settlements: (i) purchases of the claims by the National Asset Fund; (ii) purchases by the Consolidation Bank; (iii) debt–equity swaps; (iv) write-offs; and (v) settlements between debtors and creditors. While theoretically attractive, these methods pose a number of problems. First, the National Asset Fund is by law only a 'collector' of proceeds from privatisation and under no circumstances is it supposed to enter into management issues, let alone into collection of debts. Without appropriate changes in the law, the Fund would have to make its resources available for another institution such as the Consolidation Bank. Second, given the scarcity of resources the Consolidation Bank would have to be selective in the choice of debtors whose debts it would be prepared to finance. This amounts to a policy of 'picking winners' – a policy which the government has consistently rejected until now. Third, the use of debt–equity swaps is unlikely to be an effective instrument in view of the current regulations on banks which are stipulated in the Banking Law. The law restricts the bank holding of shares to 10 per cent of total assets of a given company. In addition, shares can constitute only up to 25 per cent of the bank's total capital and they can be held by the bank in question for up to two years only.

What all this means is that the process of bankruptcy proceedings will most likely be slow even though all four countries are seeking ways of making the process faster and more flexible. The process will be slow partly because of the likely recourse to the Chapter 11-type clause which protects debtors from creditors for a period of three months, as noted above, and in some cases even longer. The three months' protection period has already been found by some agencies specialising in bankruptcy proceedings to be too short for settlements of disputes and there will be pressures to extend it. In addition, the unresolved issues of the status of the National Asset Fund and the powers of the Consolidation Bank will also take time to settle. Furthermore, the courts are also likely to be moving slowly due to the lack of experience with bankruptcy proceedings and due to budgetary constraints. The unresolved balance sheet issues discussed further below will make restructuring costs unclear, which will discourage foreign investors and encourage green field investments instead, wherever possible. Commercial banks have also been found to take a more cautious approach – they tend to seek an arrangement with their debtors rather than their bankruptcy. A good example of these problems is Hungary. Out of the total member of 12 000 lawsuits between 1 January 1992 and the end of April, 6000 were thrown out of courts on the grounds of formal irregularities; 3000 cases have been pursued but the remaining 3000 cases are pending without any official explanations for the delay. The total number of actual bankruptcies has so far been only 'a few dozens'.

Other Unresolved Balance Sheet Issues

A great deal has already been said in the press about the shortcomings in accounting practices in the former communist countries. The countries under consideration in this present report are no exception. We have already discussed several issues concerning both the asset and liability sides of the balance sheets but there are other accounting differences which distort companies' balance sheets. For example, one of these issues is the value of physical capital which is shown in the balance sheets of firms in terms of highly unrealistic accounting values. Depreciation rates also have no rational economic meaning since they are typically set without much relationship to the real depreciation under market conditions. Balance sheets are typically not prepared on the accrual basis, distorting the picture about the enterprise financial position.

Conclusions and Some Policy Recommendations

Capital markets in the Czech Republic, Slovakia, Hungary and Poland are in the early stages of development. For that reason, the markets are extremely thin both for securities and for equities and they are at present far from fulfilling their main tasks. We have not seen so far much activity among companies to raise capital outside the banking sector nor have we seen much active interest on the part of investors to position themselves in these markets. But we have to emphasise that these are only early stages particularly since the privatisation process has not so far reached the momentum for which the presence of capital markets is relevant and important.

Nevertheless, all four countries have made considerable progress in establishing capital markets in anticipation of much greater activity in the future. They all now boast stock exchanges which are well staffed and equipped with sophisticated payment and settlement systems: they have established regulatory bodies, passed proper legislations, opened the room for the establishment of various non-banking financial institutions such as investment and mutual funds and liberalised conditions for entry into the market. Foreign banks have been able to open their subsidiaries in the Czech Republic and Slovakia on the basis of the 'national treatment' principle, and through them several have become members of the local stock exchanges. The conditions are slightly more restrictive in Hungary and Poland. In sum, the progress has been quite impressive and promises to attract considerable attention for future investors.

Initially, attention will undoubtedly focus on the mass privatisation in the Czech Republic and Slovakia. It is expected that privatisation will lead to a considerable interest in secondary trading of shares due to anticipated attempts of households to adjust their wealth portfolios and cash in their equities, and due to the attempts to consolidate effective equity ownerships. Once the round of such transactions is completed the activity in stock exchanges will be more dependent on primary trading.

With the exception of mass privatisation the establishment of capital markets and its related institutions is a necessary but not a sufficient condition for capital markets to be active. It must be said that in spite of all the progress made so far, the future of these capital markets in general, and from the point of view of foreign investors in particular, is not entirely clear, mainly because of the persisting difficulties of different kinds which constrain the operations of the markets at present. We have divided these difficulties into three main areas – problems of liquidity, problems related to the institution of stock exchange, such as the role of regulations and regulatory bodies, and problems related to unresolved issues of privatisation. The problems overlap in some instances and emphasise the interconnections between capital markets and privatisation.

Liquidity

There is no doubt that the demand for capital will be very strong in all of these countries. The report has discussed some of the major reasons why the interest to issue securities and equities in the capital markets will emerge quite powerfully both from the government authorities and from individual companies. What is far more unclear, however, is the supply of risk capital in the market. Risk capital is always in short supply but its scarcity in Central Europe will be particularly evident, partly because of the relative magnitude of demand for capital and partly because of the problems noted above.

The role of banks depends on the status of banking regulations. These currently restrict the equity exposure of banks in order to ensure their adequate liquidity as well as restrict the time exposure to equity holding in order to limit the banks' effective ownership and control of non-financial enterprises. The banks which have a significant amount of non-performing loans are unlikely to swap these loans for equity on a large scale, since they would lose seniority on their claims and would have to get involved in activities in which they can hardly claim expertise such as the management of industrial enterprises. Moreover, banks currently prefer to deal with money markets rather than with capital markets, which are less liquid.

The main actor in capital markets in the Czech Republic will undoubtedly be the investment funds. How far and how active the funds will be, however, will also depend on a number of factors. The current government regulations restrict the effective control of companies by restricting their investment exposure. If the maximum permissible share will not give them effective control, their demand for additional shares may be muted. In addition, some investment funds are themselves not very liquid and they will require access to bank credit. Furthermore, very few investment funds have so far even attempted to pool real savings of households. The scarcity of resources of investment funds could be a particularly difficult problem and will require clear and fairly liberal regulations on the part of the monetary and tax authorities regarding the provision of bank credit for the purchases of shares and the elimination of certain investment disincentives, as we have seen above in the text.

Foreign investors may face a specific constraint of another kind. Foreign investors are typically protected in these countries by domestic legislation and by bilateral investment protection treaties. These treaties have usually been concluded at a time when companies were planning direct foreign investment in the partner country. The protection of indirect investments is, however, surrounded by a certain amount of ambiguity. The access to capital markets may also be restricted. The legislative or regulatory system of investment protection would therefore benefit from a clear and non-ambiguous confirmation of policy which does not discriminate between direct and indirect investments, and one which minimises the number of restrictions (a 'negative list').

In addition, the supply of risk capital may be generally impeded by several institutional and policy imperfections. First, investors' security continues to be limited; currently it is provided primarily by real (fixed) assets. However, the value of such a security has been adversely affected by unreliable pricing of these assets. In general, the provision of security has also been affected by inadequate information about companies and by various unresolved issues regarding balance sheets of companies. Governments must ensure that adequate information is more widely available, and that matters such as those related to certain aspects of enterprise indebtedness or to liabilities for environmental damages are resolved.

Incentives for portfolio investors must also be modified. It appears that most countries in the region have focused so far on those aspects of tax reforms which related to indirect taxes and to income taxes. The result has been a considerable improvement in these tax regimes but rather serious distortions in the case of taxes affecting investment activities. The Czech and Slovak tax regimes, for example, do not properly allow for specific capital gains taxes, and as result the tax incidence from capital gains is almost prohibitive, as seen in section II. The structure of taxation of investment income is also distorted and will need to be changed. Another example of distortionary tax policies in the Czech system is the system of deductions from alternative costs of borrowing. Even though the countries have already had several amendments to original tax laws it is becoming evident that more changes will be necessary in order to attract new investors, especially households.

Stock Exchange Regulations

Valuation of securities has been one of the major problems in the limited experience so far. The reasons have been identified and they include insufficient quality of information about companies, in particular about the financial disclosures of companies. Sometimes the problem has been that independent audits have not been required. Other technical difficulties have included sectoral and other restrictions for foreign investors in all countries, a different regulatory environment for investment funds as compared to other financial entities in the Czech Republic and Slovakia, shortcomings in the enforcement of regulatory measures and the lack of incorporation of settlement and clearing systems into the European networks in all countries. The major policy question now is whether governments should not intervene through tougher regulatory standards to increase the amount of available information.

Whether the government should or should not intervene in this matter, however, is still a matter of dispute among experts. As indicated in the text, the case for more regulation has been disputed by several prominent experts who argue that more regulation will not necessarily mean more efficiency and that there is a better – that is, a more efficient – way of controlling investment activities – and that is, competition. On the other hand, opponents argue that perhaps only in mature and large markets may competition be a suitable way towards more efficient securities markets, and that regulation may be justified on equity grounds. Even though the matter has not yet been resolved and the 'jury is still out', the majority would argue for the case of an efficient regulatory network.

Privatisation

On the demand side, privatisation is a vital element of capital markets and it will therefore play an important role in the development of capital markets in the countries concerned. At present, however, privatisation may not provide a strong stimulus in their development in the initial stages. One reason is that the number of companies which can satisfy the strict conditions for quoting on the stock exchange is relatively limited. Another reason for the absence of relatively good candidates is the need for restructuring of many companies – a process which is slowed down by the delays in bankruptcy proceedings.

The difficulties in quoting shares of companies are related to problems discussed in the text – limited historical record and serious structural difficulties of many companies. Thus, the countries in which public companies are – or will be – privatised before being restructured must provide the conditions for private owners to acquire the effective ownership of these companies. This means that the conditions will have to be created for venture capital to step in where the state refused – perhaps justifiably so – to restructure the companies before their sales. These conditions must include the possibility for venture capitalists to obtain the majority or at least the dominant shareholding in those companies which need to be restructured. Thus, an information network and computer centres have to be created to provide potential investors with information about shares for sale and bids for purchases of shares. In the Czech Republic these centres will include commercial and savings banks and brokerage firms. A more efficient clearing mechanism must be established for the acquisition of the required percentage of shares. In the case of the Czech Republic, a decision will have to be taken about which of the two existing institutions will perform the trading in order to avoid inefficiencies. It should also be determined whether it is in the interest of efficient equity trading to release names of shareholders or potential investors.

These are primarily institutional issues which will need to be addressed but there are also policy issues to be considered. In constrast to conditions just noted which refer to the organisational arrangements of the stock exchanges, the following policy recommendations refer entirely to the policies towards privatisation. Thus, unresolved ownership rights issues will call for the government to decide the extent to which restitution rights can be modified and if so how and what legislative steps need to be taken. Unresolved liability issues will require that the government decides what policy will be adopted in clarifying the liabilities for environmental damages and for debts contracted by enterprises on behalf of the communist government. Prior government decisions may also be needed in situations when investors are interested only in a part of a large company that constitutes a holding of sister companies. In sum, the contribution of privatisation in the evolution of capital markets in Hungary, Poland and in the Czech and Slovak Republic is likely to be small outside the 'voucher scheme' in the beginning of the process. The markets will develop rather slowly particularly in situations that will require participation of foreign capital.

APPENDIX 2.A NON-BANKING FINANCIALSECTOR: MAIN LAWS AND REGULATIONS

Czech Republic

- 'Basic Conditions for the Admission of a Security to Stock Exchange Trading', issued by the Stock Exchange, 11 March 1993.
- 'The Legal Act of April 21, 1992, on Securities and Stock Exchange'.
- 'The Commercial Code', the Legal Act No. 513/1991, Col.
- 'The Stock Exchange Rules', issued by the meeting of stockholders of the Stock Exchange on 21 April 1993.
- 'The Regulations of the Shareholding Company – The Stock Exchange'.
- 'Regulations about the Stock Exchange Arbitration', issued by the Stock Exchange.
- Law about Mutual and Investment Funds.
- Foreign Exchange Law 528/1990 Col. and its Amendment of 22 April 1992.
- Law on Banks 21/1992.
- Law on Czechoslovak State Bank – 22/1992.

- On the Conditions of the Transfer of State Property to Other Persons, Act 92/ 1991 Col.,
- On the Emission and Use of Investment Vouchers, Act 383/1991, Col.

Hungary

- Amendments to Act XXIV of 1988 on Investment by Foreigners in Hungary (HRLF No. 1990/1, No. II/3 – 4, 1991, 15 February 1991).
- Act VI of 1990 on Securities and the Stock Exchange.
- Interim Correction to Act VI of 1990 on the Circulation of Securities and on the Stock Exchange.
- Unified Text of Act XXIV of 1988 Regarding Investment by Non-Residents in Hungary; Subsequent Amendments and Supplements (No. II/5, 1991, 1 March 1991).
- Law IL of 1991 on Bankruptcy Procedures, Liquidation Procedures and Final Settlement (No. II/23, 1991, 1 December 1991).
- Act LXIII of 1991 on Investment Funds (No. III/2, 1992, 15 January 1992).
- Law Decree No. 1 of 1974 Concerning Planned Foreign Exchange Policy and the Decree No. 1/1974 PM issued for its Execution in a Unified Contexture (No. III/19, 1992, 1 October 1992).

Poland

- Prawo o Publicznym Obrocie Papierami Wartosdowymi Funduszach Powierniczych, No. 155, 1991.

APPENDIX 2.B   IN CZECH REPUBLIC: MEMBERS OF STOCK EXCHANGE PRAGUE

ČSOB, a.s., Praha
tel. 2332000, 233200, fax 2355105, 2366959

Investični banka, a.s., Praha
tel. 2365934, fax 2368934

VŮB, a.s., Bratislava
tel. 07/3192267, fax 07/3192268

Česká spořitelna, a.s., Praha
tel. 2359311, 2362565, fax 225572, 2357918

Poštovní banka, a.s., Praha
tel. 6842532, 68425321.260, fax 6842539

Banka Bohemia, a.s., Praha
tel. 2362261, fax 264594

Ekoagrobanka, a.s., Ústí n. Labem
tel. 047/213111, 28267, 213584, fax 047/23787

Agrobanka, a.s., Praha
tel. 69107671, 156, fax 6911315

Komerční banka, a.s., Praha
tel. 2354955, 21222038, fax 2368289

Živnostenská Banka, a.s., Praha
tel. 21127000, fax 21127070

Interbanka, a.s., Praha
tel. 226668, 227886, fax 265658, 2350234

Creditanstalt Securities, a.s., Praha
tel. 206476, 206495, fax 296964

Credit Suisse First Boston Czechoslovakia, a.s.,
tel. 2317005, 2310426, fax 2317456

Crown Banking Corporation, a.s., Praha
tel. 2317936, fax 2311490

Elekta, spol, s r.o., Liberec
tel. 048/461389, fax 048/462716, 26997

EASTBROKERS, a.s., Praha
tel. 267339, fax 2327520

Zemská banka, a.s., Olomouc
tel. 068/22017, fax 068/23328

AB Banka, a.s., Mladá Boleslav
tel. 0326/21764, fax 0326/23769

ABN AMRO Holding N.V., Praha
tel. 2313330, 2313316, 2313362, fax 2313672

Banka Haná, a.s., Prostějov
tel. 0508/3558, fax 0508/21241

CAPITAL MARKET CONSULTING, spoi, s r. o., Praha
tel. 7152148, 7152518, fax 7152882

CITIBANK, a.s., Praha
tel. 3334222, 3334111, fax 3334613

CONSUS, poradenské družstvo, Praha
tel. 266285, fax 267778

COOP BANKA, a.s., Brno
tel. 05/24511, fax 05/27042

C.S. FOND, a.s., Praha
tel. 2362471, fax 2369348

Česká banka, a.s., Praha
tel. 268141, 264051, fax 262530

Českomoravská záruční a rozvojová banka, a.s., Praha
tel. 2963401, 566, fax 295825, 205983

EVROBANKA, a.s., Praha
tel. 9911093, fax 9911041

Fond národniho majetku ČR, Praha
tel. 225423 fax 261237, 260160

Harvardská burzovní společnost, a.s., Praha
tel. 7934580 – 85, fax 7934616

IC Banka, a.s., Praha
tel. 2361777, fax 2361776

ImAGe 1, a.s., Praha
tel. 701787, 703012/370, fax 701787

Investiční a rozvojová banka, a.s., Bratislava
tel. 07/490819, fax 07/56632, 59484

Investiční společnost Bohemia, a.s., Praha
tel. 877116, fax 887115

KIS, a.s., Kapitálová Investičnî společnost České
pojišťovny, Praha
tel. 2315060, fax 2310240

KOMERO, spol, s r.o., Praha
tel. 3114410, fax 3114410

Kreditní banka, a.s., Plzeň
tel. 019/272656, fax 019/276758, 272741

MERX, spol, s r.o. Praha
tel. 8535064, 8535447, fax 8535400

MORAVIA BANKA, a.s., Praha
tel. 2324183, fax 2320696

MOTOINVEST, a.s., Cheb
tel. 0166/267339, fax 0166/2139260

Oesterreicher a spol., s r.o., Praha
tel. 2362471, 2313896, fax 2357229

Podnikatelská banka, a.s., Praha
tel. 4152871, fax 4152624

Pragobanka, a.s., Praha
tel. 776842, fax 774564

PRO-ANO, spol, s r.o., Praha
tel. 2354086 fax. 2357065

RAXER, spol, s r.o. Praha
tel. 21422592, fax 21422588

REALITBANKA, a.s., Praha
tel. 6928080, fax 6921831

RENTIA, a.s., Brno
tel. 05/756363, fax 05/756363

Slovenská polnohospodárská banka, ú. s.,
Bratislava
tel. 07/215007, fax 07/215121

Slovenská štátná šporitelna, š.p.ú. Bratislava
tel. 07/2020305, fax 07/2020303

V.I.A., a.s., Praha
tel. 278254, fax 273520

Brněnské veletrhy avý stavy, a.s., Brno
tel. 05/3143101, fax 05/3142999

Česká národní banka, Praha
tel. 24471111, fax 2354141

UNION BANKA, a.s., Moravská Ostrava
tel. 069/2271, 2660, fax 069/211586

APPENDIX 2.C   LIST OF ISSUERS

Issuers of the Traded Shares:

Agrimpex Rt (Foreign trade)	Budapest, 1051 Nádor u. 22. Tel: 111-34-60 Fax: 153-06-58
Bonbon Rt. (Trade)	Budapest, 1072 Nagydiófa u.8. Tel: 121-44-31 Fax: 122-46-68
Budaflax Rt. (Textile industry)	Györ 9002 Pf. 110. Tel: (96) 15-108 Fax: (96) 11-274
Elsö Magyar Szövetkezeti Sörgyár Rt. (Beer industry)	Martfü, 5435 Pf. 43. Tel: (56) 50-633 Fax: (56) 50-448
Fönix Rt. (Trade)	Debrecen. 4025 Széchenyi u. 35-37. Tel: (52) 11-722 Fax: (52) 18-072

Garagent Rt.
(Foreign Trade)

Budapest, 1012
Márvány u. 16.
Tel: 156-72-55
Fax: 202-38-84

Hungagent Rt.
(Foreign Trade)

Budapest, 1023
Lajos u. 11-15.
Tel: 188-61-80
Fax: 188-87-69

Kontrax
Irodatechnika Rt.

Budapest, 1143
Hungaria krt. 79-81.
Tel: 251-48-88
Fax: 252-57-68

Kontrax Telecom Rt.

Budapest, 1149
Egressy út 20.
Tel: 251-48-88
Fax: 252-57-68

Müszi Rt.

Budapest, 1026
Érmelléki u. 13.
Tel: 135-05-87
Fax: 135-05-87

Nitroil Rt.
(Chemical Industry)

Várpalota, 8105
Pf.49.
Tel: (80) 72-750
Fax: (80) 72-345

Novotrade Rt.
(Holding)

Budapest, 1137
Katona J. u. 9-11.
Tel: 112-20-95
112-20-99
Fax: 111-30-30

Skála-Coop Rt.
(Holding)

Budapest, 1092
Kinizsi u. 30-36.
Tel: 118-93-61
Fax: 118-78-55

Terraholding Rt.
(Trade)

Pécs. 7623
Nagyvárad u. 1.
Tel: (72) 13-403
(72) 27-310
Fax: (72) 27-290

Zalakerámia Rt.
(Building Industry)

Zalaegerszeg, 8900
Széchenyi tér 5.
Tel: (92) 19-637
Fax: (92) 12-070

Issuers of Bonds (Traded Category):

Postabank Rt.

Budapest, 1051
József nádor tér 1.
Tel: 118-08-55
Fax: 117-13-69

Magyar Nemzeti Bank

Budapest, 1054
Szabadság tér 8-9.
Tel: 153-26-00
Fax: 132-39-13

CA Investment Fund (Listed Category)

Budapest, 1051
Nagysándor J. u. 10.
Tel: 269-07-11
Fax: 269-06-99

**Europool Investment Fund
(Traded Category)**

Budapest, 1052
Váci u. 19-21
Tel: 266-50-43
Fax: 117-91-74

**Budapest Investment Fund
(Traded Category)**

Budapest, 1052
Deák F. u. 5.
Tel: 118-62-09
Fax: 118-62-09

APPENDIX 2.D   POLAND: LISTED COMPANIES ON WARSAW STOCK EXCHANGE, 6 SEPT. 1993

	Name activity	*No. of shares* (in million)	*Book value* 30 Jun. 1993	*Market value* 6 Sept. 1993 (in million PLZ)	*Market/book value*	*P/E* 6 Sept. 1993
1	BIG bank	16.413	575 131	3 561 592	6.19	36.4
2	BRE bank	2	822 000	2 220 000	2.70	22.3
3	EFEKT trade, services	0.75	29 880	150 750	5.05	20.4
4	ELEKTRIM electrotech.	3	2 357 871	3 900 000	1.65	12.1
5	EXBUD constructions	1	430 229	1 025 000	2.38	12.5
6	IRENA glass	0.45	128 453	456 750	3.56	55.5
7	KABLE electr. cables	1	138 417	358 000	2.59	45.3
8	KROSNO glass	2.2	403 775	585 200	1.45	57.8
9	MOSTOSTAL Exp constructions	1.5	190 121	1 425 000	7.50	13.5
10	OKOCIM breweries	2.8	546 989	1 918 000	3.51	21.1

APPENDIX 2.D   *(cont.d)*

11	POLIFARB-ON					
	dye-stuff	3.06	508 452	2 493 900	4.90	23.8
12	PROCHNIK					
	garments	1.5	142 237	780 000	5.48	27.0
13	SOKOLOW meat					
	processing	1.75	365 955	600 250	1.64	43.3
14	SWARZEDZ					
	furniture	2.5	352 004	695 000	1.97	32.0
15	TONSIL					
	electronics	1.5	99 642	390 000	3.91	-
16	UNIVERSAL					
	foreign trade	15	379 849	1 132 500	2.98	150.0
17	WBK, bank	6.4	2 332 730	4 832 000	2.07	18.4
18	WEDEL					
	confectionaries	3.2	1 129 480	4 464 000	3.95	16.6
19	WOLCZANKA					
	garments	1.5	138 397	922 500	6.67	31.5
20	ZYWIEC breweries	2	388 194	1 900 000	4.89	20.0
	TOTAL		11 459 806	33 810 442	2.95	20.7

Notes

1.   This is a general problem in all former centrally planned economies. The problem is the result of poor accounting practices and it also reflects the fact that companies have not yet faced real market tests.
2.   See M. Mejstřík and J. Burger 'The Czechoslovak Large Privatization', Prague, Charles University, CERGE, Working Paper No. 10, p. 17.
3.   See, for example, Z. Drábek, 'Foreign Investment in Czechoslovakia: Proposals for Fine-Tuning Measures of Policy Reform', Prague, Charles University, CERGE, Working Paper No. 4, February 1992.
4.   As is well known, the views about insider-trading are not uniform. There is a small but increasingly growing number of experts who argue that insider-trading provides for a more efficient form of trade with shares. These views are not generally acceptable and they ignore, *inter alia*, equity considerations. More importantly, however, this is a general issue of regulation and the extent to which it should be used as a control mechanism. The alternative to regulation is competition. See, for example, W.J. Baumol, S.M. Goldfeld, L.A. Gordon and M.F. Koehn, 'The Economics of Mutual Fund Markets: Competition vs Regulation', cf. O. Kýn, 'The Market with Vouchers and Investment Funds', The Fifth CERGE Lecture on Practical Aspects of Privatisation, Prague, 6 February 1992.
5.   The conditions of the stock exchange are stricter than the conditions set by the Ministry of Finance.
6.   See M. Mejstřík and J. Burger, 'Voucher Privatization: Its Building Blocks in the CSFR,' *Privatization Newsletter in Czechoslovakia*, Prague, CERGE, No. 3, January 1992.

7. See *Central and Eastern European Bulletin,* 30 July 1992.

8. See *Hospodářské noviny,* Burzovní noviny, No. 11, 27 September 1993.

9. See Group of Thirty Publications, 1990 M Street, N.W., Suite 450, Washington, 20036.

10. The total debt of the non-financial sector was much higher – 94.2 billion Czech crowns at the end of the third quarter of 1992, or US$ 3.2 billion. The difference was the so-called 'secondary' indebtedness, i.e. the inter-enterprise debt. To some extent, of course, the secondary debt would, under normal circumstances, have to be replaced by primary debt.

11. The typical costs to the client in the RM-S market are: 5 Kc to purchase the trade form, 30 Kc to give the instruction to buy or sell, 8255 Kc for settlement of the transaction and 0.5% of the transaction amount exceeding 1 million Kc. The comparable costs of the transaction in the stock market are: 0.25% of the transaction, payment to the broker in the range of 0.6%–3% of the settled amount and a fee of the Centre of Securities (unknown). These figures come from an interview with Mr L. Sticha, director of RM-S in Svobodne Slovo, 27 April 1993.

12. See M. Durina, 'Jak ziskat finanči zdroje', *Hospodářské noviny,* 15 July 1993.

13. The dangers arising from the lack of regulations about disclosures and mergers and acquisitions are well understood in this part of the world. Docent Pavlat, who has been one of the main leading forces behind the establishment of the Prague Stock Exchange, has recently complained about the absence of rules to protect small investors and about the need to have a public discussion about the actual rules. See *Rudé právo,* 19 April 1993.

14. See, for example, a comparison in *Central European,* May 1992. The source refers to the Czechoslovak tax schedule before the tax reform of January 1993. Nevertheless, the reform did not lead to such changes that would fundamentally alter the conclusion.

15. These problems included, for example, political instability and lack of monetary and financial control.

16. For a review of the Polish and Hungarian privatisation programme, see, for example, Ben Slay, 'Poland: An Overview', and M. Marrese, 'Hungary Emphasises Foreign Partners', both in *RFE/RL Research Report,* vol. 1, no. 17, 24 April 1992.

17. As of the end of September 1993, the agreement existed on 195 companies of the target of 600.

18. See, for example, the Polish Security Commission Information Handout, 1993.

19. Two other groups of impediment to foreign investments should also be noted – legal and administrative restrictions and the lack of infrastructure. For details, see, for example, Z. Drábek, *op. cit.* See also the discussion of taxation and policy issues in the textbook.

Part II

Case-Studies

3 Key Issues in Czech and Slovak Banking: A Central Banker's Perspective
Miroslav Kerouš

I INTRODUCTION

In comparison with the many previous years of rigid development, the banking sector in the former Czechoslovakia underwent substantial and rapid changes during the period 1990–2 as an important part of a broad transformation process from a centrally planned economy into a market economy. The enormous range and speed of these changes have been stimulated by enormous demands from other economic sectors for financial services.

The establishment of a two-tier banking system in Czechoslovakia took place prior to any financial restructuring of the banking sector. The balance sheet of the former central bank (Státní Banka Československá) was transformed into the three ensuing commercial banks, which have taken over all original claims and liabilities of the former central bank to enterprises and to the public sector. Another four existing banks entered the new market conditions with their current portfolios.

The commercial banks have faced difficult strategic choices in the transitional period of the economy. The main factors influencing the formulation and implementation of the banks' credit policies were as follows:

The economic and financial situation of the banks' clients has direct implications for the quality of the loan portfolio. In this respect, the process of transition brought many complications in bank–client relations. For example, many clients have faced a myriad of problems, in finding new markets after the collapse of their traditional markets in Eastern Europe or in adapting to the growing competition in the domestic market. These problems have been compounded by the enterprises' management skills and motivation being predominantly oriented towards administrative procedures and to hidden speculations about ongoing privatisation. The longer this process continues, the more the banks can expect a negative impact from the process on their clients' credit performance.

Capitalisation and the technical and professional capacity of the banks represented at the start of the banking reform great internal barriers to banks' development. The existing banks were undercapitalised – the average capital/total assets ratio was 0.85 per cent – they had weak loan portfolios, as we shall see in section IV below, and they employed staff educated and experienced in a non-competitive and centrally planned economy. The newly established banks could use only the limited human resources of the traditional banks or the human resources from non-banking sectors with little professional training. The shortage of skilled staff negatively influenced the quality of credit appraisal, the loan approval process and other banking procedures related to clients.

Government policy concentrated from the beginning of the transition on the opening of the economy to private initiative. It has resulted in a broad process of privatisation based on different kinds of privatisation methods. Many of these projects have been financed by bank loans. With regard to macroeconomic policies the government of CSFR tended to favour an orthodox monetaristic policy with a very cautious approach towards industrial policy and a support of particular economic sectors. The banking sector was, therefore, no exception. The government's approach was based on the presumption that all sectors are in an equally difficult economic situation and that the banks' management should mobilise their own resources rather than rely on government support. It has been feared that government support might lead to a moral hazard for the banks and their clients.

The monetary policy of the central bank was primarily oriented towards stopping the inflationary spiral typical for countries in a transition period. The result of this policy has been relatively low inflation – 10 per cent in 1990, 53.6 per cent in 1991 under the impact of price liberalisation, and 11.5 per cent in 1992 (all in terms of consumer prices). The central bank implemented its monetary policy by utilising mainly direct instruments (ceilings on interest rates and credit volume). These instruments were removed in 1992 after the opening of a clearing centre for all inter-bank payment transactions and the settling of these transactions on the books of the central bank. This was one of the important measures that have given the central bank the opportunity to start to manage the money supply by using refinancing auctions and other operations on the open market.

Legal authority and the professional capacity of the banking supervision has been built since the beginning of the banking reform. The legal foundations of the banking reforms, the Law on the Central Bank and the Law on the Banks and Savings Banks issued by the federal parliament in 1989, authorised the central bank with the responsibility for banking supervision. Nevertheless, the central bank needed about one year for the familiarisation and incorporation of the basic supervisory procedures, the elaboration of new basic accounting standards and prudential rules, and the organisation of the information flows that are required for banking supervision. The adoption of these measures has resulted in tightening the conditions for banking business and the requirements for establishing new banks.

The complex issues of the banking sector noted above highlight the extremely difficult situation in which the banks found themselves in the beginning of the reform period. Of course, a complete analysis of the banking development is not possible within the context of this chapter, the scope of which is to focus on several key problems of the banking development process, particularly with regard to credit policies of commercial banks. Other relevant issues of the banking sector are elaborated in Chapter 4 and Chapter 5 in this volume.

The present chapter is organised as follows. The second section presents some facts about the development of the banking sector in the period 1990–2 and it gives basic information about the rapid growth of the sector. The third section elaborates the changes in the commercial banks' credit policies, and this is followed by a discussion of the problem of 'old' non-performing loans in section IV. The next two sections pay attention to the role of banking supervision (section V) and governmental policy towards the commercial banks (section VI). The special issue concerning the efficient payment system is evaluated in section VII. Finally, the chapter addresses lessons from the recent banking reforms in the former Czechoslovakia in section VIII.

The author is convinced that the experience of the Czechoslovak banking reform might be helpful for countries that have started banking reforms later. However, these lessons should be considered very carefully in view of specific conditions of individual countries. Moreover, many elements of the Czech and Slovak banking reform remain untested and particularly the years 1993 and 1994 have been a very difficult period, in which the ability of banks to assist firms in their restructuring will be tested.

The last remark refers to the time period covered in the chapter. Attention is paid to the period between 1990 and 1992, i.e. the last three years of the former Czechoslovakia. Nevertheless, I have also included a discussion of some issues of 1993, but because of the break-up of the former Czechoslovakia, these relate to the Czech Republic only.

II THE DEVELOPMENT OF THE BANKING SECTOR IN 1990–2

The reform of the banking sector in Czechoslovakia in 1992 was initiated in January 1990 by splitting the mono-bank Státní Banka Československá

(SBCS) into the classic central bank (Státní Banka Československá) and three commercial banks (Komerční Banka, Investiční Banka, Všeobecná Úvěrová Banka). In the early stages of the reform the entire banking sector consisted of the central bank, six commercial banks totally owned by the state, i.e. those three previously stated, two (Czech and Slovak) savings banks and one small bank specialising in foreign exchange operations (Živnostenská Banka). There was only one other commercial bank, which took the form of a joint-stock company (Československá Obchodní Banka) in which the capital majority was owned by the central bank as the representative of the state.

The simple ownership structure changed during the period under consideration as well as the number of banks operating in the former Czechoslovakia. The peak of the banking boom was reached in 1991 when the number of banks tripled; in 1992 the dynamic of the launching of new banks went down but still remained very high (136 per cent), as we can see in Table 3.1.

Of the 38 new banks established after January 1990, 22 banks were founded without foreign participation and the remaining 16 were founded with the participation of foreign capital. The banks with foreign participation started in the credit business but they still have a very small share of the market. In 1991 these banks provided 7.9 billion CSK in loans (1.1 per cent of total credits), and in 1992 their activity increased threefold to 22 billion CSK (2.7 per cent).

The growing banking sector has been hiring a larger number of employees. The entire banking sector (including the central bank) started in 1990

Table 3.1 Number of commercial banks (licensed banks already launched in banking operations)

	1.1.90	1990*	1991*	1992*
Banks owned by the state	6	6	8	3
Joint-stock companies without foreign participation	1	4	15	26
Banks partly foreign owned	–	1	6	8
Banks entirely foreign owned	–	–	4	7
Branches of foreign banks	–	–	–	1
Total	7	11	33	45

Source: Survey of development of banking and insurance, December 1992, State Bank of Czechoslovakia.
*End of the year.

with about 26 thousand employees, and by December 1992 it employed 55.6 thousand, in comparison with the past. However, in comparison with Austria and West Germany where there were 8.8 and 9.8, respectively, banking employees per 1000 citizens at the end of the 1980s, this ratio was in Czechoslovakia only 1.6 in 1989 and still only 3.6 at the end of 1992. A similar development has taken place with regard to the expansion of the banking network. In the beginning of banking reform, the commercial banks operated 266 branches, mostly in the regional centres. Only the two existing savings banks had a broader network of about two thousand small offices across the country. By the end of 1992 the banks were offering their services through 412 branches and 3828 small offices.

The expansion of new banks squeezed the market share of the original seven banks. Nevertheless, in 1992 the original banks still kept in their balance sheets about 68 per cent of credits of the commercial banks and more than 88 per cent of bank deposits. Allowing for the items drawn from their balance sheets and transferred to the newly established Consolidation Bank in the spring of 1992, these older, primary banks generated more than 81 per cent of bank credits and about 91 per cent of deposits. This shows that

Table 3.2   Structure of credits by main sectors

Client base	1989	1990	1991	1992
	(billions CSK)			
State	457.6	454.5	489.0	458.1
Cooperative	73.2	75.3	86.3	75.6
Private	–	3.4	71.4	214.6
Households	46.9	49.9	55.4	66.4
Total	577.7	583.1	702.1	814.7
	(in percent)			
State	79.2	77.9	69.6	56.2
Cooperative	12.7	12.9	12.3	9.3
Private	–	0.6	10.2	26.3
Households	8.1	8.6	7.9	8.2
Total	100.0	100.0	100.0	100.0

Source: Financial Statistical Information, December 1992, State Bank of Czechoslovakia.

the influence of these older banks on the development of banking credit policy was still substantial at the end of 1992.

Since 1990, the banks have faced substantially different conditions for their business in comparison with the past. This has placed considerable demands on the skills and knowledge of their staff, especially in the first years of this period. The different economic environment shifted the structure of the client base towards the private sector.

III THE MAIN FEATURES OF THE BANKS' CREDIT POLICY IN THE TRANSITION PERIOD

The transition of the economy to standard market conditions created a new environment for the commercial banks, in which the old credit policies and procedures were not sufficient to build and maintain sound loan portfolios and balance sheets of the banks. After the creation of the two-tier banking system most of the managers of both traditional and newly established banks have understood the changes in the industry and tried to manage their credit policies in a considerably more prudent fashion in order to minimise credit risk and to avoid losses from non-performing loans. In this respect the desire of banks to enter the international banking community played a positive role in strengthening bank credit policies.

One of the first steps applied by the traditional banks was the *renegotiation of old credit contracts*. This process started early in 1990 when it was obvious that the old system of fixed interest rates was over. The banks faced a strong resistance from enterprises which were trying to keep their credit contracts unchanged and maintain the interest rates at the original level, in the range of 2 to 6 per cent. In many cases the banks took the restructuring of old companies into new ones as a pretext for the renegotiations of the old credit agreements. This policy of the commercial banks was accompanied during the second half of 1990 by the suspension of loans on permanently revolving inventories, as we shall discuss further below.

Another important tendency in credit policies has been *the banks' efforts to ensure that loans are as secure as possible*. During 1990 and 1991 the banks renegotiated most of the old contracts and secured their loans with fixed assets, real estates and other kinds of property. Practically every new application for credit has been accepted only when secured by the property of debtors or by the guarantee of a third party. Sound securitisation has certainly assisted in improving the quality of banks' loan portfolios. However, the policy has proved to be a difficult barrier for many new private entrepreneurs trying to get credit from banks.

As we can see in Table 3.2, the most visible feature of banks' credit policy has been their *reorientation towards private clients*. The banks supported the government's efforts and the expectations of the public to give priority to the development of the private sector, but of course, not fully. The banks were not able to satisfy all loan applications and many proposals were turned down. The author's interviews with bankers made in the autumn of 1992 showed that there was one approved proposal for approximately every five applications in the case of domestic banks and about ten applications in the case of foreign banks, which are more cautious than domestic banks. Notwithstanding the rapid growth of loans to the private sector, the banks' credit policy has been criticised from time to time by the public and by the government for their policy of collateralisation.

The fast growing portion of credit to the private sector does not entirely diminish the importance of credit extended to state enterprises, which still represents more than one half of the banks' total outstanding loans. *Relations between state enterprises and the banks have undergone substantial changes.* Enterprise debt owned to the banks has been secured as much as possible by mortgages, liens, stocks or in equity. The management of enterprises has lost the avenue of political pressure for receiving new credit – the most powerful method of credit rationing in the former regime – since banks significantly increased their negotiating strength in comparison with the past.

Nevertheless, the heritage from the former economic regime is still very powerful and the banks are, particularly in their relations with enterprises, in a position of captives of their debtors. They hold totally or partially secured debts and in theory they could take over the property or, in many cases, the whole of an enterprise. However, they do not have the staff and skills to take over the management of enterprises. This has been the main reason for the very cautious approach by banks in resolving the issue of non-performing loans to state enterprises.

The cautious approach has also been influenced by the government's hesitation with regard to bankruptcies. The bankruptcy law was issued in September 1991, but its full implementation has been postponed twice. Under the limited power of that law it was impossible to declare bankruptcy if the firm was insolvent, so many state enterprises that were technically bankrupt did not close down but continued to survive.

One of the results of the credit contracts renegotiations and the newly implemented credit policy has been *the radical change in the loan structure in favour of short or medium term loans*. Because of considerable uncertainty about economic conditions the banks have preferred credit applications with short (up to 1 year) and medium (up to 4 years) maturities.

With the start of privatisation the banks have begun playing an important role in *offering credit facilities for privatisation*. They have been encouraged to deal with these loans when the central bank excluded the privatisation loans from the credit ceilings applied up to mid-1992. Both trends can be demonstrated as in Table 3.3.

The core of the trends discussed above reflects the changes in the loan portfolios of the traditional banks. Many of those trends are relevant for new banks as well, particularly the structure of credits preferring short or medium term maturities and the concentration on private firms, of course. Nevertheless, the situation of newly established banks is rather different in comparison with the traditional banks.

The important difference is mainly *the difficult access of new banks to the primary deposits, particularly to the long-term ones*. The new banks have been entering the market, which consists of two dominant collectors of savings from the public (Czech and Slovak Savings Banks) and several large-sized credit banks with long-term banking relations with both collectors and distributors of savings. It is apparent that the traditional banks and the savings banks have been definitely holding, in that respect, a strong competitive advantage. The savings banks in each republic have felt a certain responsibility concerning their dominant market position and have been providing funds to the new banks. However, the amount of deposit that the savings banks could make available to the new banks was limited. This was partly due to

Table 3.3   Maturity structure of credit (billions CSK)

Type of credit	1989*	1990	1991	1992
Short-term credit	123.5	161.6	272.1	299.5
– for small privatisation	–	–	0.8	1.1
– for large privatisation	–	–	–	1.1
Medium-term credit	77.7	97.3	129.7	204.9
– for small privatisation	–	–	12.9	16.5
– for large privatisation	–	–	–	6.3
Long-term credit	367.8	321.2	300.3	310.3
– for small privatisation	–	–	4.5	8.3
– for large privatisation	–	–	–	6.4
Total credit	569.0	583.1	702.1	814.7
– for small privatisation	–	–	18.2	25.9
– for large privatisation	–	–	–	13.8

Source: Financial Statistical Information, December 1992, State Bank of Czechoslovakia.
*Data refer to 31 March 1990.

the fact the savings banks launched very ambitious credit programmes of their own with the goal of becoming competitive with the traditional credit banks. In addition, they could deposit only limited amounts of their resources in each of the new banks on prudential grounds.

With the aim of increasing their share in primary savings most of the new banks began to offer new banking products such as savings books, certificates of deposit and banking bonds. This strategy has a limited success because the traditional banks offered similar products but were able to use the larger branch networks.

The central bank was aware of the problem and it tried to support the new banks through its refinancing facilities. This liberal refinancing policy of the central bank made available additional funds for new banks but the price of those funds was very high. Following its tight monetary policy the central bank could offer only a limited volume of refinancing funds whose prices were fixed in regular auctions. Since 1993 the rules for the auctions have been changed when the central bank discovered that several banks were becoming increasingly dependent on central bank refinancing. At present, any bank can borrow at most 50 per cent of offered auction funds, and the refinancing credit shall be less than 20 per cent of banks' credits to non-banking clients and less than threefold of paid-in capital of the bank.

The above discussion describes three ways of raising credit funds and it shows how the system could deliver more expensive money to small new banks while the savings banks and traditional credit banks had access to cheaper resources (deposits). This was a force which pushed the interest rate level of new banks' credits upwards and made the loan portfolios of these banks more vulnerable.

Another specific problem also related to the credit policies of new banks is *the credit exposure to the banks' shareholders*. The credit policy of new banks whose equity funds have been raised by a limited number of shareholders (mostly by private firms) is very often under pressure from those shareholders to provide credits in their favour. There are several small banks with loan portfolios burdened with too large a portion of credits provided to shareholders or to other firms that are tightly connected to the banks' shareholders. The reaction of the banking supervision to this problem will be discussed in section V of this chapter.

In reviewing the problems of banks' credit policies *the interest rate policies of commercial banks* should also be mentioned. In particular, the problem of high banking margins has been repeatedly discussed. The data related to this problem are shown in Table 3.4.

The high bank margins are typical for countries undergoing a rapid development of the banking sector, particularly in situations when

Table 3.4   Bank margins (in percent)

Interest	1990	1991				1992			
rate		I	II	III	IV	I	II	III	IV
Credit	6.2	14.7	15.1	14.2	13.9	13.5	13.7	13.6	13.3
Deposit	2.8	7.6	8.2	8.6	8.0	8.7	6.9	6.6	6.6
Margin	3.4	7.1	6.9	5.6	5.9	4.8	6.8	7.0	6.7

Note: The interest rates refer to the average nominal interest rates of credits and deposits. They may not be fully consistent with data in Table 4.4 below due to updating.
Source: Financial Statistical Information, December 1992, State Bank of Czechoslovakia.

commercial banks have to be recapitalised. It is also known that inadequate competition among commercial banks and/or within the entire financial sector will lead to the widening of bank margins.

The level of bank margins is considered too high by Czech and Slovak government officials as well as by representatives of entrepreneurs. A similar opinion was expressed by Begg and Portes,[1] who do not recommend the widening of bank margins as the appropriate primary solution in restructuring the weak balance sheets of banks. But the prevailing 'help yourself' approach favoured by the government as regards the recapitalisation of banks and the need for investment in the bank infrastructure created a strong pressure in keeping the bank margins high. The central bank in that respect kept silent and did not issue any regulation, believing in the gradual growth of competition among commercial banks themselves and from the emerging subjects of the non-banking financial sector (See Drabek, Chapter 2 in the present volume).

IV   THE PROBLEM OF 'OLD' NON-PERFORMING LOANS

The problem of non-performing loans was not discussed at the time when the banking reforms were under preparation but the issue was raised immediately after the reforms were launched. The first discussions included proposals for cleaning the balance sheets of the banks, but in 1990, when the economic situation was relatively stabilised and the government was occupied with other aspects of the economic reforms, there was not sufficient interest in dealing with the problem. The Czechoslovak authorities started to consider the problem more seriously in 1991 when

Table 3.5   The estimated volume of old non-performing loans at the beginning of 1991

Types of loans	CSK billions
Loans on revolving inventories	169
Investment and commercial loans	120
Dubious export loans to LDC	27
Housing loans	30
Social loans	30
Loans on nuclear plants	12
Loans on projects in USSR	12
Total	400

Source: Working papers of SBCS and author's calculations.

the reform package was implemented. Inflation and interest rates went up and the debtors – the state enterprises and cooperatives – signalled that they were unable to service their debt. Since that time several attempts have been made to estimate the magnitude of the non-performing loans in the balance sheets of the banks. For the purposes of this chapter it might be useful to introduce one estimation that was calculated at the beginning of 1991, shown in Table 3.5.

This estimate does not have much analytical value and should be considered only as a 'rough' estimate, according to which non-performing loans represented about two-thirds of the banks' loan portfolios. Other estimates are much lower; the lowest represents about one-third of the total loans.[2] At that time (1990–1) the wide range in the calculations was the result of aggregating the selected titles of loans that were considered primarily as non-performing. The estimations produced by the banks themselves suffered from a subjective approach and could be exaggerated because of the expectations of the banking management about possible support from the state budget. There was no further relevant and reliable data up to the second half of 1992 when banking supervision implemented the standards for classification of the loan portfolios.

The directives issued by the Banking Supervision Department of the central bank laid out the definitions of standard and classified assets. Standard assets are those in which the interest and the principal are normally paid and the creditor has no doubts about the debtor's satisfactory financial situation and/or the debt is sufficiently secured. Classified assets were defined as:

- non-standard assets, that have well-defined 'negative parameters' – for instance, loans that have not been repaid minimally 30 days after maturity;
- doubtful assets, that are not reliably secured – for instance, loans that have not been repaid minimally 90 days after maturity or claims on clients who have fallen into bankruptcy;
- loss assets, whose repayment is unlikely and insufficiently secured – repayment has been overdue for more than 360 days.

Using these standards the banks have classified their assets at the end of 1992 as shown in Table 3.6.

It should be stressed again that the first output of banking statistics relating to the classified assets should be used very cautiously. The data may not be fully reliable in view of banks' limited experience with the new evaluation methods. Further correction of these numbers might be expected after the auditing reports of the banks' balance sheets have been submitted. Also comparing Tables 3.5 and 3.6 might be misleading: the estimation from 1991 refers to 'old' non-performing loans while the 1992 figures include 'all' non-performing loans, including the new ones. The second difference concerns the loan portfolio of the Consolidation Bank (92bn CSK) that is not included in Table 3.6. On the other hand, the loan portfolio of the Consolidation Bank might not be assumed to be totally non-performing – the first evaluation of that loan portfolio done by the staff of the Consolidation Bank in the Czech Republic in the first half of 1993 classified only about 20 per cent of total loans of that bank as non-performing!

The activities undertaken to tackle the problem of non-performing loans have been done in several steps and none of them has been considered by the authorities as the solution to the entire problem. It is worth noting that

Table 3.6 Classified assets, 31 December 1992

Classified assets*	CSK billions
Non-standard assets	86.1
Doubtful assets	29.5
Loss assets	17.5
Total classified assets	133.1

* *For definition, see the text above.*
Source: Data from the Banking Supervision Department of the CNB.

the authorities had no comprehensive list of measures that should be taken in order to solve the problem. On the contrary, they tried to avoid any exaggerated expectations of banks and of their clients that government might write off all non-performing loans. In practice, each exercise was presented by the authorities as the final one to deal with the problem.

The chronology of these steps is as follows:

(a) The Conversion of Administratively Defined Loans to Commercial Loans In the autumn of 1990 the government cancelled the legal background for obligatory title of credit on 'permanently revolving inventories' (PRI). This decision was made to make it possible for the banks to adjust the administratively prescribed interest rate of 6 per cent to the market level. On 1 January 1991, the central bank set the discount rate at 10 per cent and the ceiling on the credit interest rates of commercial banks at 24 per cent. The increase in interest rates from 6 per cent to 18 per cent or 24 per cent threw many enterprises into difficulties, inter-enterprise debt went up very quickly and the government was exposed to strong pressure from business managers and the political opposition.

(b) The Establishment of the Consolidation Bank In March 1991 the government established a special agency into which about 50 per cent of credits for PRI of cooperative firms and 80 per cent of the credits for PRI from the state firms was transferred. The Consolidation Bank took over CSK 110 billion of these loans from the banks and obtained the resources to cover these loans mostly from long-term refinancing facilities of the savings banks and from the central bank. As for these enterprises, their former debt at 6 per cent interest rate and an uncertain maturity has been changed into liabilities with a 13 per cent interest rate and an 8-year maturity. Since that time, the Consolidation Bank has taken care of its ordinary debt service. The debt is slowly being repaid and at the end of 1992, the Consolidation Bank held CSK 92 billion of these loans on its balance sheet.

(c) The Supporting Activities of the State Budget Because of its cautious budgetary policy, the government has not been sympathetic to the idea of large budgetary spending to finance the writing-off of the non-performing loans. The government initiative has been highly limited in this respect. It spent 2.6bn CSK for the reconstruction and liquidation of the inventories of the military industries, 1.5bn CSK for covering the losses of enterprises with frozen foreign assets in countries under international embargoes and about 10bn CSK which the

government promised for covering the losses and debts that have emerged due to the devaluation of the domestic currency at the end of 1990.

(d) Debt Write-off Financed by National Property Funds   At the end of 1991 the three National Property Funds (NPFs), the specialised financial institutions (Czech, Slovak and Federal) responsible for the administration of privatisation proceeds and property, used part of their actual and expected revenues from privatisation to strengthen the balances of the banks with old non-performing loans. The transaction was financed by the issue of five-year bonds by the National Property Funds with the face value of 50 billion CSK at the central bank's discount rate. These bonds are redeemed from the privatisation revenues of the NPFs. The bond issue had two purposes:

(1) to write off old non-performing loans in those enterprises that had a chance to recover after this clean-up operation. The selection was placed in the hands of banks and a special advisory committee was established that was composed of representatives from ministries, the central bank and the NPFs. The committee went through the list of selected enterprises and made appropriate recommendations to the individual banks. This method enabled the write-off of about 35bn CSK of the debts.
(2) to recapitalise banks with the aim of increasing the banks' capital and thus supporting the banks' ability to write off further debts if needed. The operation required about 15bn CSK and it had a beneficial effect on the capital adequacy of the four major banks.

The evaluation of the benefits of these measures is not uniform among the Czech economists. Positive assessments can be contrasted with more frequent statements to the effect that the debt write-off has not produced the expected results, i.e. a substantial reduction in enterprise insolvency and in inter-enterprise debt. The main reason for such poor efficiency was probably the very broad selection approach of the banks. The banks did not have sufficient courage to concentrate the scarce resources on a limited number of enterprises generating insolvency among their suppliers. On the contrary, the banks tried to spread the rationed resources over too many enterprises. The reasons for that approach were probably the long-term personal connections between the bank credit officers and the business managers. The banks preferred small-scale debt write-offs tailored for many debtors rather than large-scale debt write-offs provided only for a limited number of key debtors. For this reason, the spread of their resources into many small write-offs did not bring the desired effect.

(e) The Purchase of Old Non-performing Loans by Specialised Agencies   With the expected full implementation of the bankruptcy law, government and banking circles appeared hesitant about the full impact of the law on enterprises and on banks. For this reason the authorities sought ways of avoiding the so-called 'domino effect', i.e. a chain reaction of bankruptcies. In this case the Czech government seems to be following the approach of the former federal government, that is, financing the debt by the resources of the NPF, rather than by the state budget. Proposals were most frequently focused on using the NPF's financial facilities for the support of trade in classified assets and for the subsidisation of losses suffered by financial firms specialised in purchasing and trading these banking claims.

Another proposal foresaw a trading role for the Consolidation Bank (CB) in the market with non-performing banking assets. It was suggested that the Consolidation Bank should purchase the non-performing banking loans to bankrupt enterprises up to a maximum of 75 per cent of the face value of the loans. The CB would try to sell these assets in the market. Whenever the CB realised a better sale price than the purchase price, it would declare a profit; whenever it got less, the NPF would finance the loss.

Discussions and decisions about these proposals appear more difficult than the previous measures. The ownership structure of the banks has changed substantially. The classified assets are not only those with roots in the period before 1990, but also those after, and also many companies and banks are now in private hands. The decisions are therefore more political than ever before, because any government measure of the kind discussed above is confronted with different interests of banks.

It appears that the representatives of the World Bank were right when they recommended undertaking the cleaning of the balances as early as possible while property was mostly in the hands of the state. With the diversified ownership of debt-ridden companies and the banks holding the non-performing loans, the administration of this process becomes more difficult and the use of public money for this purpose becomes more questionable.

On the other hand, the early large-scale write-off did not guarantee that the traditional banks that are entering the emerging markets would be able to keep their loan portfolios clean in the long term. The pessimists argued that such generous rescue actions might weaken the banks' own effort and that they might even raise the banks' expectations about the readiness of the government to undertake such measures in the future, if necessary.

V THE INFLUENCE OF BANKING SUPERVISION ON THE BANKS' CREDIT POLICY

At the beginning of banking reform the central bank set up the first prudential rules and the first simple conditions for the foundation of new banks:

- *capital requirement for the foundation of new banks:* 50bn CSK;
- *capital adequacy rules:* total capital/assets ratio for the banks founded before 1.1.1990 set at 2 per cent, for savings banks at 1 per cent; for banks founded after 1.1.1990 at 8 per cent;
- *liquidity rules:* for the ratio between domestic currency – the medium and long term credits and medium and long term resources were set at maximum 125 per cent.

The highly general and liberal prudential rules brought the central bank a great many problems during 1990–1, mainly in handling the licensing agenda. Seven new banks got their licences in 1990 and a further 25 in 1991. Insufficient banking services, the excess demand for credit and, of course, high margins earned in the banking business created a strong impetus for the founding of new banks. Trying to restrict entry of the weak banks, the Central Bank increased the minimal level of the required banking equity from 50 million CSK in 1990 to 300 million CSK (about 10 million US dollars) in 1992.

The opening of new banks has had positive effects: slowly growing competition and an importation of foreign know-how. On the other hand, the growing number of banks has not found the required quantity and quality of human resources in the labour market and this fact has led to a very strong demand for people with banking skills. The new banks, especially the domestic ones, have had to hire many people without banking experience and it has influenced the quality of banking services, banking management and also the quality of the relations between banks and the central bank.

The new Acts on the Central Bank and on the Banks, which came into effect in February 1992, put into the hands of the banking supervisors more authority and responsibility. Several prudential rules were introduced directly in the law, and in other cases the central bank was authorised to issue the legal regulations in the form of directives. At the end of 1992 the banking sector in Czechoslovakia worked under the basic prudential rules approximating international standards:

(a) *Minimal capital requirements:* 300 million CSK (10 million US dollars),

(b) *Capital adequacy:* A capital/risk weighted assets ratio shall reach 6.25 per cent by 31 December 1993 and 8 per cent by 31 December 1996 at the latest.

(c) *Credit risk exposure:* A set of rules has been implemented to limit the credit risk exposure towards different kind of clients:
- towards one client or an economically connected group of clients, the maximum is 40 per cent of the bank's capital by the end of 1993;
- towards a bank in Czechoslovakia and OECD countries or towards an economically connected group of debtors made up of only these banks the maximum is 80 per cent of bank's capital by the end of 1995;
- towards an entity with a special relationship to the bank or legal entities in which the bank has 10 per cent or more of the initial capital participation, or which the bank has under its control, the maximum shall be 30 per cent of the bank's capital;
- the total volume of credit risk exposure on its 10 largest debtors or economically connected groups of debtors shall not exceed 230 per cent of bank's capital.

(d) *Liquidity:* As for liquidity, the banks are obliged to ensure that they are able to keep their commitments at maturity – that means the maturity structure of the obligations shall be consistent with the maturity structure of the claims. The detailed rules have been issued in particular for open foreign exchange positions.

The implementation of the rules on capital adequacy has promoted the banks' efforts to create capital reserves that could be used for writing off their loan losses. In 1991 a standard for the creation of reserves was set at a percentage of the extended credit. In 1992, after the issuance of the guidelines for credit evaluation, banking supervision, with the approval of the Ministry of Finance, recommended rules to the banks for establishing provisions of (i) non-standard assets at 20 per cent of the accounting value, (ii) doubtful assets at 50 per cent and (iii) loss assets at 100 per cent, and rules for the establishment of reserves for general and undefined risk.

In 1992 the situation of the entire banking sector was as follows:

– Total banking assets:	1492.3bn CSK
– Capital	33.5bn CSK
– Reserve funds	37.0bn CSK
– Reserves	26.5bn CSK

The above figures demonstrate the progress made in strengthening the banks' capital base. The capital and reserves / total assets ratio reached 6.6 per cent and that means the banks have created a certain shock absorber which may be used in the process of recovering their portfolios. As regards the size of the non-performing assets it is certain that their recovery will proceed over the long term in a step-by-step process rather than a one-time write-off of all non-performing assets.

The Central Bank has made visible progress in licensing and supervising banks. Most of the basic prudential rules for the banks have been introduced with a grace period for the banks' adjustment. Issued prudential rules together with an implemented system of reporting and supervising have had significant positive effects on the decision-making process within the commercial banks. For instance, an audit based on international standards required by the banking supervision for all banks has stimulated the banks into improving their accounting, internal auditing and credit management.

VI GOVERNMENT POLICY AND THE COMMERCIAL BANK CREDIT

Since the beginning of banking reforms the government and the banking sector have been relatively independent despite the fact that all the large commercial banks continued to be state enterprises until their privatisation at the end of 1992. The government has lost the power to decide which or how much credit a certain bank or banks should give to their clients. Government influence has been reduced to personal contacts, lobbying and other methods of stimulation, plus some influence gained from the significant ownership share within the large-sized traditional banks (about 40 per cent of equity in the Czech Savings Bank, Komerčni Banka and Investični Banka).

The government continued to subsidise the interest rate of certain kinds of credit that had social implications; for instance, credit for housing co-operatives and for individual homebuilders and also credit programmes for the young and for newly weds. But since 1990 the government has reduced these subsidies significantly, which suppressed initiatives of the banks in these areas and they practically stopped issuing new credit at non-commercial interest rates. In 1993 the government of the Czech Republic refused to subsidise these loans from the budget and parliament approved a subsidy of 6bn CZK (Czech crowns) financed from the revenues of the National Property Fund.

The great uncertainty associated with loans issued to big state enterprises has led banks to require government guarantees. The government has been relatively cautious in this matter because a ceiling on the volume of these guarantees has been set by parliament and the government was under the impression that the banks were willing to bear only small risks.

On the other hand, the banks' desire for guarantees from the government sharply decreased after their first experience with payment when a financial agreement failed under the terms of the guarantee. They recognised that the government is more interested in renegotiating a guarantee for newly revolved loans than in payment of the one in effect.

To support greater access to loans for those debtors with insufficient collateral, the government has initiated the establishment of loan guarantee institutions. The Czech government, together with several of the biggest banks, founded the Czech Guarantee and Development Bank in January 1992 with the main goal to issue guarantees for privately owned companies. This guarantee bank, with a capital of 1.1bn CSK and total assets of 3.3bn CSK, initiated several guarantee and support programmes for small and medium enterpreneurs. In 1992 the bank provided more than 500 credit guarantees with a volume of 1.5bn CSK and about 950 cases of interest rate subsidies (from 4 to 7 per cent items) with a volume of 0.6bn CSK. A similar institution, the Slovak Guarantee Bank, has been developing its activities in the Slovak Republic since 1991.

The obstacles to a broader influence for these institutions are the relatively small guarantee capital and the slow and complicated administration process. More information about this topic can be found in Dědek's paper (Chapter 5 of the present volume).

A third guarantee institution, the Export Guarantee and Insurance Company (EGAP), was set up for securing and insuring export claims. At the end of 1992 it began to insure short, medium and long term export contracts against commercial and political risks. Nevertheless, already in the first half of 1993 it was clear that a broadly oriented and more powerful institution for export financing was needed. Now the Czech authorities discuss the different possibilities of establishing the Export-Import Bank, either through the expansion of the EGAP or through the creation of a new specialised bank which would be initially closely connected with the central bank.

The last indirect government influence on the banks' credit policy worth noting, is its relation to banking reserves. In spite of the verbal support for improving balance sheets of the banks, the government has been keeping a careful eye on the balance of its budget to which it gives the highest priority. The Ministry of Finance even blamed several banks for creating too high reserves in 1991 and in 1992 and thus avoiding payment of taxes and required the banks to refund the excess back to the state budget. These requests, in the amount of several billion CSK (5bn in 1991, 6bn in 1992), have been made in a highly arbitrary fashion with the goal of obtaining additional funds for the state budget. The reactions of the banks in question differed depending on their ownership structure and on the progress in the privatisation process. While in 1991 several banks agreed to pay the additional taxes, in 1993 the two newly privatised commercial banks successfully refused to meet any additional payment requirements of the Ministry.

It is hoped that the above-mentioned conflicts can be avoided in future by more precise rules for banks than those which have existed. One of these rules is in the area of taxation and it defines the maximum volume of the banking reserves that can be deducted from the taxation base. It pegs this volume to an amount of:

- a maximum of 10 per cent of the average amount of credit claims which have not been paid within the agreed maturity,
- a maximum of 2 per cent of the average amount of credit claims with a maturity longer than 1 year,
- a maximum of 2 per cent of the average amount of supplied guarantees,
- all claims on any clients going through the bankruptcy process.

Those rules are established in law which also enables the banks to negotiate with the taxation authorities a higher deduction of reserves than the law specifies.

VII THE PAYMENT SYSTEM

It is a common experience from economies in transition that immediately after the introduction of economic and banking reforms the payment system becomes the most stressed section of the banking business. The poor performance of the banks' payment systems is one of the reasons for the growing number of insolvencies of companies, especially those just beginning their operations, and it results in strong criticism of the banks by the public.

The payment system in the former Czechoslovakia began with a relatively developed system based on the ABO system (Automated Banking Operations) implemented and used since 1980 within the SBCS and on the separated payment systems of the other four banks, which were allowed to operate at that time. The banks' payment systems used to be utilised mostly for payments among the institutions, and only the two savings banks offered current accounts for individuals, with very limited services. After the banking reforms, the Central Bank and the other three ensuing banks had to share the ABO system which has been maintained by the Central Bank. There was no multilateral clearing and settlement for all banks. The development of a payment system during the banking reforms can be seen in three stages.

In the first stage, from 1990 to mid-1992, the rising number of banks and their banking clients brought an extremely rapid growth of banking accounts as well as payment settlements. The banks were in the difficult position of deciding how to serve the demand for opening new accounts for private entrepreneurs and households, especially the great demand for the opening of foreign exchange accounts. The banks' response to these demands was limited by the capacity of the existing payment systems and by the lack of qualified staff. The most stretched were foreign exchange payments, because the experienced staff was mostly concentrated in the banks that were formerly specialised in that business while other banks had to train their own staff. The most critical period was 1991 when the amount of clients and transactions, especially with foreign countries, increased fifty to sixty times among the biggest banks. It was the time when payments to and from abroad needed several weeks or months to be settled.

The second period began in 1992 when the Central Bank implemented the clearing of all bank transactions through the Clearing Centre and the settlement on books of the Central Bank. The improved payment and clearing procedures of the commercial banks made it possible to shorten the time for moving payments from one client to another. At present, the several big banks are able to provide domestic payments within their own network in one day. When the payments go to a client of another domestic bank they need a minimum of three days (all banks and the Clearing Centre, too, need one day to provide the payment). The payments in foreign currency take longer. The best banks state that they are able to provide those payments approximately within 8 to 12 days, but there are still cases that need more time, particularly in situations in which the relationships between the banks conducting the transactions are not yet firmly established.

The third period began in the second half of 1993, when the old ABO system was removed and all banks using that system implemented their own payment systems. This action has opened more possibilities for the supply of banking payment services, which had been limited by the old ABO system. We expect that the banks that are the cornerstones of the banking sector will become more flexible and will offer many more new services. We expect that the banking sector will focus on these serious problems that concern the future development of the payment system. For instance, it remains to be decided whether to invest in a payment system based in cheques or to concentrate on the implementation and development of the paper-less products such as card systems and on-line transaction systems.

Reviewing the history of the payment systems in the process of the banking reforms in Czechoslovakia, we reach several conclusions:

(1) The ineffective underdeveloped and accordingly slow and inefficient traditional payment systems need time to adjust. During the period of adjustment there will be a shortage of banking capacity for opening and maintaining accounts and for making reliable payment transfers. The typical reaction of clients, especially entrepreneurs who are vitally dependent on prompt money transfers, is an orientation to cash payments which offer faster and more certain payments despite the lower security connected with that type of transactions. Of course, there are also other reasons for the growing preference for cash, for example the use of 'dirty' money or tax evasion.

(2) The great stress under which the banks had to operate in this period of growing demand for payment services has led to an inability of the commercial banks to cooperate effectively on the elaboration of a new general payment system. When all the banks were concentrating on their own payment problems, there was still only one authority – the Central Bank – that could prepare and implement the needed clearing system. The decision of the Central Bank at the beginning of 1991 to make the investment in the Clearing Centre was very useful and made progress in that area.

(3) The establishment of the clearing centre by the central bank has not completely determined further developments of the payment system. Emerging problems, such as the securities payment transactions and their clearing, might require the development of locally based and private clearing systems in addition to present systems.

(4) It has been confirmed that the biggest progress has been made in the banking markets where competition has been functioning. It has been the corporate banking on which most banks have focused. On the other hand, in retail banking most business is still controlled by the two

Republican savings banks and development in customer services has been delayed. It seems that the splitting of these massive and less flexible saving banks into several competitive retail banks could have had a more supporting effect on the development of retail banking, including the payment systems.

VIII LESSONS FROM RECENT BANK REFORMS IN THE FORMER CZECHOSLOVAKIA

The development of the banking sector in the former Czechoslovakia can be evaluated as relatively successful in the period 1990–2. In spite of the expanding number of commercial banks and their range of operations there were no banking failures requiring intervention by the central bank or the state authorities. The reason for this can be explained as follows:

– The initial structure of the reformed banking sector was based on a relatively small number of large banks creating the core of the sector and the entries of new banks into the sector have been under the control of the continuously improving banking supervision by the central bank.
– The relatively tight and prudent budgetary and monetary policy did not allow an extreme expansion of banking credit. The initial small number of pivotal large banks allowed the Central Bank to implement monetary policy directly through negotiations and gentleman agreements with the top managers of these banks.
– The relatively strong independence of the central bank and the commercial banks from government influence saved the banks from the political and governmental pressures concerned with the easing of the banks' credit policy.
– The unwillingness of the government to promise a total and once-for-all recapitalisation of the banks at the beginning of the banking reform induced banks to seek their own measures for securing the loan portfolios and the fast implementation of standard credit evaluating methods.
– The establishment of National Property Funds as institutions financially independent of the state budget enabled the use of revenues from the privatisation for recovering the balance sheets of the banks without using taxation revenues or budgetary deficit for financing that need.

It should be added that the above-mentioned experience offers several *negative* lessons too:

- The retention of a significant part of the non-performing loans and the balance sheets of the original large banks and the insufficient capital base for write-offs of these loans pushed the banks to revolve the credit lines and to accept only interest repayment with an aim to avoid failure of the client, especially the big companies.
- The strongly oligopolistic structure of the banking sector in the initial period of the banking reform exposed the new, mainly domestic banks into a high dependence on credit facilities provided by savings banks and the central bank. The difficult access to the primary sources pressed their credit interest rates up and it increased the riskiness of their credit contracts too.
- The weak activity of the banking supervision at the beginning of the banking reforms allowed the emergence of several small banks whose capital strength and the quality of the staff were high, but their credit activities grew dynamically and often not sufficiently prudently, many times under pressure from the corporate banks' shareholders who expected preferences in credit rationing and tended to influence the management of their banks in that way.
- Every postponement or lengthening of the privatisation process in Czechoslovakia, a country in which privatisation has proceeded relatively fast, preserves the banks' traditional behaviour towards their non-performing clients. Also the postponement of a full effectiveness of the bankruptcy law has had a negative influence on the payment discipline of debtors.

The evidence indicating progress in the banking sector achieved in the former Czechoslovakia in the period 1990–2 must be assessed very carefully. From a current point of view, it was only comparitively recently that the banks were adjusting to standard market conditions, and the consequences of the banking reforms are not yet apparent. More important and significant systemic changes continue. The new tax, social and health insurance reforms were implemented in 1993, and individual shareholders, investment funds and other kinds of institutional investors have received the shares obtained through the first wave of voucher privatisation. In addition, two capital markets have started to operate and expand, and the bankruptcy law is effective. The cumulative effect of these systemic changes have become more evident since mid-1993. The future development of the banking sector will become perhaps even more complicated than any time before, particularly in connection with growing competition within the entire financial sector.

Notes

1. D. Begg and R. Portes, 'Enterprise Debt and Economic Transformation: Financial Restructuring of the State Sector in Central and Eastern Europe', CEPR Discussion Paper no. 695, June 1992, London.
2. CSFR Financial Sector Review, World Bank, Memo, 31 March 1991.

4 Capital Accumulation for Long-Term Economic Growth in the Czech Republic
Jan Klacek

I INTRODUCTION

Any long-term economic forecast for an economy in transition from a centrally planned regime to a market-type one has to address the shape of transition proper as well as the development issues that are partially interlinked and partially represent a new phase that follows. The fundamental institutional changes in the economy combined with a completely new international environment within which the changes are effected tend to produce uncertainty and, indeed, indeterminacy as regards the feasible paths of economic growth and development which are expected to start once macroeconomic stabilisation is achieved.

On the other hand, given the dimension of present economic depression in the Czech Republic, the need to analyse the conditions not only for economic recovery but also for long-term economic growth cannot be stressed enough. As extrapolations of past trends are almost useless in the face of rapid change in all economic structures, one can resort to the analysis of the starting conditions for economic growth experienced by other economies that have been subject to more or less similar economic, political and social upheavals in the recent past and managed to generate relatively fast economic growth. These are the newly industrialised countries of the Far East, and Spain and Portugal in Europe. All these countries had to reform their economic development. They could be taken as reference points, though the Czechoslovak case differs in that the initial level of industrialisation was high. On the basis of this analysis some scenarios could be derived – both optimistic and pessimistic – for a country like the Czech Republic.[1] In this respect the author draws on studies by Rollo and Stern (1993), Summers (1992) and the Economist Intelligence Unit (1993). These approaches are modified as far as the required capital accumulation is concerned; allowance is made for obsolescence of the existing capital stock, and the issue of domestic accumulation of capital is introduced. Two implications are then discussed:

(1) for the financial sector to generate sufficient domestic savings and channel them to new investments;
(2) for fiscal and monetary policies to adopt a more active role in initiating and shaping the process of economic growth.

II PROSPECTS FOR ECONOMIC GROWTH AND CAPITAL ACCUMULATION

The scenarios of future economic trends can be derived when the necessary and sufficient conditions to begin a catching-up process in the countries of Central Europe are clarified. Under optimistic assumption, Rollo and Stern postulate the process of catching-up for former Czechoslovakia, Hungary and Poland to start in 1993–4, peaking in the late 1990s and then decelerating up to 2010 (see Table 4.1).

Under this scenario – probably more deductive than realistic – CSFR could reach the GNP level of Spain by the year 2010. The imperatives for capital accumulation required to start a catching-up with the EC economies are, however, demanding. Under this optimistic scenario, assumptions on the availability of capital and on the catching-up potential are based on a forecast that the sum of foreign official and private financing flows to six countries of the region of Central and Eastern Europe would reach US$33.7 bn by 1995, i.e. roughly 2 per cent of the countries' GNP. Later in the 1990s, the foreign capital inflow is assumed to be stopped and reversed. Hence, the capital accumulation must be based primarily on domestic sources. As a reference point one may take the estimated DM 750 bn of investment required for East Germany up to 2005 to catch up with West Germany by 2005.

If we take the optimistic scenario as a basis for more realistic projections of the catching-up process the forecasts must reflect more adequately:

Table 4.1   Optimistic scenario for economic growth in CSFR, Hungary and Poland (annual average growth rates of GNP)

	1991–1995	*1995–2000*	*2000–2010*
CSFR	0.6	10.0	5.0
Hungary	2.0	10.0	5.0
Poland	1.9	10.0	5.0

Source: Rollo and Stern (1992).

(1) the possibilities for using initial capital stock in the future;
(2) the rate of scrapping due to obsolescence in technological, ecological and economic terms of existing structures and machinery equipment;
(3) the resulting incremental capital–output ratio (ICOR).

If a greater part of the initial capital stock proves to be obsolete and subsequently is scrapped, the value of ICOR will be high and can reach the level of, say, 4, at least in the first phase of the catching-up process (see Tables 4.2 and 4.3). On the other hand, if the bulk of the initial capital stock can be employed further, the calculated value of ICOR for the 1990s will be much lower, around 2. In any case, the required increment in the fixed capital stock for the CSFR could be estimated in the range of US$400–540 billion (in 1991 prices). A corresponding figure for the Czech Republic after the split of Czechoslovakia is US$300–400 billion.[2]

Table 4.2   Intensity of turnover of machines in the manufacturing sector of the Czech Republic
(in percent)

	1981–85	1986–90
Gross investment Fixed capital stock	6.93	6.45
Replacement investment Fixed capital stock	1.44	1.40

Source: D. Hanzlová, 'Evaluation of the Starting Conditions of the Privatized Companies in Manufacturing Sector of the Czech Republic', *Finance a úvěr*, June 1993.

Table 4.3   Average fixed capital turnover period and average age of machines in the manufacturing sector of the Czech Republic
(in years)

	Average turnover period		Average age
	1985	1990	1990
Manufacturing	25	26	10.0
Chemical industry	30	31	11.2
Machinery and electronics industry	27	29	10.3

Source: As for Table 4.2.

The value of ICOR coefficient of 4 does not seem too high in the light of other forecasts. For example, Lawrence Summers (1992) in his forecast for East Central Europe in the 1990s projects 3–4 per cent GDP growth rates with a given investment rate of 20 per cent. The implied value of ICOR is in the 5–7 range. In this respect, it is not so much the shortage of capital but a very low return to capital that may represent the major bottleneck.

The emerging picture for the longer-term economic prospects of the economies in transition seems to be that of a wide spectrum of possible outcomes. A successful entry into the process of catching-up will be determined also by the rate of technological advance. The rate of technological advance depends on the human capital, availability of resources for accumulation, on investment policy (embodied technological change) as well as on institutional factors promoting the adoption and introduction of innovations by enterprises (disembodied technological change).

Here we have to distinguish between the process and product innovations of predominantly domestic origin and the effects of technological change stemming from the spillovers from the most advanced economies. Both the propensity to save and the introduction of systemic changes conducive to fast assimilation of technological and managerial know-how will differ among the countries of Central and Eastern Europe. The traditional assumptions behind the theory of economic development can be applied with due attention to the specifics of a transition period. This is reflected in the latest Project Link World Outlook (1992) forecasting a strong growth of investment starting from 1993 onwards only in three countries of the region.

Hence the reform of the financial sector should be viewed from the standpoint of whether it makes the sector responsive to the need of the mass-scale accumulation of capital and whether the financial sector will be capable of channelling new savings into new investments. This raises the issues of time structure of credits and level of interest rates.

III   DEBIT, CREDIT AND DISCOUNT RATES

The necessary investments in the new fixed capital and human capital should be stimulated by the appropriate interest rate policy of the banking sector. However high interest rates and credit squeeze have been typical components of restrictive monetary policies in the economies in transition. Had the interest rates been lowered by the monetary authorities, demand for credit by firms and households would have increased. This would have stimulated the growth of aggregate demand above the level to which it was depressed at the time of stabilisation. Lower interest rates would undoubtedly make the financial position of the new, mostly private firms, less critical. Thus, a higher level of economic activity in the Czech industry, currently at 40 per cent below its 1989 level, could have been reached as economic recovery would have eventually closed a three-year-long period of negative rates of economic growth.

As it is well known, more significant is the indirect Keynesian multiplier effect that is brought about by the increased wage income and the corresponding higher aggregate money demand generated by the initial increase of demand on the part of wage earners. The initial increase of aggregate money demand induces further increments of output through the higher sales of subcontractors, higher wage incomes of workers employed by them, etc. Finally, when the chain reaction is completed, the total increment of aggregate demand is equal to the multiple of the initial injection. The chain reaction can continue for as long as the capacity (or, more realistically, the potential output) constraint allows.

The most serious arguments behind the calls for interest rate cuts are those in favour of economic recovery. Determination of the interest rates by the commercial banks proceeds as follows. Banks tend to maximise a difference between the costs and the revenues subject to certain constraints. If we leave aside the other non-credit transactions the costs incurred are the interest paid to clients (deposit interest rates) and the interest payments to banks by debtors (lending interest rates) represent the revenues.

Looking at the data we find that in May 1993 the average deposit interest rate on all deposits of the banking sector of the Czech Republic reached 14.8 per cent annually (see Table 4.4).

While in the last quarter of 1990 the difference between the borrowing and lending interest rates – the so-called interest rate spread – amounted to 4.3 percentage points, in May 1993 it reached 7.8 percentage points. The deposit rate declined and the lending interest rate was increased in spite of a sharp deceleration of inflation. However, the level of the average deposit interest rate was lower than both the actual and expected rates of inflation. As the expected rate of inflation for 1993 ran at about 19 per cent, the banking sector and especially the saving banks gained from the negative real interest rate on their deposits. This tendency towards a negative real interest rate is likely to be reversed in 1994 when inflation is expected to decelerate close to a single-digit rate.

High profits of banks in the period of 1991–3 have been partially financed by the *de facto* devaluation of the stock of savings of households and the stock of companies' financial assets. This conclusion is drawn on the aggregate level of the banking sector and by implication the position of individual banks may differ.

Table 4.4 Average lending and deposit interest rates of commercial banks
(percent)

Czechoslovakia

	1989	1990				1991				1992			
		I	II	III	IV	I	II	III	IV	I	II	III	IV
Credits (lending rates)	5.7	5.4	5.4	5.6	7.6	14.7	15.1	14.2	13.9	13.4	13.7	13.6	13.3
Deposits (deposit rates)	2.5	2.6	2.6	2.8	3.3	7.6	8.2	8.6	8.0	8.6	6.9	6.6	6.6
Margin	3.2	2.8	2.8	2.8	4.3	7.1	6.9	5.6	5.9	4.8	6.8	7.0	6.7

Czech Republic

	1992				1993					
	I	II	III	IV	I	II	III	IV	V	VI
Credits (lending rates)	13.9	13.4	13.4	13.2	13.7	14.2	14.4	14.6	14.8	14.8
Deposits (deposit rates)	7.9	6.7	6.1	6.3	6.8	6.9	7.2	7.3	7.5	7.0
Margin	6.0	6.7	7.3	6.9	6.9	7.3	7.2	7.3	7.3	7.8

Note: The data may not be fully consistent with data in Table 3.4 above due to updating.
Source: Czech National Bank, Financial Statistical Information.

What was underlying this interest rate policy was the expected wave of bankruptcies by both state-owned and privatised companies and the resulting negative impact on the balance sheets of the banks. The banks claim they will have to write off some loans, allocate more funds into reserves and they expect that their profits will shrink. Nevertheless, most analysts of the developments in the banking sphere more or less agreed there was an absence of effective competitive pressure (see, e.g., OECD Survey on Czech and Slovak Federal Republic, 1991). This is evidenced by the extremely high profits of banks, the low standard of banking services and the limited range of banking products. As the main source of these profits was the spread between the banks' lending and borrowing interest rates, the argument was that just due to the low competitive pressure these spreads could be maintained significantly higher than the customary 1–2 percentage points on competitive money markets of developed economies.

While the banks' profit margins showed a decreasing tendency in the course of time, the interest spreads mostly further increased, though in a diverging rate across individual banks. Hence there is scope for a reduction in the lending rates by commercial banks without any impact on the deposit rates which are in fact negative in real terms. However, the scope for the central bank to function as a price maker on the money market seems to be rather limited nowadays. The discount rate determined by the Board of the Czech National Bank applies directly only to refinancing credits the central bank provides to commercial banks. The share of these credits in the total amount of credits extended is estimated to represent 12 per cent. But even if the central bank were the price maker in the money market and a lower discount rate made a standard for all credits by the commercial banks,[3] the fundamental issue of adequate funds to match future demand for credits remains open.

Formation of the new domestic savings has been disproportionately low compared to the need for massive new investment into manufacturing industries, infrastructure, education and the health sector. In addition, the rate of savings by households has been declining since January 1992 (see Table 4.5). The lack of domestic savings will persist, unless the economy enters a phase of robust recovery. In the meantime, the inflow of direct foreign investments may prove decisive but any over-optimistic expectations about the extent of capital inflow are unlikely to materialise. Hence, the sources of accumulation of capital are to be found primarily in the domestic economy.

In this context economic policy measures stimulating a higher propensity to save, cautious budget deficit financing and institutionalisation of the state debt should be considered. Exchange rate policy generating current account surplus through undervalued domestic currency is beneficial for the balance of payments but should also be viewed from the longer-term perspective; the present current account surplus represents export of scarce

Table 4.5   Rate of savings of households in the Czech Republic, 1992–93
(in percent, monthly rates of increase)

	1	2	3	4	5	6	7	8	9	10	11	12
1992	16.7	22.4	11.4	11.1	11.9	11.9	11.3	12.0	10.8	10.4	9.7	11.1
1993	-5.9	1.1	3.5	5.6	6.1	6.1	6.5	7.2	6.8	7.4	8.1	10.6

Note: Data on savings include time and demand deposits, cash balances, deposits on hard currencies account and securities bought by households. Incomes are defined as disposable money incomes (after taxes) by households.
Source: Czech National Bank.

domestic savings. In the short run, both monetary and fiscal policies should result in lower lending rates of interest by the commercial banks. New forms of savings like savings for housing, pension schemes and corporate savings should be encouraged.

IV   THE ROLE OF FOREIGN INVESTMENT IN THE CZECH REPUBLIC

Though domestic capital is to be stimulated as the major source of capital accumulation, the role of foreign investment is significant, too. Foreign direct investment (FDI) may bring both modern technology and managerial skills to the countries in transition. That is why the impetus for the unleashing of supply side responses in the current stage is being associated in all the transition economies with the progress of privatisation and with the hoped-for increased flows of foreign direct investment. The Czech Republic might be expected by this reasoning to be heading for an efficiency and performance 'leap' in the near future. Although the economy was almost entirely 'socialised' by the late 1980s, with no private sector and negligible foreign investment, the situation has been recently reversed in both respects. As the process of privatisation of state-owned domestic industry picked up momentum at the end of 1991 and in 1992 in particular, the opportunities opened up for foreign investors, including the acquisition of existing Czechoslovak firms.

The legislation governing joint-ventures and FDI has undergone a significant liberalisation in the last few years, and the regime is already mostly deregulated, including profit and capital repatriation. A promising trend in FDI in Czechoslovakia is reflected in Table 4.6.

This record in FDI, however, fell short of that in neighbouring Hungary with an inflow of US$900 million and 1500 million in 1990 and 1991, respectively. Czechoslovakia, and the Czech Republic in particular, nevertheless ranks among the top priorities of foreign investors. This was reflected by the recent upgrading of the Czech Republic to investment grade by Moody's and the Standard and Poor's as the only country in transition to a market-type economy.   The most important examples of foreign direct investment in Czechoslovakia are shown in Tables 4.7, 4.8 and 4.9.

V   CONCLUSIONS

(1) The reform of the financial sector should be viewed in the context of whether it makes the sector responsive to the need of the mass-scale

Table 4.6   Foreign investment in Czechoslovakia 1989–93
(in US$ millions)

1989	1990	1991	1992	1993
256	181	607	1085	550

Source: Czech National Bank.

Table 4.7   Major FDI in Czechoslovakia

Name	Year	Product	Foreign participation	
			Country of Origin	Share
Dow Chemicals Co.-ChZ Šokolov	1992	Chemicals	US	36%
Volkswagen-Škoda Mladá Boleslav	1990	Cars	Germany	31%
Siemens-Škoda/ Energo	1992	Energy	Germany	67%
LIAZ and Mercedes	1992	Vehicles	Germany	31%
SIOT*	1992	Pipelines	Italy	n.a.
Philip Morris-Tabák	1992	Tobacco	US	30%
Siemens-Škoda	1992	Vehicles	Germany	51%
Rhone Poulenc-Chemlon	1992	Chemicals	France	52%
Nestlé/BSN-Čokoládovny	1992	Food	France	43%
US West-Tesla	1991	Telecom-munications	US	n.a.
Glaverbel-Sklo Union Teplice	1991	Glass	Belgium	n.a.
Air France-Czechoslovak Airlines	1992	Transportation	France	40%
Linde-Technoplyn	1991	Gas	Germany	n.a.
Procter and Gamble	1991	Detergents	US	100%
Volkswagen-BAZ Bratislava	1991	Cars	Germany	80%
Renault-Karosa	1993	Buses	France	60%

*The deal has been concluded with the Czech government.
Note: The abbreviation n.a. means that data are not available.

Table 4.8 Total foreign investment in Czechoslovakia by country origin (end of 1992)

Country	% of total
Germany	39
USA	21
France	14
Austria	7
Belgium	7
Others	13
Total	100

Source: Czechinvest.

Table 4.9 Total foreign investment in Czechoslovakia by industries (end of 1992)

Industry	% of total
Vehicles and transport equipment	26
Construction	14
Foodstuffs	11
Banking	10
Others	39
Total	100

Source: Czechinvest.

accumulation of capital and whether the financial sector will be capable of channelling new savings into new investments.

(2) The sources of accumulation of capital are to be found primarily in the domestic economy. Economic policy measures stimulating higher propensity to save, combined with cautious budget deficit financing and with measures to institutionalise the state debt are to be considered. The present current account surplus represents export of scarce domestic savings. In the short term, both monetary and fiscal policies should be used to lower lending rates of interest by the commercial banks. New forms of savings like savings for housing, pension schemes and corporate savings should be encouraged.

(3) The role of foreign investments is significant, too. Foreign direct investment may bring both modern technology and managerial skills to the

countries in transition. The Czech Republic might be expected to be heading for an efficiency and performance 'leap' in the near future.

Notes

1.   The scenarios for future economic growth were derived for Czechoslovakia. After the split of the federal state the long-term conditions for the Czech economy to complete the transformation and to catch up with the EU countries have improved.
2.   GNP of the Czech Republic is forecast to increase three times by 2010 when GDP is expected to reach US$200 billion (in 1991 US$). The value of ICOR is assumed to be high, with a gradual decline from 1995 on.
3.   In June 1993 the Czech National Bank reduced the discount rate from 9.5 to 8 per cent which was followed by only marginal reductions of the lending rates by the commercial banks.

References

Begg, D., *Economic Reform in Czechoslovakia: Should We Believe in Santa Klaus?*, London: Centre for Economic Policy Research, 1991.

Bohatá, M., Pohled na výkonnost dnešních průmyslových podniků, *Politická ekonomie*, 1, 1991.

Economist Intelligence Unit, *Czech Republic: Country Forecast, 3rd Quarter 1993*, London, 1993.

Griffith-Jones, S., A. Marr and A. Rodriguez, 'The Return of Private Capital to Latin America; The Facts, an Analytical Framework and Some Policy Issues', paper for Forum on Debts and Development (FONDAD), The Hague, 1992.

Hare, P. and G. Hughes, *Competitiveness and Industrial Restructuring in Czechoslovakia, Hungary and Poland*, London: Centre for Economic Policy Research, 1991.

Klacek, J., 'The Role of Industrial Restructuring in Economic Reforms in Czechoslovakia', Conference at The University of Southampton, 1991.

Klacek, J., 'Longer-Term Prospects for the Countries of Central and Eastern Europe', Conference on Perspectives for the World Economy up to 2015, The Hague, 1992.

Memorandum to the International Monetary Fund, *Týdenîk Hospodářských novin*, 13, 1991.

OECD, Positive Adjustment Policies: Managing Structural Change, Paris: OECD, 1983.

OECD, *Economic Survey of the Czech and Slovak Federal Republic*, Paris, 1991.

Rollo J.M. and J. Stern, *Growth and Trade Prospects for Central and Eastern Europe*, London: National Economic Research Associates, 1992.

'Scénář ekonomické reformy', *Hospodářské noviny*, 4, 1990.

Summers, L., 'The Next Decade in Central and Eastern Europe', in C. Clague and G. Rausser (eds.), *The Emergence of Market Economies in Eastern Europe*, Oxford: Blackwell, 1992.

5 Problems of Financing Small and Medium-Sized Enterprises in the Czech Republic
Oldřich Dědek

I INTRODUCTORY REMARKS

This chapter endeavours to address seemingly simple interrelated questions: How does the financial sector in the Czech economy, itself undergoing the deep process of transformation, contribute to the growth of small and medium-sized enterprises (SMEs)? Does the flow of funds from financial intermediaries to the SME sector match the priority attached to the promotion of the latter? Are there any major gaps in the financial infrastructure which slow down SME performance? What is and should be the role of government agencies and particularly their money in the process? Do established channels direct government funds to SME borrowers in an efficient way or is there room for recommending better solutions?

Many economists would argue that the SME sector provides important public goods, which are conducive to the healthy development of an economy:the creation of employment opportunities, the founding of entrepreneurship, enhancement of the competitive environment and innovative capacity of the economy.[1] As the growing body of literature suggests market forces may not provide for an optimum level of public goods. For this reason, the SME sector may fill the gap and may need to be encouraged.[2]

As the first period of economic reform in the former Czechoslovakia was about to start, considerable attention was paid to sociological arguments. Some economists asked who was the force behind radical economic reform: a workforce corrupted by non-existent unemployment and low and stable prices, an exuberant and powerful state bureaucracy, or the emerging middle income group of craftsmen and small businesses.

Later on, when the privatisation process took off, the main SME issue centred around the access of small and medium business to the large-scale privatisation scheme.[3] According to a government scenario, which focused on the fast restoration of property rights, incumbent managers of state-owned enterprises were expected to propose and elaborate privatisation projects. As a result, proposals to conserve existing production units would have prevailed. On the other hand, many people argued that a breakup of big units into smaller parts, or sales of liquidated firms to emerging entrepreneurs, would become a more efficient way of promoting SME development. The pressure finally opened the way to the possibility of preparing competing privatisation projects.

At the start of 1993, another controversial issue attracted the attention of the general public. The government was blamed for the fact that, with the introduction of the sweeping tax reform, the total tax burden had reached extremely high levels, notably in the SME sector. There is some empirical evidence about adverse effects on small businesses, which was reflected in the high number of exits from the sector.[4]

The above episodes document several dimensions of the problem of the SME development in transition economies. A complex analysis should cover topics, along with those already mentioned, such as dissemination of information for SMEs, the role of advisory and consulting agencies, technical assistance extended in the so-called technology parks and incubators. Furthermore, the importance of broader underlying factors such as macro-economic stability, with a non-inflationary environment and a stable exchange rate cannot be emphasised enough. The SME issues have to be seen against the stringent need to restore financial discipline of large enterprises that are plagued by bad debts (see Kerouš in Chapter 3 above); against the introduction of private ownership of banks and other financial institutions (see Drábek in Chapter 2 above); against the need to master business skills on the part of all economic agents and to complete a legal and juridical framework for a market-oriented economy, including the establishment of a regulatory framework.

Viewed from this perspective, some commentators may consider the subject of this chapter, which concentrates mostly on financial issues, as unduly restrictive. Nevertheless, the questions which we are going to address lie at the core of the topic, as financial problems do represent a special source of concern for SME development. (see Table 5.1).

The chapter is organised as follows. The following Section II reviews some facts from the past and recent history in order to emphasise the relatively small importance of the SME sector until the early 1990s. Section III identifies factors which influence the supply of commercial credit to the SME sector. Section IV evaluates the credit guarantee scheme operating in the Czech Republic. The general lack of long-term financing brings out the importance of development banking and venture capital facilities. These

Table 5.1   Impediments to faster growth of small firms
(results of a survey of small entrepreneurs)

Bad legislation, directives	87.6
Financial problems	66.8
Underdeveloped infrastructure	57.6
Unskilled employees	55.8
Business premises	53.6
Problems on demand side	49.3
Problems on supply side	46.7
Local authorities	45.3
Monopoly of state sector	43.4
Lack of contacts, experience	38.8

Note: Represents percentages of answers stating definitely yes or probably yes.
Source: *Hospodářské noviny*, 3/1992.

issues are discussed in Section V and VI of the chapter. The final section (VII) addresses the question regarding the role of government in the SME development process and the way in which government money should be channelled to the SME sector.

II   SOME FACTS FROM PAST AND RECENT HISTORY

The importance of the SME sector in the Czech Republic is better understood when we take into account the broader historical perspective. In the former Czechoslovakia the communist regime was one of the most orthodox in fighting 'the remnants of bourgeois capitalistic society' by means of a massive nationalisation programme. In the late 1940s, not only large and medium enterprises were targets for waves of nationalisation but also small private business was almost liquidated.

The shrinkage of the small business sector, in terms of both the number of units and people employed, is shown in Table 5.2. Beginning in the 1960s, only a limited number of self-employed traders survived.

Table 5.3 shows that the pace of forced socialisation in agriculture was equally vigorous. The so-called socialist sector with its two basic forms (cooperatives and state estates) continuously grew bigger, acquiring more than 90 per cent of arable land.

During the socialist episode the Czechoslovak economy closely followed the logic of the centrally planned economy based on large-scale production. The bias in favour of large-scale production plants, fostered for the convenience of planners rather than on the grounds of economic efficiency,

Table 5.2   Small business in Czechoslovakia, 1948–60

	1950	1952	1956	1958	1960
Plants	249 582	91 289	47 135	22 000	6553
Employment	428 540	108 652	49 834	22 557	6601

Source: Průcha (1974).

Table 5.3   Socialisation in the Czechoslovakia agriculture, 1950–70

	1950	1955	1960	1965	197
Arable land (%)	20.1	43.2	90.9	93.1	93.1
Cooperatives acreage (hectares)	–	270	420	608	63.8

Source: Průcha (1974)

left little room for small, independent and responsive small firms. As a result, the Czechoslovak economy entered economic reform with a highly concentrated and administratively monopolised industrial structure. Distortions in size distribution are even more conspicuous when compared internationally. The average size of a firm in Czechoslovakia was almost ten times larger than that in West Germany (See Table 5.4).

Table 5.4   Size distribution of manufacturing firms in Germany and
Czechoslovakia, 1986
(shown as percentages)

	Number of firms		
	20–499	500–990	1000 and more
Czechoslovakia	8.9	21.1	70.0
Germany	94.2	3.1	2.7
	Number of employees		
Czechoslovakia	1.3	7.5	91.2
Germany	39.7	10.4	49.9

Source: Izak and Zemplinerová (1991).

The dismantling of the communist regime in November 1989 opened the way to a market-type economy and the development and support of private enterprise and small business. The process gained momentum by means of denationalisation and demonopolisation which took the form of small and large privatisation, restitution of property and liquidation of some government enterprises.

All empirical evidence shows that the dynamic development of the private sector has been instrumental in easing the adjustment in 1990–1992 (see Table 5.5). This is reflected mainly in the activities of small and medium enterprises as it was too early for the large-scale privatisation to have any significant effect.[5] Compared to the decline of 16 per cent of real GDP in 1991, the output of the private sector during the same period increased by 28 per cent.

In the Czech Republic, the number of individuals with entrepreneurship as a main activity reached, as of December 1992, 411 000 persons, which represents 343 per cent increase since the beginning of 1991. The number of small organisation of all forms of ownership (under 24 employed) rose between the beginning of 1991 and December 1992 by 707 per cent. Accordingly, employment in the SME sector has increased in the same period by 715 per cent.[6] In terms of employment the small sector was responsible for 16.3 per cent of the available labour force in 1992. The number of firms with 100–499 employed increased by 11 per cent between January and November 1992.

The end of 1992 and beginning of 1993 was marked by some deceleration of the process. This decline may be attributed partly to the decrease in initial enthusiasm and partly to rising competition. Nevertheless, there is evidence of an impressive come-back of small and medium enterprises. Further impetus may be expected from the completion of large-scale privatisation as many privatisation projects consider breaking up big units into smaller parts. The liquidation of a number of state-owned enterprises will also lead to the creation of small firms.

Table 5.5   Private sector in the Czech Republic
(percentage of GDP)

1990	1991		1992					1993
	I–III	*I–IV*	*I*	*II*	*III*	*IV*	*I–IV*	*I*
4.0	7.0	11.0	17.8	18.5	20.0	21.5	19.5	29.9

Source: *Indicators of Monetary and Economic Development*, no. 17, Czech National Bank.

III   COMMERCIAL BANKS AS A SOURCE OF SME LENDING

Commercial banks play a very important role in the life of SMEs. Very small enterprises working primarily in local markets normally restrict their business with banks to transfers and payments and to making small deposits and credits. As the enterprise grows and turns towards more distant markets, the need for more credits and other banking products increases, and the enterprise may to a large degree use the bank as a partner and consultant.

In general, several facts may explain the dominant position of commercial banks in SME lending. In particular, the branch network permits knowledge of local conditions and personal contact with entrepreneurs. Commercial banks are able to offer a broad variety of banking services tailored for specific clienteles. They have accumulated experience in debt collection and enforcement of honouring obligations. The everyday operations enable them to acquire skills in risk assessment and evaluation.

Empirical evidence in transition economies, however, invokes some qualifications to the general framework. First, the commercial banking sector has inherited a relatively high degree of monopolised structure. Only a few large banks may base their business on the branch network, which allows them to be close to potential customers and, most importantly, attract savings. In contrast, many small banks, find themselves in a difficult position. They are short of locally raised funds but have high costs associated with starting operations. Competitive pressures may even push them close to the limits of prudent behaviour. But they are determined to play a role and, despite their competitive disadvantages, their local impact on improving competitiveness is perceptible and promising.

Second, the quality of banking services lags behind in transition economies. As discussed in Chapter 3 of this volume, the Czech commercial banks are often exposed to criticism for usurious interest rates, a bureaucratic approach to clients, long queues at the counters, an insufficient set of banking products and a sluggish execution of payments. There is undoubtedly a point in these complaints. Nevertheless, experience seems to show that things are improving, although slower than expected. Despite all criticism the skills of the commercial banking sector tend to move upwards along the learning curve.

When pondering failures of commercial banks in the provision of financial services to SMEs, it is important to distinguish between transitional or non-systemic failures on the one hand and permanent or systemic features which one can encounter even in developed market economies.

Many economists tend to argue that lending to the SME sector is perceived by commercial banks as particularly risky investment.[7] The riskiness may be supported by data which show the high number of bankruptcies within one or two years after starting operations, and losses incurred by banks. The rational response to the increased risk exposure on the part of commercial banks is to charge risk premia, so that interest rates paid by SMEs tend to be on average higher. Second, commercial banks are reluctant to lend on a longer-term basis, showing strong preference for short-term credits.

With some minor exceptions, the outlined framework may be observed in the Czech Republic. The interviews made with bank officials reveal a strong preoccupation with the risk issue. They have almost unequivocally pointed to the absence of track records for small entrepreneurs which makes it impossible for them to use standard risk assessment techniques; the low quality of submitted projects is allegedly caused by unclear business plans; the projects neglect the supply–demand linkages in local markets; there is insufficient knowledge of accounting procedures, tax laws and other administrative prerequisites.[8] In other words, banks' representatives say that if it were not for a feeling of social responsibility among banks, plus the fact of an anti-bank mood in society, the banks themselves, adhering purely to standard risk assessment criteria used in market economies, would probably supply the SME sector with less credit and at higher costs.[9]

Of course, the above arguments may be played down as being intertwined with the vested interests of banks. Unfortunately, it has proved extremely difficult to collect empirical evidence that would assess excess riskiness in SME lending. First, the banks are extremely unwilling to reveal information about losses incurred due to bad loans. Partly they consider these data vital for the goodwill of a bank, concerned that their disclosure may distract potential savers if the real figures were worse than that of competitors. Higher rates of losses or endangered credits may be interpreted by the general public as an unprofessional job done by bank personnel, making banks unsafe places for savings.

Second, the reason why it is so difficult to obtain a clearer picture about the riskiness of SME lending is the simple fact that it is too early for many banks, particularly for new ones, to create objective standards of comparison. Because many banks have only been in business for a short time, their accumulated knowledge about failures, write-offs of losses and debt collection is limited. Experience shows that the time period needed to create relevant benchmarks may be two or more years.

Due to this lack of reliable statistics it could be argued that the claims of commercial banks about excess SME riskiness is largely preconception rather than a true proposition borne by facts. On the other hand, one can interpret these claims as rational expectations inferred from limited experience which, on average, are going to be fulfilled.

When assessing the risk of SME lending, two circumstances should be taken into account. First, riskiness is a relative measure; the same risk may look different in different underlying environments. In particular, the degree of risk of SME lending may be perceived to be smaller in the face of large default risks involved in lending to the rest of the economy as the case may be at present. The expected wave of bankruptcies and the infancy of the capital market in transition economies make lending to larger enterprises a no more secure investment. Second, to point to the poor quality of submitted projects, which may reveal low entrepreneurial skills among many small businessmen, is a dubious argument. Badly prepared projects entail almost no risk for banks as it is very easy to identify their intrinsic flaws. Much more difficult is the assessment of supposedly sound projects against the background of broader regional and national uncertainties (e.g. absorption capacity of local markets, macroeconomic outlook, currency risks) which need developed bankers' skills and represent the real source of potential losses.

Analytically, banks have not seemed to grasp the procedures for charging explicit risk premia. The idea of risk measurement is employed in a very rough manner, having been based more on the subjective discretion of local evaluators rather than on some explicit ranking scale. So tensions may arise, as is often the case, if an SME borrower does not understand the link between his or her individual project and the interest rate surcharge. Making evaluation procedures more comprehensible for SMEs should be a top priority. The banks ought to prepare and follow written guidelines which would determine the decision on granting and managing credits. The evaluation of both the business plan and the customer in terms of risks involved should be well documented. Some relevant information may be missing due to non-existent track records (management's personal character or ability to fulfill credit obligations, analysis of the enterprise's market strength and ability to survive in bad market conditions). On the other hand, the balance sheet and cash flow analysis may reveal much valuable information (e.g. leverage ratio, ratio between current assets and short-term liabilities, cash reserves as a percentage of turnover). Customers should be divided according to some scoring techniques into risk categories that will be the guidance for the bank's credit limits and for collateral and pricing policy.

Another problem with SME customers is that they represent higher administrative costs of lending as low-volume credits are allocated among a large number of clients. As a result it may be difficult for a bank to cover all SME customers on an individual basis. These large numbers should result in a simplified handling in the bank procedure and in the employment of standardised techniques for assessing business plans. Even the standardisation of forms for credit application, achieved in some Western countries, would be extremely helpful to the SMEs in the Czech Republic.

To summarise basic points, the relation between commercial banks and the SME sector in the Czech Republic brings forth both standard and non-standard problems and produces a lot of criticism. So it is no surprise that many people, even among the top policy-makers, tend to see the way in which commercial banks provide finance to the SME sector as highly unsatisfactory with symptoms of a market failure. However, government should maintain an impartial view in evaluating arguments of both sides of the dispute, i.e. banks and their SME clients. It would not be conducive to the development of a healthy banking sector to employ policies that inter-vene in their commercial assessment of credits. Government measures must assure that commercial banks find the SME financing a profitable part of their portfolio, interest rate policy must allow an appropriate margin to cover risks and administrative costs and government assistance should not weaken the motivation of commercial banks in the mobilisation of savings.

On the part of commercial banks there will be an active learning process that will eliminate many present tensions. There is already promising evi-dence that banks do improve their banking skills and that they are willing to invest resources into raising the standards of their services. In some cases their behaviour is probably more conservative and precautionary than one would consider necessary for the Czech transforming economy. On the other hand, the argument regarding the high risks of SME lending should not be played down as the SME sector itself is undergoing a substantial learning process of market economy.

IV CREDIT GUARANTEE SCHEME

As summarised by Levitsky and Prasad (1987), credit guarantee schemes for small and medium enterprises are set up with the purpose of encourag-ing financial institutions and particularly commercial banks to lend to SMEs with viable projects and good prospects of success but which are unable to provide adequate collateral or which do not have a suitable record of financial transactions to prove that they are creditworthy. The authors put forward the list of associated questions which can be used as a guidepost for evaluating workability of guarantee schemes in the Czech Republic.

The need for a network of financial institutions devoted to guarantee business is well understood. The SME sector has generic problems with securing loans. The value of SME collateral tends to be inadequate to attract the necessary amounts of external finance. Moreover, due to the low degree of confidence and unsettled financial discipline in transforming economies, banks tend to be reluctant to accept as collateral movable assets (accounts receivables, inventories, trucks), which means that SMEs are able to offer as security for loans only their houses, and these are inadequate in many cases for their borrowing needs. Many SMEs do not even own houses. Banks may also expect big problems in cases of default and the seizing of collateralised assets, mainly because courts are overloaded with business disputes. Some commentators even argue that due to the amount of collateralised houses, the banks are now in the position of estate agents exposed to big losses in the event of a slump in the property market. The recent British experience provides a warning in this respect. All of these facts underline the importance of efficient and accessible guarantee activities operating on a big enough scale.

The establishment of the Czech-Moravian Guarantee and Development Bank (CMGDB) in March 1992 is an important step in filling the gap. The bank runs the following guarantee scheme. In 1992, there were five programmes set up that formulate general criteria to be met when applying for CMGDB facilities. The programme START is designed for small-business-launching entrepreneurs with a weak capital standing. Another programme – DEVELOPMENT – should contribute to the needed structural changes in the Czech Republic. The programme REGION aims to promote economic activity in depressed and underdeveloped areas and to create new employment opportunities. PATENT is designed to encourage technical progress within the SME sector. Finally, AESCULAP has been initiated with the aim of promoting a private health service. All programmes are sponsored by the Ministry of Economy. In addition to this, the CMGDB administers the GARANT scheme which is part of the EC assistance extended under the programme PHARE.

In 1993 four additional programmes were launched: CONSULT (advisory service for SME), REGENERATION (reconstruction of historical objects in cities and towns), TRANSFER (introduction of domestic and foreign technical and technological advances), PARK (setting up technology parks).

At present CMGDB offers three types of services: (i) guarantees on credits extended by cooperating commercial banks (up to 70 per cent of a loan payable within 4 years, when AESCULAP allows for an 8-year redemption period); (ii) financial subsidies for interest rates (up to 7 per cent); (iii) short-term loans for bridging the period of financial difficulties. The upper size limit for a firm to be eligible for CMGDB assistance is generally 500 employees, if not stated otherwise in individual programmes.

There are several issues which deserve attention. In principle, two options are available in financing guarantee schemes – for profit and non-profit. Provision of guarantees may be operated in a manner used by insurance companies, i.e. to set up appropriate premiums covering all costs of the scheme. As a result, the guarantee agency tends to display profit maximising behaviour in charging market rates for assumed risks. The legal status of CMGDB is likely to support this arrangement as the main shareholders are the major commercial banks. The government's share of ownership at the level of 30 per cent may put them in a minority position against commercial banks' coalition.[10]

One can question whether the guarantee business for the SME can be satisfactorily run on a purely commercial insurance basis. According to Levitsky and Prasad, at least ten years' records on loan repayment behaviour under similar conditions are needed to reach any valid statistical conclusions. The risks involved in lending may induce too-high risk premiums, factually cutting off SME borrowers from guarantee facilities. That's why many schemes both in developed and developing countries are funded by government, and the agency entrusted with the administration of the scheme is expected to behave as a non-profit organisation. For the time being, there is no apparent serious conflict in the fact that profit maximising commercial banks own would-be non-profit institutions. Moreover, CMGDB have not yet manifested a strong desire to move towards other activities of development banking which offer no direct use for main shareholders or may even compete with them.

The guarantee scheme adopted by CMGDB is based on risk sharing between the borrower, the commercial bank extending credit, and the guarantee agency. Under this arrangement the borrower takes the risk that he will be deprived of his or her collateral if the project fails. The commercial bank assumes the risk of losing part of its money as a result of faulty project assessment. Finally, the guarantee agency is exposed to the possibility that claims will have to be paid. This philosophy has a sound basis. It precludes any sort of automatic government insurance of loans and invites thorough independent risk assessment and double checking of project proposals by both financial institutions.

There is a natural tendency for commercial banks to transfer as much risk as possible on the guarantee fund. CMGDB offers guarantees up to 50–70 per cent of credit value with which, as interviews have revealed, some banks are unhappy, pushing for the higher involvement of CMGDB. On the other hand, commercial banks are interested in cooperation with CMGDB which suggests that the part of risk shared by commercial banks does not surpass the point that makes the guarantee scheme unattractive. It's noteworthy that programme AESCULAP allows for 100 per cent guarantees and that the 70 per cent risk-sharing limit was relaxed in the 1993 programme. The near future will show whether a more generous commitment by CMGDB represents a retreat from the risk-sharing principle. In any case, the phasing away of this principle or considerably suppressing it should be strongly avoided.

There are a lot of questions about the efficiency of the present guarantee scheme which can be answered only after some experience has been accumulated. For example, how smooth in terms of administrative costs will be the process of handling claims? Are there any safeguards against abuse, e.g. the right to reject a claim and refuse payment against a guarantee if it can be shown that a bank has not taken all reasonable precautions against default? Will the present prices charged by CMGDB be sufficient to recover eventual losses? Will the loss rate be acceptable? What obstacles are going to complicate the foreclosing on collateral? Will the realised price of collateral be substantially lower than the original estimate?

Despite many unknown variables, there is no doubt that the establishment of a guarantee scheme run by CMGDB is an important step in the promotion of SME development. The design of the scheme that consists of selected programmes with well-defined goals will probably enhance the broader view about the usefulness of government industrial policies in transition economies.

The controversial issue is the scale of the scheme. In 1992 (as of 30 November) the CMGDB, having been slightly more than half a year in existence, accepted 1352 requests for support, of which 782 were approved, 141 rejected, 50 withdrawn and 377 undecided at that time. The scale of support, both in absolute and money terms, is shown in Table 5.6.

Despite a relatively vigorous start, typically plagued with administrative hurdles, many economists suggest that the scale of the above support schemes, dependent substantially on government resources, lags behind the efficient absorption capacity of the SME sector. By the efficient absorption capacity we mean the total of projects that are considered viable by CMGDB and would be granted assistance if the bank was not constrained by the lack of funds allocated for the SME support schemes. Thus, the money constraint

Table 5.6   The scale of guarantee (CMGDB) activities
(November 1992)

Type of support	Number	Million CSK
Credit guarantees	400	1085.0
Interest rate subsides	772	483.6
Short-term loans	34	16.8

Source: Internal material of CMGDB.
Note: CMGDB stands for Czech Moravian Guarantee and Development Bank.

imposed by the government by its balanced budget philosophy has been actually binding (many requests for interest rate subsidies were rejected in the 1993 programme). More generous government financial involvement is even more necessary if the schemes are to cover privatisation demands of small entrepreneurs and new private farmers. Of course, there are many competing ends for government money. On the other hand, the SME sector is quite likely to capture opportunities in product markets and more likely to respond to financial injection with supply increase rather than with inflationary pressures typical for state-owned enterprises.

Another problem is the underdeveloped locational pattern of the guarantee scheme, which is operated by only one bank with practically no local branches. It implies a long trip for a customer to reach the scheme. Deconcentration of some activities (e.g. interest rate subsides) should be achieved in the near future. Bringing guarantee services near to customers and increasing the number of their providers is going to strengthen the competitive mood in the banking sector.

V   DEVELOPMENT BANKING

One of the most voiced complains of SMEs is that commercial banks do not provide loans with maturities of more than four years. At the same time, they point to the need for long-term financing for many lines of business activity. Commercial banks reply that the increased supply of longer-term credit has to be matched by the increase of longer-term savings; the tendency of the latter to decline as a reflection of the overall risky environment in the economy makes it impossible to expand the former. The lack of funds, combined with a high degree of risk involved in SME borrowing, makes the costs of long-term credit prohibitively high. In other words, the majority of SMEs could not afford to pay the price if charged on a purely commercial basis.

Institutionally, various forms of development banking arrangements are supposed to alleviate the above constraints. Their design should secure sufficient financing for projects with benefits spread more into the future. In the Czech Republic this gap is meant to be closed, as the name suggests, by the recently established Czech-Moravian Guarantee and Development Bank, as discussed above. But CMGDB is fully involved in guarantee business for the time being, and development banking activities are only in a preparatory stage.

The absence of development services for SMEs represents an important drawback of the present financial infrastructure. This in turn poses the question of what can be done and what are the chances of removing the gap in the foreseeable future.

As for the problem of domestic saving mobilisation, one can envisage opposite tendencies.[11] The development of the capital market and other financial institutions is going to enhance savings and investment opportunities. Provision of long-term capital may be related to the anticipated expansion of mutual funds, pension schemes, insurance companies and similar institutions which are important providers of long-term capital in Western economies. However, some economists express doubts about smooth intermediation of emerging capital markets in the Czech Republic (see, for example, Drabek in Chapter 2 above). Notably, policy-makers may be confronted with monopoly power seized by dominant investment funds in the course of voucher privatisation or the wave of ordinary shareholders striving to sell voucher shares for ready money. An unsettled environment may detract or slow down the inflow of foreign long-term capital which waits until things become less uncertain. But even though the initial turmoil would not manifest itself with the intensity projected by some economists, the question remains whether additional long-term capital will reach the SME sector. Big and newly privatised enterprises will need to finance their reconstruction and modernisation plans. Dominant commercial banks will be under no pressure to allocate their long-term funds to the SME sector as long as they are faced with problems discussed in previous sections.

It seems that the government should play a more active role in establishing an appropriate financial infrastructure. This should be augmented as a part of regional policy by a system of municipal banks engaged in long-term development of local communities. A specialised institution should be devoted to the development needs of the agricultural sector. A more general issue arises as to whether the best way to fill these gaps is to set up new financial institutions or accommodate facilities of existing ones. The acute shortage of experienced staff imposes constraints on extending the number of home-based banks.

A shortage of domestically raised funds should stimulate exploration of assistance coming from abroad. The evidence shows that this source of financing is by no means the least significant.[12] There are both private and official foreign institutions prepared to extend funds for SME development. It depends on the ability of transition economies as to what extent they will succeed in creating an efficient environment capable of seizing open opportunities.

Foreign lenders can be divided into two categories. The first category includes loans approved by foreign lenders themselves. It means that the Czech bank only acts as an intermediary. Experience shows that there are high administrative costs with this procedure. Small entrepreneurs face costly approval procedures and disclosure obligation, and it is difficult for many to prepare financial statements and other required paperwork in a foreign language. At the same time, for a commercial bank it is less burdensome to match the loan with a few larger projects rather than with many smaller ones.

The second category of foreign lenders agrees to trust money directly to the selected Czech bank and this bank itself conducts project appraisal. The problem is that the foreign creditor usually demands government guarantees and even if these are provided the price of credit is close to that obtained in market terms. This kind of investor will probably not be satisfied unless high-quality guarantees are offered to him. According to CMGDB, the solution is seen in seeking surrogate guarantees (e.g. banks' guarantees or guarantees of local authorities). Great emphasis is put on the idea that, together with financing, the development of banking know-how is extremely desirable as an efficient way of raising standards of local project evaluators.

VI VENTURE CAPITAL

Venture capital arrangements in developed market economies are an important source of fresh finance to small and young enterprises in the early stage of their life. A venture capitalist is defined as a person or a body engaged in investing his money into promising projects, and usually prepared to assume substantial risks and incur losses which are outweighed by outstanding gains. Venture capital schemes are designed to provide long-term equity financing; accordingly they represent an alternative to development banking. This form of financing alleviates substantially the problem of collateralising the loans. For a small entrepreneur, entering into a venture capital agreement enables him to overcome the disadvantage of using the equity market in which the low volume of equity issue does not usually cover issuing costs. Venture capitalists are agents specialised in dealing with risks inherent in firm creation. They closely monitor the initial effort of new firms and encourage profitability of their business.

The absence of risk-capital facilities in the Czech Republic may be considered as another gap in the present financial infrastructure. Several factors may explain why this form of raising capital lags behind.

First, there is psychologically motivated reluctance of the part of SMEs, which can be overcome only gradually. Giving an ownership stake to someone else may be viewed as a limitation on one's own abilities and personal freedom. Letting a partner in means offering a part of profits which many small firms would be reluctant to do.

Second, the general lack of domestic capital means that the counterparts of major suppliers of risk capital in modern market economies (banks, insurance companies, mutual funds, wealthy individuals) are undercapitalised and for the time being demonstrate no clear intention of locking themselves into long-term ownership of small risky firms. CMGDB mentions in its Charter this line of business. But one can expect only a limited amount of money and effort allocated to venture activities and only after the main domain of guarantees is consolidated. Accordingly, one should not expect a steep take-off of venture capital business in the Czech Republic, which implies that its role in launching SME activities is going to be less important in comparison with developed market economies.

The shortage of domestic venture capital can be alleviated to some extent by attracting funds from abroad. Related problems are very similar to those of development banking. Potential investors are shopping around for profitable projects, but very often hit barriers of insufficient legal and financial infrastructures.

A more active role should be played by entrepreneurial associations. As is usual in market economies, they should assist in the creation of venture capital institutions by subscribing equity capital. Seen from that perspective the ongoing discussion whether membership of the Chamber of Commerce should be compulsory or voluntary, the compulsory solution would mean more money for these purposes.

Government policy should be aimed at making enough room for private initiative. The voucher privatisation has led to the creation of an array of private investment funds. In the face of sharp competition many of them (notably the smaller ones) will have to reconsider their position within the financial sector. It is worthwhile encouraging with tax and other concessions their interest to become venture capitalists.

The banks may also find merit in risk capital. As a partner they have direct control of the collateral. They should be encouraged in setting up subsidiaries specialised in venture capital operations.

VII FINANCIAL ASSISTANCE FROM GOVERNMENT

Promotion of small and medium enterprises is proclaimed as one of the top priorities of government economic policy. 'Put your money where your mouth is' is one pertinent saying. In other words, the role of government should not be restricted to the creation and preservation of a macro-economic framework only. A more active position is expected. Related to this, two relevant questions may be asked: (i) How big should the flow of assistance be in order to ensure its efficient absorption by the SME sector? (ii) How should government funds best be intermediated?

The power of government to raise money for SMEs is well understood. Direct budget appropriations is not the only source. There are other government agencies (e.g. the National Property Fund responsible for proceeds from privatisation) which are capable of financially sponsoring various programmes of assistance. The creditworthiness of government makes it able to attract funds from abroad.

It should be noted that the activities of the Czech government towards SME development are relatively extensive, when compared, for examples, to regional, export promotion or industrial policies. Nevertheless, there are many who would claim that the volume of government assistance is still limited and lacks coordination. The dispute often boils down to the argument that a special government agency or a foundation should be established in order to take over and execute all government functions: formulation of SME development policies; identification of existing barriers; encouragement of incubator centres and technology parks; administration of the database about the SME sector; financing of educational programmes, etc.

There is nothing intrinsically wrong in this area. But some proponents maintain that the agency should also take on some financial services: short and long-term credits, credit guarantees, interest rate subsidies, overdraft facilities. It is argued that the prospective agency is in a position to replace, at least partially, with its financial activities supposedly expensive and low-quality services of commercial banks. The agency is expected to be able to secure a reliable inflow of funds (e.g. appropriations from government budget, equity tax levied on state-owned enterprises, government borrowing abroad) independently of profitability of individual investment projects.

This is turn allegedly will allow proper attention to be paid to the quality of projects, thus providing finance to riskier but promising innovative ideas at reasonable cost. Credits will be made cheaper and accessible to a larger clientele.

The idea of a government institution that performs some banking functions but largely avoids the deficiencies of the commercial banking sector, is flawed for several reasons. First, examples which point to similar arrangements in some developed market economies (notably the Japanese experience with substantial government involvement in banking may be appealing) are difficult to apply; the shortage of trained banking staff is one of the main reasons. While in reference countries the private banking sector tends to supply skilled professionals to the government sector, in transition economies trained people are one of the most scarce resources even within the relatively well-paid banking sector. So a bureaucratic rather than a rational economic approach may be expected to prevail in the semi-bank government agency. Second, it is questionable whether it is a sound policy to make credit cheaper by ignoring or undervaluing risk in project assessment. Such an approach is going to lead inevitably to misdirection of limited resources.

The magnitude and the expected long duration of the restructuring of the banking sector may tempt many not to wait for its results and to create government funds for on-lending to SMEs. Even if the concern for speedy creation of lending facilities for SMEs may be justified, one should seriously caution against such an idea. Government funds in the form of direct credits, guarantee schemes or interest rate subsidies should be channelled through the banking sector using and enhancing professional experience of bankers in project evaluation.

Of course, it does not preclude more active government initiatives. The allocation of government funds may become a powerful instrument in promoting competition within the banking sector itself. Entrusting the administration of SME funds to small banks would strengthen their position. However, the bias to cooperate mostly with large banks demonstrates that the government prefers short-term economies of scale and convenience to longer-term effects of increased competition in the banking sector. For the time being, government money reaches only a limited number of banks (in terms of administration of foreign loans with government guarantees, government interest rate subsidies). Why should not the interest rate subsidisation scheme, similar to that run by CMGDB, be operated by a broader range of banks? Government assistance may become a vehicle for improving the performance and standards of small banks. Together with receiving funds from the government the banks may be required, as *quid pro quo*, to observe patterns of prudent behaviour consistent with general policy objectives.

VIII CONCLUSIONS

The conclusions of this study that has been concerned with the problems of SME financing in the Czech Republic must be seen as tentative, for the following reasons: (i) lack of statistical data, which are collected irregularly or treated as confidential information; (ii) insufficient accumulated experience which does not allow the proper evaluation of many financial arrangements; (iii) unsettled behavioural patterns of economic agents.

Nevertheless, there are some crucial points which deserve attention:

– The institutional infrastructure of financial facilities reveals several gaps in comparison with developed market economies: notably, there are no providers of long-term finance – venture capital business and development banking – and guarantee schemes are taking off only gradually.

– Commercial banks will remain the principal source of external finance for the SME sector, which underlines the importance of credit policies of the former for development of the latter.

– Many tensions observed between commercial banks and their SME clients are not to be interpreted as a market failure, invoking regulatory measures that would intervene in credit allocation on a commercial basis. SME financing must remain a profitable part of banks' portfolios, and interest rate policies must allow an appropriate margin to cover risks and administrative costs.

– Despite statistical and conceptual problems of measurement one should recognise the risks involved in SME lending and give proper merit to the precautionary policies of banks. Both banks and SME entrepreneurs are moving upwards along their learning curves. This learning process is going to mitigate many of the present bottlenecks.

– Shortage of collateralised assets makes the workable credit guarantee schemes indispensable. One should not retreat from the presently adopted risk-sharing principle between a commercial bank and a guarantee agency which precludes automatic government insurance of loans and invites double checking of project proposals.

– The scale of guarantee facilities should be enlarged to also cover privatisation demands of SMEs and agriculture. Deeper financial participation of government is indispensable for a larger impact of assistance schemes.

- The most efficient way of channelling government support is via the banking sector; the idea of a government institution taking on some banking functions is likely to lead to the undervaluation of risk in project assessment and may lead to misdirection of limited resources.
- The allocation of government funds may become a powerful instrument in promoting competition within the banking sector itself and improving standards of prudent behaviour.

Notes

1. See McDermott and Mejstřík (1991) for a broader evaluation of the role of small firms in transition economies. See also section IV in the text below.
2. As Levitsky (1986) makes clear, there is also negative experience with ill-managed support schemes which in the eyes of some economists may even question the desirability of SME assistance.
3.   The small-scale privatisation scheme, conducted mainly through public auctions, was extremely conducive to the growth of small firms. From the beginning of the process more than 23 000 small units (shops, local services, restaurants) have been privatised. Also restitutions contributed extensively to the take-off of the SME sector (by the end of 1991 more than 30 000 claims have been met under the law of restoration of small assets expropriated in the 1950s).
4. It has been estimated that due to new registration requirements and the introduction of social and health insurance, 18 000 people left the sector of firms with less than 25 employees in the first half of 1993.
5. The SME Government Support Act (passed in April 1992) defines a small and medium firm as that with up to 500 employees. For statistical purposes the category of 1–24 employees has been introduced.
6. See Beneš (1993).
7. See Levitsky and Prasad (1987), Paulson (1992), and Stijn (1992).
8. According to Vrbská (1993), the most frequent deficiency of SME business plans is the undervaluation of costs and overvaluation of revenues together with low marketing skills of small entrepreneurs.
9.   According to Paulson (1992), in Norway the average annual credit losses on small and newly established enterprises was historically restricted to a level of 1–2 per cent of total credits with a recent increase up to 5–6 per cent. In this prospect, the recent announcement of the Director General of Česká Spořitelna (Czech Savings Bank), the major and most experienced lender to the SME sector, that the Bank's share of the so-called endangered credits is 1 per cent, may look surprisingly low.
10. It is symptomatic that the bulk of CMGDB guarantees have been granted to the clients of CMGDB shareholders. As of 30 September 1992 the guarantees relating to credits of non-owner commercial banks did not exceed one-fifth of the total of guarantees.
11. For more detailed discussion, see J. Klacek, Chapter 4 above.
12. In 1993 four main programmes of foreign assistance aimed at supporting SME sector were as follows: (1) Programme PHARE financed from EC

funds. It consists of the programme GARANT (credit guarantees for SMEs), the programme of small loans (up to 300 000 crowns, 3-year maturity) and the programme PALMIF (restructuralisation of the labour market); (2) The loan from the European Investment Bank extended to Czech National Bank (85 mil ECU) for SME investment projects in selected industries; (3) The loan from the Export Import Bank of Japan extended to the Czech National Bank; (4) Czech-American Entrepreneurial Fund (the so-called Bush Fund).

References

Beneš, V., 'Small and Medium Enterprise in Numbers', Prague, *Ekonom*, no. 3 (1993) (in Czech).

Charap, J., 'Entrepreneurship and SMEs in the EBRD's Countries of Operation', unpublished paper, 1993.

Horkel, V., 'Small and Medium Enterprises Need Assistance', Prague, *Národní hospodářství*, no.2 (1993) (in Czech).

Izak, V. and A. Zemplinerová, 'Monopoly and Economic Policy', *VP*, EÚ ČSAV, Prague, no. 391 (1991) (in Czech).

Klvačová, E., 'Activities of Czech-Moravian Guarantee and Development Bank', Prague, *Ekonom*, no.48 (1992) (in Czech).

Konečná, M., 'Barriers to SME development', Prague, *Ekonom*, no. 22 (1992) (in Czech)

Levitsky, J., 'World Bank Lending to Small Enterprises', *The World Bank, Industry and Finance Series*, vol.16, 1986.

Levitsky, J., and R.N. Prasad, 'Credit Guarantee Schemes for Small and Medium Enterprises', The World Bank, *Industry and Finance Series*, no. 58, 1987.

McDermott, G.A. and M. Mejstřík, *The Role of Small Firms in the Industrial Development and Transformation of Czechoslovakia*, CERGE, Prague, 1991.

Paulson, H., 'Norwegian Commercial Banks as Source of Financing of SMEs', EFTA workshop on financing SMEs, Prague, 1992.

'Present State of Private Enterprise in CFSR, Its Promotion and Development.' working material of Ministry of Economy, April 1992 (in Czech).

'Problems of SME Development', internal material of the Centrum for supporting small and medium enterprises, 1992 (in Czech)

Průcha, V., *History of Czechoslovak Economy in 19th and 20th Centuries*, Prague, Svoboda (in Czech), 1974.

Slifirczyk, K., 'Financing of the Small and Medium Size Enterprises in Poland', EFTA workshop on financing SMEs, Prague, 1992.

Small Business Situation in Japan, Japan External Trade Organization, March 1986.

Stijn, A., 'Development of SME Financing in Central and Eastern Europe', EFTA workshop on financing SMEs, Prague, 1992.

Vrbská , D., 'Experiences with the Realization of Government Support of Small and Medium Enterprises', Prague, *Poradce podnikatele*, no. 10 (1993) (in Czech).

6 Development of the Financial Sector in Hungary During the Transition Period

Rezsö Nyers and Gabriella Rosta Lutz

The most important economic reform measures of the 1980s were introduced in the financial sector. Of the main reform measures, the following deserve to be mentioned:

- the re-establishment of trading in securities from 1982 on, followed by the development of the organisational structure and institutional framework of the capital market (1980–90), the enactment of the Law on the Issue of and Trade in Securities, the relaunching of the Stock Exchange (1990);
- the establishment of a two-tier banking system in 1987; the creation of independent commercial banks;
- the activation and growing autonomy of monetary policy and, in close connection with this, the enactment of the fundamental financial laws. Among these, the Law on the National Bank of Hungary of 1991 deserves mention. It declares the relative autonomy of the Central Bank and its monetary policy, and was followed by the enactment of the Banking Law of 1991, the Accounting Law (1991) and the Bankruptcy Law (1991), all in conformity with international practices.

I TWO-TIER BANKING SYSTEM IN HUNGARY

Since 1 January 1987, Hungary has again operated a two-tier banking system. As a result of the banking reform of 1987 involving about two years of preparation, the divisions of the National Bank of Hungary dealing with company financing were separated from the NBH and three large commercial banks were set up out of these divisions. The new commercial banks took over the outstanding loans of, and lending to, the business

127

sector from the NBH. (Earlier, the NBH – Hungary's Central Bank – had dealt with company financing in addition to its central banking functions. Household financing had formerly been the task of the National Savings Bank and the 260 savings cooperatives, which they performed with limited autonomy.) The banking reform separated the central and commercial banking functions also institutionally.

The reform of the two-tier banking system has throughout been characterised by a gradual approach. The years between 1987 and 1990 were spent 'practising' the new tasks and with the gradual expansion of the commercial banks. The taking over of enterprise financing was followed by the free choice of banks in 1987, i.e., companies deciding, at their own discretion, with which bank to keep their accounts. The decentralisation of household banking activities took place in 1987–8, and foreign exchange transactions had been liberalised by 1990.

The fifth year of the operation of the two-tier banking system, 1991, can be regarded as the year of legislation, as it was in that year that parliament enacted the laws establishing the fundamental legal framework of the operation of the financial institutions, such as the Banking Law, the law on the National Bank of Hungary, the new Accounting Law effecting the basis of the operation also of the financial institutions, the Law on Mutual Funds and a whole range of other laws with a bearing on the financial institutions.

By the end of the fifth year of the two-tier banking system, the up-to-date legal–institutional framework determining, to a large extent, the activities of the financial institutions and adopting international standards, can be said to have been established. The year 1992 and foreseeably the first half of the 1990s will be characterised by the building up of the 'supplementary' institutions of the banking system (e.g. loan guarantee, loan insurance institutions, export guarantee institutions, etc.) and by the enhancement of the capital strength and operational security of the banking system.

II   THE MAIN CHARACTERISTICS AND STRUCTURE OF THE BANKING SYSTEM

Since 1 January 1987, the establishment of the two-tier banking system, the main elements of the banking system have been the following: the National Bank of Hungary (the Central Bank of the country); commercial banks with universal licences; specialised financial institutions with a limited scope of activities; and savings cooperatives. Act LXX of 1991, the Banking Law, does not regard insurance companies, various financial brokerages, securities trading firms, mutual funds, etc. as part of the banking system.

At the end of 1992, the banking system consisted of 37 commercial banks and specialised financial institutions and 258 savings cooperatives. (See Table 6.1.)

In 1990, seven, and in 1991, six new financial institutions were established, in contrast to the total of three new banks set up between 1987 and 1989.

The number of banks increased continuously until 1991, and their services and licences expanded. In 1992, however, the growth of financial institutions came to a halt. Even though new banks – exclusively with foreign ownership – were established in 1992, as well, some financial institutions discontinued operations in 1992. The liquidity of certain minor banks and saving cooperatives was shaken because of poor or irresponsible management and partly because the severe recession of the economy and the transition made their effects felt – not least due to the new financial laws – in the banking sector, too, in the grave deterioration of portfolios and the lack of risk reserves, by 1992.

At the end of 1991, the banks had 726 branches, the savings cooperatives had an additional 1800 offices and branches. The Postabank offices functioning at 3200 post offices also provide banking services for the Postabank. That is, the financial institutions had more than 2500 branches and offices, and together with the Postabank offices, more than 5700, by the end of 1991; their number approached 6000 in 1992.

Table 6.1   Number of financial institutions 1987–92

	1987	1988	1989	1990	1991	1992
1. Commercial banks	15	16	16	23	32	30
– Large banks	5	5	5	4	4	4
– Medium banks	9	10	9	17	26	24
– Retail banks	1	1	2	2	2	2
2. Specialised financial institutions	6	8	8	8	5	7
Financial institutions (total 1+2)	21	24	24	31	37	37
Of this: with mixed and foreign ownership	3	3	8	9	15	18

Source: Central Bank of Hungary.

In Hungary, there is one bank office for 1500–2000 people. The banking system presently employs between 30 000 and 35 000 employees, that is, only 3–3.5 bank employees per 1000 inhabitants. This indicator lags way behind the West European average.

At the end of 1991, the banks kept nearly 550 000 current accounts (accounts of businesses); their number increased to 620 000 in 1992. It has been an important feature of the Hungarian banking reform that commercial banks and especially large banks should not be specialised into sectors or certain banking operations; rather, they should be financial institutions free of sectoral or operational constraints, able to provide the full range of banking services. This approach was reflected by the structural changes taking place between 1987 and 1992, even though the concentration of the banking system is still strong.

In 1991, the combined total assets of the commercial banks and specialised financial institutions amounted to HUF 2117.7 billion; this figure was HUF 2354.3 billion in 1992. The combined 1991 total assets constituted 212.5 per cent of the 31 December 1987 figure and exceeded the level of the preceding year by 30.7 per cent; in 1992, the amount of the total assets made up 236 per cent of the 1987 value. Nearly half of the combined total assets of the banking system were made up of the liabilities of the four large banks (see Figure 6.1), with the National Savings Bank also representing a considerable share. At the same time, the share of the total assets of the specialised financial institutions did not even reach 1 per cent in 1991, (see again Figure 6.1).

A structural analysis of the banking system indicates that the strong concentration has somewhat improved in the past few years, even though the four large banks are still playing a determining role, especially in the financing of the business sector.

In recent years, the most typical feature of the development of the banking system has been the fast growth of the number and share of the medium-sized banks. This process – the expansion of medium-sized banks specialised in various operations and clienteles, yet able to provide complex services at the request of their customers – can be observed in international practice as well.

Between 1987 and 1991 the share of the group of medium-sized banks in the combined total assets increased from round 5 per cent in 1987 to 25–30 per cent in 1991. Nevertheless, the Hungarian banking system is still, in the seventh year of the operation of the two-tier banking system, characterised by a strong fragmentation:

– in corporate financing, the share of the four largest commercial banks exceeds 55 per cent;

Figure 6.1   Share of the total assets of the groups of banks in 1991

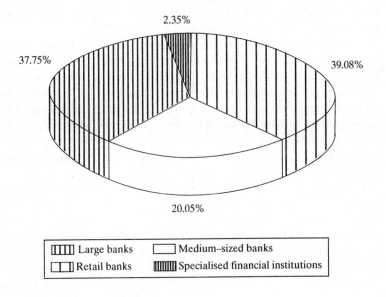

2.35%

37.75%

39.08%

20.05%

| Large banks | Medium–sized banks |
| Retail banks | Specialised financial institutions |

Source: Central Bank of Hungary

– in retail banking, the share of the National Savings Bank is nearly 90 per cent;
– in foreign exchange operations, the four large commercial banks represent about 70 per cent.

III   THE LIABILITIES OF THE BANKING SYSTEM

Within the liabilities of the banking system in 1991, internal liabilities made up some 10 per cent, external liabilities 80 per cent and 10 per cent was the share of other liabilities that could not be categorised into either of the former groups (e.g. interest costs of deferred liabilities, other passive settlements). (See Table 6.2.)

The Internal Liabilities of the Banking System

In 1991, the internal liabilities – founders' equity, accumulated capital, reserve capital, untaxed provisions – made up 10 per cent of the total

Table 6.2   Liabilities of the banking system and their composition (HUF billion)

	1987 Amount	1987 %	1988 Amount	1988 %	1988/1987	1989 Amount	1989 %	1989/1987
I. Internal liabilities (Equity)	60	6.03	75.5	7.38	125.75	93.9	7.69	156.43
II. External liabilities	794.3	79.72	787.6	76.99	99.16	921.1	73.85	115.98
(a) Deposits	520.8	52.27	564.2	55.16	108.24	662.8	53.14	127.27
(b) Loans	263.9	26.48	208.5	20.38	79.01	235.4	18.87	89.22
(c) Securities	9.6	0.97	14.9	1.46	155.33	22.9	1.80	238.34
III. Other liabilities	142.0	14.25	159.9	15.83	112.59	232.3	18.62	163.58
Total liabilities	996.3	100.00	1023.0	100.00	102.68	1247.3	100.0	125.2

	1990 Amount	1990 %	1990/1988	1991 Amount	1991 %	1991/1987	1992 Amount	1992 %	1992/1987
I. Internal liabilities (Equity)	122.4	7.55	203.85	209.7	9.9	349.18	262.3	11.14	437.17
II. External liabilities	1240.8	76.55	156.19	1870.0	78.86	210.27	1835.3	77.96	231.06
(a) Deposits	886.7	54.72	170.27	1204.0	56.85	231.2	1373.7	68.35	263.77
(b) Loan s	309.9	19.12	117.43	351.3	16.59	133.14	308.6	13.1	116.9
(c) Securities	44.0	2.71	457.87	114.7	6.42	1194.43	153.3	6.61	1596.88
III. Other liabilities	257.5	15.9	181.38	238.0	11.24	167.61	256.5	10.9	180.63
Total liabilities	1620.5	100.0	162.66	2117.7	100.0	212.57	2354.3	100.0	236.3

Source: Central Bank of Hungary.

liabilities. The share of internal liabilities by itself is not low in an international comparison and it increased considerably both in 1991 and 1992.

The fast increase in internal liabilities – especially in the case of the large banks – can be traced back to the initial situation in 1987, when the new banking system and primarily the large commercial banks were characterised by an inadequacy of internal liabilities and by undercapitalisation, on the one hand; on the other hand, to the vigorous efforts of the large banks – especially in 1991 and 1992 – to increase their internal liabilities, motivated by the need to adjust to the requirements of the Banking Law and to the international practice of provisioning.

The internal liabilities of the large commercial banks created in 1987 consisted of the shareholders' equity only; they had no reserve capital and practically no provisions. In view of this, the increase of the share of their internal liabilities to nearly 10 per cent must be considered a major achievement on the part of the banking system, even if – as will be discussed later – lending risks also increased dramatically in the meantime. The fact that the value of internal liabilities increased fourfold over the six years means that the net assets of the banking system also expanded considerably in real terms.

The comparison of the share of internal liabilities in the total by groups of banks reveals that the specialised financial institutions have the largest share of internal liabilities in the total (32.50 per cent) while the retail banks had the lowest share (5.71 per cent). (See Table 6.3). These ratios characterised the development of the internal liabilities of the groups of banks throughout the period 1987–92.

The internal liabilities of the financial institutions under study rose from HUF 60 billion in 1987 to HUF 210 billion in 1991 and, by 1992 – according to preliminary data – to about HUF 260 billion.

Table 6.3   Internal liabilities to total liabilities by groups of banks (%)

	1987	1988	1989	1990	1991
Large banks	6.23	8.75	8.94	7.79	11.69
Medium banks	24.39	21.87	17.44	15.07	12.32
Retail banks	1.39	1.18	2.14	3.07	5.71
Commercial banks, total	5.34	6.61	6.92	7.08	9.73
Specialised financial institutions	49.09	37.09	27.88	29.94	32.50
Financial institutions, total	6.03	7.38	7.53	7.55	9.90

Source: Central Bank of Hungary.

The opposite tendency can be observed in the case of the medium-sized banks: relative to 1987, the ratio of their internal liabilities to the total was practically halved. This can be attributed partly to the fact that four specialised financial institutions with relatively small prime capital were granted commercial banking licences in 1991 and were thus admitted to the group of medium-sized banks, and the new medium-sized banks had only a relatively short period of time to reach the adequate level of capitalisation; when launched, they only had the minimal prime capital required for foundation. Also, this tendency expresses the fact that the more active business operations of the medium-sized banks necessarily involve the mitigation of the former relative 'overcapitalisation', to the extent that will equally satisfy the requirements of risk reduction and profitability.

Within the net assets of the banks, founders' equity has the largest weight. Whereas in 1987 founders' equity (prime capital) made up 83 per cent of net assets, it only reached 56 per cent in 1991. This also indicates that in 1987 the two-tier banking system began its operation practically without reserves.

The major shareholders of the banks are the state, the foreign financial institutions and investors, domestic institutions, companies and, to a negligible extent, Hungarian private investors.

At the end of 1991, the state, through the State Property Agency (SPA), had direct shareholdings of 40.85 per cent on average, in nine banks; its holding in the entire banking system represents 36.6 per cent. It has a 100 per cent holding in one bank, a 50 per cent holding in another bank; the state share in the other banks was below 50 per cent. At present, the state holds shares in twelve financial institutions.

At the end of 1991, 25 per cent of the founders' equity of the banks was in foreign hands. Four financial institutions are held by foreigners in full.

As a result of the Banking Law coming into force at the end of 1991, in that year the fastest growth rate was recorded in the case of provisions; their share in net assets exceeded 23 per cent. The fast increase in provisions continued also in 1992.

The External Liabilities of the Banking System

There is a significant and continuous rearrangement in the composition of external liabilities compared with 1987. The share of deposits (within this, forint and foreign exchange deposits) is basically unchanged, while that of central bank liabilities (refinancing loans) is continuously declining. Increasingly, the role of central bank liabilities is taken over by commercial bank securities issues. The shares of the three major groups in the combined total liabilities of the banking system represent 57 per cent, 17 per cent and 5 per cent, respectively.

In 1991, the large commercial banks collected 39.1 per cent of the total deposits and the retail banks collected 39.2 per cent – that is, essentially the same amount. These two groups of banks have been characterised by deposit collection of nearly the same proportions since 1987, although the growth rate in the case of the large commercial banks was faster in recent years, which is related to the extension of retail banking licences to commercial banks outside the National Savings Bank.

The medium-sized banks hold about one-fifth of the deposits. The most dynamic development was observed in this group of banks with respect to both the growth rate and its ratio.

The changes in the liability structure of the banking system were marked by the continuous reduction of the refinancing loans extended by the Central Bank and the fast increase of deposits (particularly foreign exchange deposits) and especially of securities liabilities during the period under study. The high level of real interest rates evolving due to a stringent monetary policy caused a dramatic increase in savings and a decline in investments and in the demand for credit. The external financial position of the country improved because of the reduction in domestic demand and a policy that, at first, kept inflation within manageable limits and, from the middle of 1991, reduced its rate (manifested in the surplus of the current account and the fast increase in the inflow of direct foreign investment); this, coupled with the decentralisation of foreign exchange operations, led to a sudden increase in the foreign liabilities of the banking system.

IV   CHANGES IN THE ASSETS OF THE BANKING SYSTEM

Naturally, loans and loan-type assets have the greatest weight within the total assets of the banking system. The combined loan portfolios of the financial institutions under study changed, in a breakdown by years and groups of banks, as shown in Table 6.4.

The combined loan portfolio of the financial institutions increased by about 65 per cent in the period 1987–92, while the value of the loan portfolio in real terms decreased. The stringent monetary policy, which had kept interest rates at a relatively high level until the end of 1992, played the decisive role in the relatively moderate growth of the loan portfolio. This, coupled with the real economic processes of the transition (fall in output, market reorientation, change in ownership, structural changes), considerably restrained corporate and household demand for credit. Changes in

Table 6.4 Changes in loan portfolios in 1987–91

	1987		1988		1989		1990		1991	
	HUF Bn	%	HUF Bn	%	HUF Bn	%	HUF Bn	%	HUF Bn	%
Large banks	450.8	100.00	415.9	92.96	469.5	104.16	610.3	135.38	648.0	143.74
Medium banks	32.4	100.00	37.9	116.90	56.6	174.52	144.4	445.63	291.6	900.12
Retail banks	296.6	100.00	331.6	118.81	124.2	41.89	223.7	75.44	284.3	95.86
Commercial banks, total	779.8	100.00	785.4	100.72	650.3	83.40	978.4	125.47	1223.9	156.95
Specialised financial institutions	7.4	100.00	14.6	197.04	21.4	287.30	15.6	210.46	6.1	82.58
Banks and financial insititutions, total	787.2	100.00	800.0	101.63	671.7	85.32	994.0	126.27	1230.0	156.25

Source: Central Bank of Hungary.

arrangements also played a part in the slight expansion of the loan portfolio. Such a change was the replacement of the formerly extremely low-interest, preferential housing loans by bonds in 1989, followed by their removal from the portfolio of the National Savings Bank.

Lending activity has, however, been vigorously growing in the case of the medium-sized banks. This group has increased its loan-type assets some tenfold since 1987, attributable to the growth in the number of medium-sized banks as well as to the active, expansive business policy of this group of banks.

At the end of 1991, short-term lending (maturing within a year) accounted for more than 40 per cent of the combined loan portfolio of HUF 1.230 billion, some 50 per cent in 1992.

Considerations of prudence arising basically from the recession of the economy played the most important role in the growth of short-term lending. The fall in output, high market rates, the uncertain position of businesses forced the banks to tighten their rating systems. Consequently, the number of business organisations applying for loans for the financing of development projects with a safe return decreased radically. Creditworthy, prosperous businesses, however, shun Hungarian commercial banks because of the lending rates, which are high even without the risk premiums; these – mostly jointly owned – businesses are raising credit directly from abroad at lower interest rate levels. (In 1992 the amount of direct borrowing abroad by enterprises was some US$ 500 million.)

The share of long-term lending in the total declined from 60 per cent to 30 per cent.

The above data also support the change perceptible in the lending practices of the banks: owing to the recession, the range of low-risk clients has been continuously shrinking, while the demand for long-term loans on the part of the former state enterprises and cooperatives has been severely constrained by their uncertain future due to the transformation and the high interest rates.

V SUBSTANDARD LOANS IN THE BANKING SYSTEM

Right from the very establishment of the two-tier banking system, the presentation of substandard loans in the balance sheets of the commercial banks has been required by Ordinances of the State Banking Supervision and the Decrees of the Minister of Finance. Up to 1991 – the passing of the Act on Financial Institutions – however, the rating of the assets of the banks differed widely from international practice, as did the former

Table 6.5   Bad debt, total and as a share of total assets 1987–92*(Ft Billion)

	Large banks	Medium sized	Retail banks	Spec. fin. instit.	Banks total
1987					
Bad debts	2.7	0.1	–	–	2.8
Total assets	579.5	46.6	354.6	15.6	996.3
per cent	0.5	0.2	–	–	0.3
1988					
Bad debts	6.5	–	–	–	6.5
Total assets	544.8	58.6	389.9	26.1	1019.4
per cent	1.2	–	–	–	0.6
1989					
Bad debts	21.1	1.1	–	0.3	22.6
Total assets	640.3	128.4	488.9	26.6	1284.2
per cent					
1990					
Bad debts	38.8	3.2	0.6	0.7	43.3
Total assets	781.2	222.7	582.9	33.7	1620.5
per cent	4.96	1.4	0.1	2.0	2.6
1991					
Bad debts	45.0	14.2	26.6	1.7	87.5
Total assets	897.1	468.3	736.3	16.0	2117.7
per cent	5.0	3.0	3.6	10.6	4.1
1992					
Bad debts	–	–	–	–	305.8*
Total assets	911.2	464.5	871.4	57.6	2354.7
per cent					12.9

*Numbers for 1987–91 are based on the regulations in force at the time. 1992 numbers reflect the new standards for determining bad debt which conform with international norms.
Source: Central Bank of Hungary.

differences in accounting systems. Thus, the recent substantial increase in substandard loans presented in the balance sheets (See Table 6.5) can partly be attributed to the fine-tuning of the rules.

In 1991–2, the issue of substandard loans – not least as a result of the Banking Law and also because the tensions of the real economy made their effects felt in the financial sector as well – became the single most important problem of the commercial banks.

Until 1990, only overdue debts counted as substandard loans. Obviously, this was only one element of the actual risk, of the potential lending loss, especially as the banks did not refrain from prolonging loans in order to present a higher, although only fictitious, profit figure; to put it in other terms, they preferred to prolong loans rather than write them off as losses.

The practice of rating loans, followed until 1991, was laden with a number of problems. It gave far too large a scope to the subjective judgements of the banks and did not link the rating of time assets with provisioning.

The Banking Law came into force in December 1991, and radically changed the practice of loan qualification, introducing an internationally acceptable rating system that was much more differentiated than the old one. Accordingly, the financial institutions were required to group their loan assets into four categories: standard and substandard loans, doubtful and bad debts. Pursuant to the Banking Law, the banks are required to set aside adequate provisions based on the rating. (See Table 6.6).

The amount of substandard loans carried in the balance sheets has considerably increased in every group of banks since 1987. The large commercial banks owned more than half of the total stock of substandard loans in 1991–2, but the substandard loans held by the medium-sized and small banks and the retail banks increased by a multiple, too.

As discussed above, to cover their substandard loans carried at a total of HUF 100 billion in the balance sheets, the banks had HUF 209.7 billion in internal liabilities at their disposal, nearly half of which was the founders' equity. In accordance with the then prevailing accounting regulations, the substandard loans presented in the 1991 balance sheets embraced only a part of their actual lending risks.

Pursuant to Par. 23 of the Banking Law, financial institutions should have reached a weighted asset to risk ratio of 8 per cent by 1 January 1993 (7.25 per cent by 1 January 1992 – a requirement in conformity with generally accepted international practice. The State Banking Supervision had the power to grant exemptions from meeting the capital adequacy requirement.

In 1992 and 1993 it became apparent that an ever-widening range of the debtors of the banking system become qualified debtors in the process of restructuring and the period of stabilisation, and that the deterioration of the quality of bank portfolios, the capital inadequacy of banks, and especially large banks, is so extensive that it makes it impossible to settle the situation of banks without specific help from the state. State intervention is further justified by the macroeconomic desirability of strengthening the lending activities of banks, thereby funnelling savings to investments in this key restructuring period.

The so-called loan consolidation scheme, to be implemented with government assistance, serves to clean up the banks' portfolios and the preparation of the banks for privatisation. The scheme reduces the burden on

Table 6.6   Problem loans

	1987 HUF Bn	1987 %	1988 HUF Bn	1988 %	1989 HUF Bn	1989 %	1990 HUF Bn	1990 %	1991 HUF Bn	1991 %	1991 %
Large banks	2.7	94.87	6.5	98.56	21.4	94.61	38.8	89.57	57.5	57.5	2129.6
Medium banks	0.1	4.85	0.1	0.92	0.8	3.72	3.2	7.32	14.2	14.210	428.84
Commercial banks, total	2.8	99.72	6.6	99.48	22.2	98.33	42.6	98.36	98.3	98.3	3510.7
Specialised financial institutions	0.007	0.28	0.1	0.52	0.4	1.67	0.7	1.64	1.7	1.7	21661.58
Banks and financial institutions, total	2.8	100.0	6.7	100.0	22.6	100.00	43.3	100.00	100.00	100.00	3571.4

Source: Based on data from Hungarian Central Bank.

the financial institutions resulting from their bad and doubtful debts and improves the quality of their portfolios, and this can facilitate, *inter alia,* the stimulation of lending activities and could indirectly contribute to the reduction of high interest rates.

The gravity of the problem is demonstrated by the fact that at the end of December 1992 doubtful and bad debts made up 22.2 per cent of the outstanding debts of the banks, more than HUF 264.4 billion. (See Table 6.7).

Table 6.7   Distribution of the outstanding debts of the banking system in a breakdown by risk, 31 December 1992

	Debt rating in HUF billion	*Stock in percentage*
Standard	888.43	74.4
Substandard	41.1	3.4
Doubtful	98.1	8.2
Bad	166.6	14.0
Total outstanding debt	1194.1	100.0

Source: Central Bank of Hungary.

Scope of the Bad Debt Problem

In December 1992, the stock of non-performing loans in the Hungarian banking system totalled Ft 305.8 billion compared with Ft 43 billion in 1990 and under Ft 3 billion in 1987. As a percentage of total assets, bad debts rose from 0.3 per cent in 1987 to 2.6 per cent in 1990 before jumping to 12.98 per cent in 1992.

The enormous increase can be attributed to several factors. Primarily, *the most important factor* was the serious *economic downturn.* Lending became increasingly risky as the impact of the economic recession and the collapse of the East European markets led to the deterioration of the financial position of the business sector. Second, as monetary policy and the financial regulation were fine-tuned and became more and more sophisticated the range of loans classified as non-performing increased rapidly. Third, the Hungarian banking regulation, in particular the system of loan classification in place between 1987 and 1991, both underestimated and aggravated the bad debt problem. It gave an incentive to banks to prolong loans, through automatic roll-overs or capitalisation of interest, instead of writing them off. Furthermore, classification of debt as 'bad' under the regulations in effect until 1991 was not linked to any requirement to set aside adequate reserves. Thus the regulations, in accordance with the prevailing accounting practice, allowed banks to hide potential losses and oriented them toward declaring high and, in part, fictitious profits. The large jump in non-performing debt after 1991 reflects in particular the new loan classification system at the end of 1991. And last but not least, the deep economic recession not only downgraded the financial situation of previously creditworthy firms but also depreciated the value of collateral held by the banks.

Another worrying aspect of the problem is that bad debts are highly concentrated in the three largest commercial banks that were split off from the NBH in 1987. Despite the rapid increase in the number of banks in Hungary since 1987, these three banks *still account for 70–80 per cent of total corporate lending.* Not surprisingly *they also held nearly 60 per cent of the total non-performing loans of the banking system.*

The recent data show that the required amount of risk reserves was HUF 222.5 billion, but the banks only set aside HUF 104.5 billion at the end of 1991. According to the latest estimation the required amount of risk reserves, or capital, was more than 200 billion Ft at the end of 1992 (and almost 250 billion Ft for the end of 1993). The lack of required risk reserves and capital characterise primarily the largest banks.

Evolution of Hungarian Policy to Restructuring Bank Balance Sheets

The approach of the Hungarian government to the bad debt problem has evolved substantially since 1987, from an essentially gradual approach relying on the banks themselves to take the necessary measures, to an approach which contemplates an increasingly important role for the government. The government's initial gradual approach was based on the assumption that the amount of bad debt on the banks' books was manageable and that the banks could 'grow out' of the problem, naturally with a relatively limited financial support given by the government. Strong growth of assets and profit, made possible partly by inflation, would allow the banks to increase their reserves sufficiently so that the eventual write-off of non-performing loans would be covered. The government needed to take action to facilitate reserve creation.

There was a second, very important element of the original Hungarian approach: the illusion of a quick stabilisation and transition of the economy. Assuming the start of economic recovery, a slight real growth from 1991 to 1992, and supposing a further reduction of the inflation, the original government forecasts took into account an improving financial position of the enterprise sector. That assumption was an illusion. The stabilisation and the transition, creating the market economy, needs longer time than was expected.

The real economy had to be faced with different types of shocks on the demand and the supply side. The introduction of the bankruptcy law has caused in a few thousand cases liquidation or bankruptcy of companies. The recession in the developed countries and the collapse of the former COMECON market led to a sharp decline in the export and in the total output of the economy. The domestic aggregate demand had to be reduced because of the stabilisation.

The structural adjustment of the industry and agriculture can only be a long-term process. Therefore, the extent of the problem loans is growing continuously, and the extent of the bank portfolio problem is larger than it was estimated earlier. Furthermore, the bad loan problem is linked to the structural difficulties of the real economy. It means that neither the portfolio problems of the financial sector nor the structural difficulties of the real economy can be solved separately.

Government Measures since 1991

The first response was in mid-1991, when the government decided to guarantee Ft 10.5 billion for about half of the inherited pre-1987 bad debt in order to reduce the size of the banks' required risk reserves. In addition, until the banks had built up the necessary reserves and the capital adequacy ratio requirement according to the Banking Law, the banks were told to reduce their dividends to their shareholders (primarily the state and state-owned enterprises) to about 8–9 per cent of 1990 profits, in contrast to the 15–20 per cent paid in the previous years. The after-tax profits remaining after the payment of dividend were then to be used to increase bank capital. The banks, however, themselves began to explore various ways to transfer debt off their balance sheets by establishing specialised firms to buy and manage their problem loans.

The large jump in non-performing loans in 1992, despite the measures taken in 1991, forced the government to find new methods for a more effective financial support.

The second step was the loan consolidation in 1992. The aim of Hungarian credit consolidation was to assist the normal functioning of banks and to substantially improve their economic and financial indexes (for example, capital adequacy) to reduce the interest margins together with interest rates on credits; to facilitate the privatisation of those banks with considerable state ownership (mainly via increasing their capital); and to support the reorganisation of debtor companies (at least to establish the necessary conditions).

The basic elements of the 1992 loan consolidation scheme were the following:

- The cost incurred must be met by the future incomes of banks, that is, indirectly by the owners, over a prolonged period of time.
- Claims excluded from the banks' balance sheets must be treated by methods of the market economy.
- The direct financial role of the state must be limited to compensate banks' potential loss of assets.
- Credit consolidation should be linked to company reorganisation programmes.
- The 1992 loan consolidation scheme was transitory due to the quickness with which the portfolios were sorted out, and hurried solutions were implemented.

The main features of the 1992 model were the following:

- Banks took part in the consolidation voluntarily (11 commercial banks).
- A part of non-performing assets was separated from banks and concentrated to a state-owned specialised financial institution (Hungarian Development and Investment Company).
- The form of the loan consolidation was the issue of special treasury bonds and exchange of them for bad assets. The total value of the special treasury bonds, issued in 1992, was almost 100 billion Ft. The value of non-performing assets, involved in the 1992 loan consolidation scheme was almost 140 billion Ft.

In order to avoid substantial loss of assets, banks were given interest-bearing and tradeable government bonds after the debts are sold or transferred to the market organisations. The combined value of risk reserves and the transferred bonds cannot exceed 90 per cent of the nominal value of 'bad' debts or 50 per cent of 'doubtful' debts.

The 1993 model could be characterised – in a wider sense – as a *bank* consolidation programme, linked to enterprise restructuring as well. The main features of the model include:

- Voluntary bank participation in the consolidation.
- Claims can be transferred indirectly or directly to market organisations (companies); they will collect on their claims to debtors through agreements partially cancelling the debt, rescheduling it, or through the

transfer of ownership. It is an opportunity, too, for the banks to further manage those assets;
– The state may undertake a part of the nominal value of the claims in order that the banks do not suffer losses, but the banks in exchange are subject to certain fees for a period of 20 years.

The credits that are allowed to participate in the 1993 credit consolidation are those which were extended before 30 September, 1992 and will be rated 'bad' or 'doubtful' by 31 December, 1993.

In the framework of the 1992 credit consolidation, bad debts were bought by the state, taking into account given risk reserves, for 50 per cent, 80 per cent, and in certain cases 100 per cent of the nominal value. In 1992 there was not enough time to establish market organisations which could have assumed responsibility for the debts. The state paid for these claims through interest-bearing and negotiable bonds.

In the framework of the 1993 bank consolidation, banks can sell their 'doubtful' or 'bad' assets directly to the market organisations at a market price.

The most important feature of the 1993 model is that the participating banks will get capital from the state as financial support. It means that the bank consolidation programme in 1993 is aiming at the recapitalisation of given commercial banks, instead of – as in 1992 – separating non-performing assets. In the first step of recapitalisation the capital/adequacy ratio of participating banks will be improved on a 4 percentage point level. In the second phase it is planned to increase the ratio further with 2–3 percentage points through capital investment by the state.

Privatisation of the Banks

One of the driving forces behind the government's strategy regarding restructuring bank balance sheets was the government's desire to accelerate the privatisation of the large banks which was supposed to have begun in 1992. The growing bad debt problem was seen as a major factor delaying the process, since bank privatisation is integrally connected with the condition and value of a bank's loan profolio. While the government has to reduce its stake in the banks to no more than 25 per cent until 1997, it hopes to accelerate bank privatisation through the sale of a strategic stake (in the order of 25 per cent) to a foreign investor as an optimal way to shore up bank capital, as well as promote modernisation of both bank management and technical skills. All the four large commercial banks are being prepared for privatisation and have hired international investment banks as advisors.

VI   THE PROFITABILITY OF THE BANKING SYSTEM

Development of Earnings

The comparison of some of the main economic indicators unambiguously shows signs of 'overheating' followed by 'cooling', of inflation accelerating and then slowing down, as well as the necessary manifestation of these in the earnings of banks. (See Table 6.8).

Table 6.8   Hungarian economic indicators

	1988	1989	1990	1991	1992
GDP volume	99.9	99.8	96.0	88.9	95.0
Industrial price index	105.4	114.6	120.9	131.5	114.0
Money supply M2	112.0	116.0	129.0	125.8	127.0
Growth rate of the total assets of financial institutions	102.7	121.9	129.9	130.7	111.2
Banks' earnings	123.7	142.0	127.4	56.1	0–5[*]

Note: Numbers express the proportion of the preceding year's figures.
[*] At less than 5 per cent of the level of the previous year, pre-tax aggregate earnings of banks after provisioning was minuscule in 1992.
Source: Central Bank of Hungary.

The changes in the results of the banks reflect the economic downturn, even if the former accounting regulations enabled the banks to present unrealised profits and the 1991 and 1992 results were considerably reduced by vigorous provisioning.

The profits of the banks reached their peak in 1990 with HUF 63.3 billion; in 1991, this fell to 56 per cent of the preceding year's figure due to the reasons referred to above and, in 1992, the combined result of the banks decreased to a minimal value.

Another factor contributing to the reduction of profits was that in 1991 a further shift could be observed in the composition of the liabilities of the banks towards more expensive funding. As a result of all these factors, in 1991 the profits to combined total assets ratio did not even reach the 2.8 per cent level of 1987, being only 1.7 per cent. (This ratio was 3.4 per cent in 1988 and 3.9 per cent in 1989 and in 1990.) In 1992, fundamentally owing to the vigorous efforts of the banks to set aside provisions, the result after provisioning relative to the combined total assets of the banking system sank to below 1 per cent.

The profits to net assets ratio also points to the severe changes affecting the banks' results. The results in 1991 represented 16.9 per cent of their net assets; within this, the value of the ratio was 25.8 per cent in the case of the medium-sized banks, 17.9 per cent for the retail banks, 12.3 per cent for the large banks and 4.2 per cent for the specialised financial institutions. In comparison with 1987, only the medium-sized banks and the specialised financial institutions were able to improve their profits to net assets ratios, while the ratio declined in all other groups – in the case of the large banks, to about a quarter of the 1987 value. (See Table 6.9.)

Table 6.9   Profits to net assets (percent)

	1987	1988	1989	1990	1991
Large banks	50.7	44.7	45.1	50.5	12.3
Medium banks	20.2	28.8	32.9	33.2	25.8
Retail banks	151.0	182.9	161.6	108.6	17.9
Commercial banks, total	53.4	51.0	56.9	54.7	17.3
Specialised financial institutions	3.9	14.7	20.3	18.6	4.2
Banks and financial institutions, total	147.2	46.4	53.0	51.7	16.9

Source: Central Bank of Hungary.

In 1991, the profits to sales ratio of the banks and financial institutions reached 5.8 per cent (see Table 6.10), which is only about a quarter of the 1988 figure. The decrease demonstrates that, in parallel with the increase in the banks' sales revenues, their costs also rose substantially. The average 5.8 per cent was exceeded only by the medium-sized banks: their profits to sales ratio was 12.2 per cent. The lowest ratio, 3 per cent, was measured in the case of the retail banks, as this group of banks bore the highest costs and expenditures in 1991.

VII   CONCLUSIONS

The overall development of the Hungarian banking system in the period 1987–2, following the banking reform, can be evaluated as follows:

Perhaps the establishment of a functioning and progressing two-tier banking system involved fewer jerks and hitches than expected. In view of the fact that in a good number of West European countries the dismantling

Table 6.10   Profit to sales ratio

	1988	1989	1990	1991
Large banks	27.1	25.0	18.9	5.4
Medium banks	31.7	22.1	23.0	12.2
Retail banks	10.9	15.0	12.5	3.0
Commercial banks, total	20.0	20.1	16.7	5.8
Specialised financial institutions	33.3	69.0	20.9	3.9
Banks and financial institutions, total	20.3	20.7	16.8	5.8

Source: Central Bank of Hungary.

of government restrictions on the financial sector and the reinforcement of the banks took 10–15 years – and in some places the liberalisation of the financial sector is still an unfinished business – it is hard to exaggerate the significance of the fact that by the early 1990s Hungary has an independent, functioning financial sector with viable commercial banks and real money and capital markets, even though they have numerous problems.

On the whole, the financial sector adequately performs its financial mediatory functions in the difficult period of the transition, laden with serious macroeconomic tensions.

The Hungarian banking system operates within an adequate legal framework; the Banking Law and the Accounting Law adjusted to international practices, both were adopted in 1991, and in effect since that same year, adopted international standards also to the Hungarian banking system. The financial institutions are licensed – and able – to perform most banking operations. This is worthy of appreciation, even if the standard of the banking services and the choice of banking products lag far behind those of the advanced countries.

The fast development of the financial sector worldwide sets higher requirements for the Hungarian banking system, as the fundamentals had to be established simultaneously with catching up with the rest of the world.

The main tasks can be summarised as follows:

Especially after 1991, in the context of the economic downturn together with the tremendous restructuring efforts, the high interest rates and high lending risks, the lending activities of banks have become more and more restrained. The phenomenon of the credit crunch is not unknown in international financial life, as it has appeared also in other countries at times of recession. Within the triple grip of restructuring, economic stabilisation and the institutional development of the financial sector, the promotion of lending and thereby funnelling savings to investments constitutes particularly significant challenges for Hungarian monetary policy.

One of the fundamental issues of monetary policy in the forthcoming period is therefore the promotion of the lending activities of the banks, with a view to facilitating the launching of economic growth. This requires, *inter alia*, the setting-up of the 'background institutions' improving the security of lending, and playing an important role in reducing risks (e.g. guarantee funds, credit information systems, institutions dealing with bad debts on a business basis); but first of all it requires the strengthening of the capitalisation and risk-bearing capabilities of the banking system, while also expanding the range of creditworthy customers. Therefore, bank consolidation is a key issue, together with the reorganisation of the enterprise sector.

The overall direction of the change in the structure of the banking system has been sound: the heavy fragmentation of the financial sector of the money markets has lessened somewhat. The share of the formerly 'overbearing' large banks has been reduced in all respects, and a substantial group of medium-sized banks has come into being. The money market, however, is still heavily segmented: whether in corporate lending, retail banking, accounts or foreign exchange operations, 4–5 banks of the 37 play the decisive role (with shares of 60–80 per cent). At the same time, certain institutions, such as building societies, mortgage lending institutions, network of rural banks, etc. are still missing from the Hungarian banking system.

One of the decisive, characteristic features of the past years was the withdrawal of banks especially from investment lending. This is attributable fundamentally to the recession, the increased lending risks and the liability structure of banks. However, the present situation is unacceptable. Of course the problem is not simply the consequence of the lack of long-term funds.

The challenges of the day ensue from the development of the two-tier Hungarian banking system so far. The greatest challenges include the satisfaction of the qualification and provisioning requirements of the Banking Law, and, closely related to this, the adaptation of the requirements of the Accounting Law based on international accounting standards; the reduction of the high share of bad debts, to a smaller extent inherited but mostly related to the economic downturn; and the enhancement of the capital strength and of the risk-bearing capabilities of the Hungarian banks. The further liberalisation of the financial sector is a formidable challenge, requiring that the technical equipment of Hungarian banks and the skill of their employees make them capable of competition with financial institutions of foreign ownership, which in turn should help increase the quality of service. Following the creation of the basic financial markets, it is going to be a serious task to prepare for financial derivative transactions. This requires an improvement in the quality of technical background and personal conditions.

7 Financial Sector Development and Macroeconomic Policy in Poland in 1990–3
Tadeusz Lamacz

I INTRODUCTION

This chapter consists of four sections. Following this Introduction section II shows the transition process from a socialist to market economy in Poland, which is analysed as having proceeded in the three following areas:

- macroeconomic stabilisation,
- institutional changes,
- microeconomic restructuring of production capacity.

Section III contains a presentation of the evolution of the Polish banking system, from one in which the monobank (NBP) played the role of a budgetary branch, to the two-tier system, with the NBP assuming the functions of a central bank and a group of commercial and specialised banks. It was found that the stabilisation package launched in January 1990 contributed to substantial profits of banks in 1990. Later, due mainly to the adverse effects of stabilisation measures and lagging systemic changes, as well as failing the microeconomic adjustments, the performance of banks sharply deteriorated. As will be shown, the main policy response to the banks' problem is incorporated in the Programme of Financial Restructuring of Enterprises and Banks. In this chapter, less attention is paid to the capital market, which was non-existent at the beginning of the transition process, and since 1991 has been slowly growing and is still being limited by the slow pace of privatisation and securitisation of assets.

Section IV focuses on:

- possible consequences of the 'systemic shock' to the financial sector triggered off by mass privatisation and financial restructuring of enterprises and banks, and

– the growing domestic debt and even larger foreign indebtedness.

II   THE ECONOMIC TRANSFORMATION PROGRAMME IN POLAND AND MAJOR ADJUSTMENT ISSUES

Although some market-oriented reforms (limiting price control and widening the scope of the self-sufficiency of state enterprises) were launched in Poland in 1980s, the transition to a market economy from the systemic point of view started in 1989. Among 25 Eastern and Asian countries undergoing the process of systemic transformation, Poland is at the most advanced stage of change due to a comparatively long experience of changing the centrally planned system, and starting fully fledged reforms as early as 1989.

The transition process has been taking place in these areas:

– macroeconomic stabilisation,
– institutional changes,
–   microeconomic restructuring of production capacity.

Macroeconomic stabilisation, launched on 1 January 1990, consisted of mainly orthodox measures of the IMF-type programme, namely:

– reduction of the budget deficit from 6.6 per cent of the GDP in 1989 to the planned 1 per cent of GDP in 1990, through both tax increases and the elimination of most subsidies;
– liberalisation of almost all prices, and a threefold increase in the prices of hard coal, crude oil, electricity and natural gas;
– introduction of positive interest rates, in real terms, on both old and new debts, allowing part of the increased interest payments to be capitalised;
– devaluation of the zloty by 31.6 per cent, freeing the exchange rate for at least 3 months, and introducing internal convertibility of the zloty;
– imposition of drastic limits for wage increases, through a high and progressive excess wage tax, whereby wage indexation was assumed at a very low level of 0.2 in January and 0.2 in February 1990.

Institutional changes, preceded by the formation of a legal basis for the economy, consisted of the following main actions:

– raising barriers of entry and exit to and from economic activity (The Revised Act on Economic Activity from 28 December 1989);

- introducing a constitutional guarantee of private property (amendment to the Constitution from 29 December 1989);
- revalidity of the Commercial Code of 1934 regulating the development of the private sector, and the reintroduction of the Bankruptcy Act of 1934;
- introducing the practice of investigation and enforcement of competition law (The Antimonopoly Act of February 1990);
- far-reaching liberalisation of foreign trade: abolishing the state monopoly of foreign trade, guaranteeing equal treatment of domestic and foreign activity, lifting nearly all quantitative restrictions on exports and imports, and adopting low tariffs (trade-weighted average tariff estimated at 10 per cent) and suspension of duties for numerous items;
- creation of a two-tier banking system;
- creation of capital market (opening of the Warsaw Stock Exchange in April 1991, and earlier – passing of the Act on Public Trading in Security and Trust Funds of March 1991);
- opening up several paths of privatisation under the Law on Privatisation of August 1990 (i.e. small privatisation, privatisation via liquidation, capital privatisation and mass privatisation);
- adopting a liberal law on foreign investments (July 1991).

The third area of transition, *microeconomic restructuring*, is of vital importance since it concerns the development of the private sector and the changing behaviour of state-owned enterprises in the new economic environment, characterised by free prices, drastically reduced subsidies, positive interest rates in real terms, as well as growing competition from the private sector and foreign firms.

Anticipating further analysis, it must be stressed that although Poland has recorded a measured success in privatising its economy (see Table 7.2), considering the share of the private and state sector in GDP and especially in industrial output, it still has a fundamentally socialist economic structure (see Table 7.1).

This very fact implies that Poland's economic performance since 1990 was strongly influenced by the behaviour of the state-owned industry. This also means that the so-called 'shock therapy', tantamount to macroeconomic stabilisation, was applied to an economy which was not only far from being a market one, but also reluctant to adapt to rapid systemic changes. The question which remains is whether the restrictive stabilisation measures have helped to accelerate or to slow down the desired systemic changes.

The on-going reforms in Poland should be considered as a process of interlinked changes in the three areas mentioned above. Its most important feature

Table 7.1   Share of private sector (in percent)

	1989	1990	1992
Share in GDP			
(fixed prices 1984)			
(incl. agriculture)	28.4	35.0	45.0
Share in employment	44.3	45.8	58.0
Share in output:			
industrial production	16.2	17.4	28.4
construction	33.4	32.2	76.8
agriculture and retail trade	55.4	61.2	80.8

Source: *Statistical Bulletin*, Central Statistical Office, Warsaw, February 1993.

is that the stabilisation measures have preceded a break-up of multifactory state monopolies, mass privatisation, creation of financial markets and the enforcement of real property rights. From the outset of the stabilisation programme an almost entire liberalisation of foreign trade together with the granting of free access to economic activity, was achieved in the systemic sphere.

The stabilisation package has been imposed on an economy that was neither centrally planned, nor a market one. It was aimed at eradicating the hyperinflation of 1989, which exploded as a result of erroneous and panic reforms of the last communist regime (the decrease of corporate income tax rates, the introduction of the 'dywidenda', a kind of property or capital tax abolishing the system of advanced payments of due taxes, import liberalisation, partial liberalisation of prices and full wage indexation), and was perceived by the Solidarity-led government as an acute illness which was to be cured instantly.

The stabilisation measures applied in the first six months brought about a rapid improvement in the budget outcome (i.e. a fiscal surplus of 7.4 per cent of overall budget revenues). At that time the profitability of state enterprises was high due to the inflationary shock caused by the price liberalisation. Those banks which operated with positive real interest rates, high spreads, charges and commissions also prospered. Measured success was achieved in combating inflation. After high corrective price increases in January and February 1990, the rate of inflation was slowed down to 70 per cent in the whole year, compared with approximately 1000 per cent at the end of 1989.

The immediate results of the changes commenced in 1990 were also:

-   strong growth of exports to the West, the EEC in particular, due to the sharp devaluation, s.c. 'distress sales' and the abolition of the state

Table 7.2 Number of economic units (end of quarter)

| | State enterprises | Commercial law partnerships | | | Religious organisations | Foreign small-scale enterprises | Cooperatives | Social and political organisations | Foundations |
		of Treasury*	Joint-ventures	Private					
30 June 1991	8591	283	2 840	38 516	151	856	17 308	1628	183
31 December 1992	8209	764	10 131	55 551	473	716	18 284	1404	296

Source: Statistical Bulletin, as in Table 7.1.
*Joint-stock companies with the sole participation of the Treasury.

    monopoly in foreign trade – resulting in the trade surplus of 2.2 billion US$ in 1990;

- a sharp decline in output (GDP fell by an official estimate of 11.6 per cent in that year); while private sector output increased by around 17 per cent a year, state sector output declined by 20 per cent. The latter was due to growing indebtness, when high interest rates were imposed on old and new debts. The state sector decline was also due to falling real demand; decrease in inflationary profits, from March 1990; limited inventory build-up; rationalisation of production in some industries, and cutting down on pollution. State enterprises were expecting government support and the easing of monetary and fiscal constraints. Their attitudes were shaped by disincentives both to adjust and to restructure. State enterprises were 'doomed' after the privatisation programme was initiated, and fiscal preferences for private firms applied (in contrast to the state enterprises, private firms do not pay 'dywidenda' and the excess wage tax), but the privatisation process has been long and hard;

- as far as monetary development is concerned, the 'corrective inflation' of January and February 1990 helped to absorb the 'monetary overhang', so that by March 1990, price levels has been adjusted sufficiently to bring money holding into line with the supply of available goods; according to the OECD analysis, the equilibrium achieved at the end of March 1990 can be seen as the benchmark for monetary development later in 1991–2.

    As a result of liquidation of the 'money overhang' the nightmare of queues disappeared. Shops were stocked-up. Cheap imports, as well as the 'small privatisation' (mushrooming private retail establishments) were the other factors which contributed to rapid stock improvement.

    The prevalence of the positive effects of the stabilisation programme in the first quarter of 1990 aroused the expectation that the country was on the threshold of an economic improvement. To meet the upturn of the economic cycle half-way, the government decided to cut the refinancing credit interest rate and to increase the coefficient of wage indexation, and initiated discounting enterprise bills as a remedy for growing inter-enterprise debts, as well as launching the programme of support for agriculture. To some extent these moves were interpreted as signals that the government would intervene in favour of the state sector in the economy, although the degree of relaxation was small.

    In 1991 and 1992, growth of output did not follow. Further economic development in Poland was held back by two unfavourable phenomena, namely contraction of output and growing fiscal deficit. These two factors were exacerbating social discontent and engendering a critical assessment of the stabilisation package, and *especially the reform sequencing*.

After an approximately 12 per cent decline in 1990, GDP recorded an 8 per cent slump in 1991 and a 2 per cent contraction in 1992. Thus, the decline is fading. After the contraction of industrial production by about 40 per cent from 1 January 1990, output is on the rise again. Between March and December 1992, in real terms, was 5–6 per cent higher compared with the same period in 1991. Yet in 1992, GDP fell again mainly as a result of further contraction in agriculture due to, *inter alia*, the severe drought of that year.

As for the fiscal balance, contrary to the GDP decline, in the wake of the stabilisation programme the budget deficit is growing. Having achieved a surplus of 0.4 per cent of GDP in 1990, the deficit amounted to 3.8 per cent of GDP in 1991 and 8.1 per cent in 1992. In 1993, the budget deficit was restrained to 81 trillion zloty (about 5 billion US$) or 5 per cent of GDP.

Any serious presentation of the macroeconomic framework of Poland in 1990–93 should clarify the reasons for the output collapse and the fiscal disaster. There seems to be a rather broad consensus of opinion that in the three consecutive years a continuous decline of output can be attributed to the mismanagement of the state sector and to the slow pace of privatisation. These two factors are working hand in hand. Tough policy toward the state sector (i.e. higher taxes than those charged to the private sector; withdrawal of most subsidies and a high interest rate on the old debts), coupled with a deficiency of competent governance over them, might not have contributed to the heavy breakdown of output if ownership changes had proceeded faster. In other words, the parallel introduction of tough, monetary and fiscal policy towards the state sector, coupled with a dynamic process of privatisation, may have not been as disastrous for the level of output as the uncoordinated stabilisation and systemic policy was. This argument seems to be strengthened by the recent pick-up of industrial production which contributed first of all to the private sector performance. Therefore, it seems that effective privatisation is a priority which is to be accomplished in the process of transition. Taking into consideration the fact that even in market economies public enterprises take several years to become privatised, and that privatisation covers a wide continuum of possibilities between denationalisation on the one hand and market discipline on the other, making the choice of proper techniques extremely difficult in countries in which the economy was almost totally state controlled, the slow pace of privatisation in Poland should not be seen as an error in policy. Apart from the factors mentioned above, the fall in output should also be imputed to the breakdown of the CMEA markets. The exogenous factor has narrowed the margin for macroeconomic manoeuvres, as well as accentuated 'tender spots' in the economic programme.

Fiscal deficit stems from the contraction of output and narrowing of the tax base, as well as from the construction of the stabilisation package and the continually prevailing socialist-type mechanism of national income distribution. Stabilisation measures have obviously influenced the negative changes in output. Also a particular disharmony between constraints imposed on the state enterprises and the slow pace of privatisation were important factors of the decline. As for the construction of a stabilisation package, a high tax component is necessary. High direct taxes levied on the state enterprises (the main corporate taxpayers in the post-socialist country), together with high interest rates working as a quasi tax since the central bank's profits (both outstanding from 1989 and due in 1990) were transferred to the budget and contributed to its surplus.

When in the following years these transfers dried up, and, at the same time, the high average tax rate pushed the economy to the sloping side of the Laffer curve (i.e. total tax proceeds began to decline), the revenue side of the budget worsened significantly. Moreover, the emerging private sector was not only granted tax privileges, but the fiscal authorities were strangely helpless in coping with huge tax evasion in this sector. This means that the sector which could positively contribute to the fiscal balance was not fully utilised, while the ineffective and partly dismantled state sector had to bear the main fiscal burdens.

The high tax components (directly through taxes, indirectly through interest rates) of the stabilisation package has helped to inject monies into the socialist-type budget which is characterised by an enormously extended sphere of social financing and administrative costs. Special importance can be attributed to the budget expenditure on insurance funds (workers', farmers' and the Labour Pension Funds) which in 1993 reached 21.8 per cent of the budget expenditure. Other items such as financing of medical and social care, education, subsidies for housing construction and appropriations for agriculture reached a further 42 per cent.

In Poland one-third of GDP is being distributed through budgetary channels. In the period 1989–92 the share of budget expenditure in GDP increased by about 8 points. This poses a real threat to sustained growth for several reasons:

- less efficient financing of insurance, medical and to some extent also educational services through the budget, in comparison with direct financing by final consumers, is tantamount to partial wastage of tax revenues; it means that the reduced demand and investment ability of taxpayers is not offset by delivery of the required services by the public sector to the extent justified by taxpayers' renouncements;

– high average tax rate, wrung by expenditure, hampering investment possibilities of enterprises and consumer spending;

– overburden public sector expenditure makes the efforts to curb the budget deficit extremely difficult from a political and social point of view (the threat of instability);

– with still underdeveloped capital markets, the deficit is financed mainly by the banks, and thus threatens monetary control and engenders a crowding-out effect;

– with high interest rates, the budget deficit contributes to the increase of the domestic public debt (in 1992 domestic debt increased by 106.7 per cent, compared with the previous year, to 239.2 trillion zloty or 20.9 per cent of GDP, whereby 95 per cent of the debt is due to the banking sector).

The initial stabilisation package had been modified slightly; however, its very core, namely the strong fiscal measures, generally positive interest rates and wage restraint, were still maintained. The exchange rate of the zloty, initially strongly devalued, had been kept fixed against the dollar for 17 months until May 1991. The nominal anchor strategy lost its sense, since the appreciation of zloty in the period January 1990 to May 1991 contributed to the worsening of the competitive posture of enterprises. In October 1991 a fixed peg was finally abandoned in favour of a crawling peg. Nevertheless, the zloty was devalued by a further 12 per cent in March 1992.

It seems that the pace of depreciation of the zloty enabled both the easing of competitive pressure on exporters and acted as a constraint on enterprises' ability to raise prices due to rising prices in imports. The latter effect was important since in 1991 tariffs were increased from 5 per cent average trade weighted to around 18 per cent. The zloty had to be slightly overvalued in order to defeat inflation.

In the course of the transformation programme Poland is being supported by external lending, although – due to the low absorption of limited resources from foreign loans – the role of external financing in the economic and systemic turnaround is rather small. Up to December 1992, total loan commitments of international organisations and bilateral creditors reached the level of approximately US$8.5 billion, whereby actual disbursements to Poland – expressed as a percentage of total commitments – amounted to approximately 19 per cent. In the case of the World Bank credits the percentage of actual disbursements is estimated at about 21 per cent.

The performance of the foreign loans portfolio deteriorated in 1992. Various factors have been limiting disbursements of foreign loans to Poland so that the percentage of total commitments is low. Due to high risk assessments, credit agreements are provided with numerous safeguarding clauses making it difficult to draw up credits. A further impediment for credit absorption is the condition of bilateral credits of imports from a lender's country; credits from international organisations are 'tied up' with specific projects and areas which make them highly immobile. Finally, problems arise due to the highly inflexible stance of foreign creditors with respect to the Polish banking system (e.g. insistence on guarantees issued by the largest commercial bank Bank Handlowy S.A.). As for the Polish side, potential borrowers suffering the effects of recession and excessive debts are often not creditworthy; there is also a lack of experience in putting together investment packages; complex and time-consuming bank requirements can be mentioned among other important impediments (e.g. procurement rules). Furthermore, the Polish banking system itself, having meagre own funds, is not able to onlend more than 30–100 million dollars for a project. Moreover, the difference between high interest on short-term domestic credits and low interest on long-term lending in foreign currency does not work in favour of the latter.

The Polish economy is under the strain of a large foreign debt which in 1992 was in excess of 50 billion dollars.

In April 1991 agreement was reached in the Paris Club that Poland's debt to official creditors in the West (amounting at the time to some 32 billion dollars, or over 65 per cent of total Polish external debt) would be written down by 50 per cent in present value terms. The principal features of this debt-forgiveness operation are as follows:

(1) 30 per cent debt write-off would be effective immediately, with the remainder coming into effect in April 1994 on condition that the International Monetary Fund completes its review of Poland's extended fund programme by the end of 1993.

(2) Poland undertook not to provide more favourable terms to non-Paris Club creditors (including in particular private banks) than has been agreed with the Paris Club creditors. Western banks have generally not been satisfied with this condition, and in the resulting impasse Poland is continuing not to service its bank debt. (In fact, Poland stopped payment on this debt in 1989.)

(3) Paris Club members agreed that forgiveness would be structured so as to ensure that Poland would not need to repay principal for five years, and that interest payments for the first three years would be limited to

no more than 20 per cent of interest due on the whole stock of debt before any debt reductions. Beyond this, individual creditors and the Polish government were to decide bilaterally on the precise modalities through which the 50 per cent present value reduction was to be achieved (e.g. whether by debt write-off, reduced interest rates, or interest deferrals).

As the result of the Paris Club agreement, the external constraint on Poland is substantially eased until 1994 compared to what it would have been if the debt had not been reduced. The agreement helped to restore the confidence of foreign creditors in the Polish economy. The commitments by the World Bank and other international institutions, and a number of bilateral credit lines with foreign governments, insured by them through their export-credit insurance agencies, are in place. However, the condition not to provide more favourable terms to non-Paris Club creditors produced an impasse in the negotiations with Western private banks, to whom Poland owes about 13 billion dollars, since the banks are wary of the scale of the debt reduction approved by the Paris Club.

In 1993 the economic situation in Poland was characterised by high and growing domestic indebtedness of both the state and the corporate sector, and some signs of economic recovery. Growth scenarios for Poland are not unequivocally optimistic. On the one hand, the social costs of transformation are rising, the fiscal balance is deteriorating and becoming unsustainable, and renewed inflationary pressure is emerging. On the other hand, it is argued that after difficult years of adjustment, Poland has entered the path of a sustained growth of output and private consumption, and this and the convergence of Poland's inflation with international levels are two key macroeconomic objectives, the prospects for which are reasonably good.

There is, however, a rather broad consensus among different experts that the policy measures applied in order to achieve the goal of anti-inflationary growth in Poland in the medium term have to be focused on the following key areas:

- measures for external balance and a sustainable macro-framework;
- the need for fiscal reforms and for a substantial strengthening of public administration;
- removing supply bottlenecks, by accelerating the pace of privatisation and improving corporate governance while awaiting privatisation;
- solving the problem of non-performing loans in the banking sector;
- strengthening the social security network;
- establishing the means of financing the necessary infrastructure.

III   POLISH FINANCIAL SECTOR DEVELOPEMENT

Institutional and Financial Restructuring of the Banking sector

The objectives of a well-functioning banking system are at least fourfold:

- generation of higher domestic savings to finance development;
- improvement of efficiency of allocation of scarce resources to competitive enterprises;
- imposition of financial discipline on enterprises by banks through debt enforcement and liquidation, if necessary;
- evolution of financial instruments to improve monetary management through the market, instead of credit directives.

How far did the country succeed in accomplishing the purpose of having such a banking system?

The reform of the banking system, having been launched in 1991, consisted of two elements: transforming 9 branches of the NBP (National Bank of Poland) into 9 commercial banks having the status of joint-stock companies (in the beginning all shares were held by the state); and, secondly, liberalisation of entry for new banks, including ones with non-state capital.

The number of banks grew rapidly. At the end of 1991 there were 75 commercial banks, of which 30 had a majority private share, 7 banks with foreign capital involvement, more than 1500 cooperative banks and 5 specialised banks.

At the end of 1992 more than half of the banks in Poland were held in private hands. However, the role that the state-owned banks play in the Polish economy remained substantial, and still accounts for nearly 90 per cent of the credit market.

The important element of the reforms in the banking sector is the actual transfer of ownership from the state to the private sector. This process consists of two steps: the commercialisation of banks, and offering the shares of the bank for sale to individual private investors. The former process means that the state-owned banks are transformed into joint-stock companies with sole participation of the Treasury; it means that the bank receives recognition as a legal entity with a structure similar to those found in Western economies. The commercialisation as described above allows an ownership transformation without stripping the bank of its rights, and maintains all of its contractual obligations.

The latter process (the offering of shares of the bank for sale to private investors) involves drafting a strategy after which such a transfer would follow. The current strategy assumes that the privatisation process should incorporate the following principles:

- foreign strategic investors will initially acquire a minority stake, but combined with a management contract; the acquisition of a larger stake may be possible in the future;
- the State Treasury is likely to retain approximately 30 per cent of equity, but may limit its control rights to those analogous to a 'golden share' designated to protect strategic interests. It is the intention of the government to further dilute its stake in the future;
- Polish as well as foreign investors, both retail and institutional, are offered an opportunity to participate in the privatisation through a flotation or a combination of flotation and private placement.

Given the parameters mentioned, the initial future ownership structure of the commercial banks may be envisaged as follows:

- foreign strategic partner or a core group of investors: 20–30 per cent
- State Treasury: 30 per cent
- employees: 5 per cent
- other investors: 35–45 per cent

The whole Polish banking system has remained small; its total own funds are lower than that of one leading Western bank (at the end of 1991, ca 40 trillion zloty = 3.5 billion US$). The system also remained rather monopolistic with about 70 per cent of deposits placed in the five leading banks and the majority of credits allocated to big state enterprises.

Financial restructuring of the Polish banks is tightly connected with an IMF type stabilisation programme which started to be realised on 1 January 1990. In 1990 and early 1991 banks thrived. Despite the high level of mandatory reserves imposed on them, their profitability (measured as the ratio of net profit to total cost) was high (127.5 per cent for nine commercial banks; 65.6 per cent for all banks). The exceptional increase in profitability was also high and contributed to the increase of gross capital and reserves of the nine banks to 15 per cent of total assets (July 1990) compared with 5.9 per cent before. This situation could be attributed mainly to positive real interest rates, being the leading component of the stabilisation package, imposed, however, on a socialist-type economy, far from being ruled by market forces. A non-competitive environment allowed banks to apply high spreads (average margin between 12-month lending rates and 12-month deposit rates fluctuated widely up to as much as 5 per cent per month) and high charges and commission rates. Since new private banks were less profitable due to high start-up costs, the nine commercial banks which seceded from the NBP were the main gainers, but also the inheritors of old debtors, mainly large socialist enterprises, which were economically ineffective and had accumulated arrears. Banks began to charge penalty rates when enterprises were in arrears in their servicing for more than 30 days, but at the same time about 80 per cent of working capital require-ments of these firms were rolled over automatically. The picture is not a completely clear one, but it may be stated that the high profits of banks in 1990 did not stem from a sound portfolio, but from the rapid transition from a sharply negative real interest rate and credit rationing to a positive interest rate as the main instrument for restricting credit demand.

The portfolios of the biggest commercial and specialised banks were and still are burdened by:

- loans to big socialist-type enterprises which have lost their financial credibility;
- formerly highly subsidised housing loans;
- the financing of central investments.

Therefore, in spite of some windfall profits at the early stage of the stabilisation programme, both the slightly changed 'banking culture' and the unrestructured, highly indebted post-socialist enterprises credited by banks soon caused substantial difficulties in the banking sector.

In 1991 the situation worsened. The proportion of bad and doubtful loans increased dramatically. Profit margins of banks declined on average to 24 per cent, and 40 per cent for the nine commercial banks. In August 1991, the stock of irregular credit increased to about 18 per cent. The cap-ital ratio norm for some important banks (measured as: own capital – losses in previous year – outstanding loans for which no reserves were pro-visioned/risk-weighted assets) such as the PKO BP and the BGZ, had fallen down to nearly 0 per cent. In 1992 banks' profitability worsened further (estimated at 18.5 per cent in the first six months of the year).

The share of bad loans in the leading banks' portfolio is presented in Table 7.3. According to the rules imposed on the Polish banks by the NBP, credits are being classified as normal, credits under special observation, credits to borrowers facing difficulties, doubtful loans and losses (the latter two categories are considered to be 'bad loans').

As seen from Table 7.3, the bad debts' share varies from bank to bank and according to different periods. The specialised bank 1 has the highest proportion of bad debts which is a result of a high concentration of credit

Table 7.3 Bad debts of nine commercial banks and two specialised banks granting together ca 95 per cent of credits for business and individuals

	June 1991	December 1991	March 1992	July 1992	September 1992	June 1993
9 commercial banks in trillion zloty	18.72	17.51	18.90	20.00	–	30.33
share in their credit portfolio (%)	23.7	20.0	21.4	19.8	–	30.6
Specialised bank 1 in trillion zloty	–	2.672	–	–	2.633	2.35
share in its credit portfolio (%)	–	52.6	–	–	75.3	72.1
Specialised bank 2 in trillion zloty	2.799	4.077	5.552	–	8.288	8.311
share in its credit portfolio	12.5	13.7	18.4	–	26.1	26.9
Total credits for business and individuals (in trillion zloty)	154.5	193.8	208.3	223.8	230.4	290.4

Source: Collated from banks.

financing on a limited number of big socialist enterprises. The nine commercial banks have a lower share of bad debts, but in the first half of 1993 this rose significantly. It may be added that for the whole banking sector, bad debts accounted for 31.7 per cent in June 1993 compared with 31.4 per cent at the end of 1992. Hence the general picture remains rather gloomy.

The second important observation is that the old bad debts (granted before 1990) are owed mainly by industrial complexes (socialist 'dinosaurs') while new bad loans have been accruing in agriculture. This very fact reflects both the slow pace of adjustment in agriculture and the high protectionism of Western markets, making the export of agricultural products to the West difficult.

Three factors caused a deterioration in the banks' performance in 1991 and the first half of 1992, namely:

- a lack of radical improvement in management and the functioning of state firms, as well as the slow pace of restructuring agriculture, fragmented and dominated by small-scale farms;
- a perverse effect of the stabilisation programme which, after the period of windfall profits of banks and enterprises, pushed the economy into deep recession and fiscal imbalance, and, after deteriorating economic performances, contributed to a slower-than-expected progress in transition and reforms;
- the passive stance taken by banks which were too cautious and tardy in their proper assessment and risking of new investments.

Policy Response

By now, the most complex policy response to all the above-mentioned problems faced by the Polish financial sector is the Programme of Financial Restructuring of Enterprises and Banks (PFREB), part of the Enterprise Pact signed in February 1993. The proposed operation (also called 'privatisation through debt relief') consists of four steps:

(a) The first step is to capitalise state and State Treasury banks in the form of an allotment of bonds amounting to 25 trillion zloty. Under the Memorandum of Understanding of 28 December 1992, setting forth the mutual understanding of the NBP, the Ministry of Finance, and the Government of Poland, with the former donors to the Stabilisation Fund, the Polish Bank Privatisation Fund was established. The purpose of the PBPF is to provide resources to support the payment of interest and a principal of long-term, zloty-denominated debt

securities (GOP bonds) in support of the recapitalisation and privatisation of the nine Polish state-owned banks. The principal is
expected to be in an aggregate amount of up to 1.41 billion dollars,
equivalent to 21 trillion zloty as determined by the mid-range dollar–
zloty exchange rate at the NBP on 25 November 1992. As described
in the Memorandum, the proceeds of drawing on the PBFB resources
will be disbursed by the Government of Poland after it has issued the
GOP bonds and one or more of the nine Polish banks has been privatised. The PBFB resources are an integral part of the PFREB,
which also involves the commitments of the IBRD in the form of the
two-tranche quick disbursing adjustment loan totalling 400 million
dollars.

The banks' own increased funds and reserves will act as a 'cushion'
against the risks faced by banks in the process of privatisation and
restructuring. The Ministry of Finance is to lay down the principles of
the bond allotment and terms on which the banks start handling
indebted enterprises. The banks will have the options of entering into
conciliatory proceedings, disposing of all dues owed by an enterprise
by selling them off at market value, going to court to wind up a debtor,
or entering into bankruptcy proceedings.

(b) The second step is to allow a debtor to initiate conciliatory proceedings. This action is aimed at both the privatisation of an indebted
enterprise and its debt relief. The subsequent agreement between a
bank and an enterprise should define the debtor's activities as tending
towards restructuring the enterprise. It should further define the creditor's activities (debt restructuring, giving new funds, etc.) and contain institutional guarantees for putting the agreement into effect. In
some cases the bank can pay off part of the enterprise's debt and take
over the claims of a satisfied creditor (this solution may help to clear
some inter-enterprise debts).

(c) The third step is the commercialisation of dues owed by the enterprise
under the procedure. The bank can sell its claim on the enterprise at
market value. In this way 'bad debts' can be eliminated from the
banks' assets at the cost of losing a part of their claims, but reserves
created at the first stage of the operation will ensure their 'soft
landing'.

(d) The fourth step is the conversion of debt into equity. Creditors to whom
enterprises owe at least 30 per cent of their debts may enter into a swap
arrangement provided that these liabilities are due and payable. This
conversion might, however, not be carried out, regardless of the
employees' right to acquire 10 per cent of preferential shares.

The programme is intended both to complete the process of the formation of a modern commercial banking sector, and to advance privatisation of the state-owned enterprises.

The initial results of the measures undertaken to form a modern commercial banking sector were encouraging (i.e. the nine state-owned banks were turned into joint-stock companies with the sole participation of the Treasury; the MOF has commissioned regular portfolio reviews and financial audits; it has also given strong guidance to the newly appointed supervisory boards of the banks and steered bank managers to accept comprehensive foreign assistance to build up their banking skills). The MOF therefore decided that the recapitalisation of banks would occur on an ex ante basis, rather than ex post based on actual collection performance. The MOF that worked out the programme seems to be convinced that without an injection of government funds to rebuild the banks' capital, the banks' behaviour threatens to inhibit the still weak but clearly discernible recovery in the economy. However, whether this procedure will, on average, provide sufficient new capital for the banks while maintaining incentives for them to reach constructive restructuring solutions for their non-performing debtors remains to be seen. One cannot miss the point that, until the banks are privatised, civil servants from the MOF will take a series of steps, including mandatory action, to be imposed on the banks and ensure their close monitoring by the MOF. Thus the independent nature of commercial banking is to be violated, and 'banking culture' can only be insufficiently improved in the course of the operation.

The semi-market form of the PFREB is underlined by the role the ministries are to play in the 'privatisation through debt relief'. Apart from the actions the MOF has already launched and still intends to launch, the Ministry of Ownership Changes is to decide which enterprises are eligible for debt/equity swaps and what the discounted purchase price of indebted assets is.

One cannot expect that the debt securities issued under the programme will be in great demand unless foreign investors acquire a substantial amount of equity offered. Also, banks do not seem to profit much from acquiring the assets of ailing enterprises. Even assuming that the low discounted purchase price of various equities does not undermine the banks' solvency, new venture investments pose a challenge to the banks to behave more as investment than as commercial banks. Whether such a re-profiling of the banks' activities will be possible on the scale imposed by the bad debts figures remains to be seen. The success of commercialisation and debt/equity swaps depends a lot on foreign-capital inflow and the role foreign strategic investors will play in the process. Foreign capital participation is, therefore, the crucial element in any auspicious 'privatisation through debt relief'. Since the Polish economy still remains 'inflationary fragile', the fiscal absorption of the 'bad assets' via monetary expansion cannot be seen as a reasonable alternative to foreign capital involvement.

One can be far more optimistic regarding the privatisation performance envisaged by the programme. The law allows banks to require the commercialisation of state-owned enterprises, or their liquidation through privatisation, as a precondition for concluding a conciliatory proceeding. The government expects that, under the new incentive framework, bank managers will have a strong interest in seeking the commercialisation, and simultaneous or subsequent privatisation, of the great majority of their customers, so as to maximise their banks' intrinsic value.

The other important element of the government's strategy for instilling stability, discipline, and confidence into the financial sector is a deposit insurance system approved already by the parliament. The risk-averse, joint-stock entity with the resources and credibility for guaranteeing public deposits at domestic branches of qualified banks is to insure zloty-denominated population deposits, up to an inflation-indexed maximum of 35 million zlotys per depositor per bank. The creation of the deposit insurance system stems from the line of thought that state intervention is indispensable in achieving two difficult goals simultaneously, namely underpinning the weak but clearly discernible economic recovery and making commercial banking stable, disciplined and effective. Hence, the governing body of the insurance association is a Supervisory Board comprised of representatives including those from the NBP (central bank) and the Ministry of Finance, and the newly created entity will also monitor and examine member banks, and conduct, or participate in conservatorship, liquidation and bankruptcy proceedings of banks. On the other hand, the deposit insurance system incorporates some refined market mechanisms. Continued funding after the start-up of operations of the entity will come from annual premium assessments on the insured deposits of member banks; but the plan envisages the payment of premium rebates to member banks using a risk-based distribution method, if the coverage ratio of the fund exceeds a pre-defined limit. The other refined element of the plan is the provision for a Modified Purchase and Assumption liquidation of failed banks. Unlike a traditional Purchase and Assumption transaction in which all depositors, insured and uninsured, receive full payment on their claims, the MP and A gives uninsured depositors a pro rata claim on the economic value of a bank's assets, after all insured deposits have been transferred to an acquiring bank.

Some evident positive effects can be expected from the deposit insurance system mentioned. First of all, a social benefit is the provision for safety for small depositors and the prevention of widespread deposit runs and the damage such runs cause to the financial sector. Further, since the government's explicit guarantees on deposits at state-owned banks have been substantially reduced, the scheme will encourage continued bank privatisation. Moreover, the method of continued funding of the deposit insurance system, the foreseen premium rebates to member banks, as well as the provision for a Modified Purchase and Assumption liquidation of failed banks, introduce a sound market calculation into a risk management system.

Evolving Indirect Instruments of Monetary Policy

The transformation of the NBP from the only communist-type bank into a central bank in a market economy was the leading component of the institutional changes in Poland in recent years. In its new role, the NBP applied the set of instruments available to a central bank (refinancing, reserve ratio policy, interest policy, exchange rate policy, open market operations, supervision). The main features of the evolving instruments mentioned are:

(a) the NBP refinancing rate is the key instrument of the interest rate policy, and has a major influence on lending and deposit interest rates;
(b) the mandatory reserve and the issue of the NBP's own bills make the control of the banking system's liquidity more efficient;
(c) discretionary methods of monetary control include the regulation of the size of the commissions charged by the banks.

Since January 1991 the indirect tools of monetary control had been (although supplemented by a temporary corset) an administrative guidance over credit expansion by the commercial and specialised banks.

Concurrently, the NBP made a large contribution in improving its function as a regulator and supervisor of the banking system. Since 1980 the NBP issued recommendations relating to the principles of awarding credit; the qualification of loan portfolio credits; the required capital adequacy ratios; information and financial reporting on large debtors; and bank liquidity measurement standards. However, in 1990–1, effective control over the banking system was rather loose, resulting in the foundation of private banks poorly equipped with capital and skills, and also in dubious, sometimes mafia-type, connections among banks and enterprises. In that time, some scandals shook the banking community. It appeared that some banks' guarantees were committed against bribes, credits were allocated without proper securities for them, and interest was paid two times or more on the same deposits. Such activities can be attributed partly to the deliberately free access to economic activity assured by the liberal reformers, partly to interstices in the banking legislation and procedures.

Both the dismissal of the then president of the NBP and the amendments to the Banking Law of 1989 which came into life on 9 April 1992, were aimed to trim the course. New definitions and limits on the concentrations of exposure to one client, or a group of mutually dependent clients, were imposed. The new law places a limit of 15 per cent of the bank's own funds (defined as the share capital plus reserves) on the bank's total exposure to one, or a group, of interdependent clients. Also a limit of 10 per cent of the bank's own funds is placed upon any given exposure arising out of a single agreement.

According to the amendments pertaining to the Banking Law of 31 January 1989, banks are required to make known their audited balance sheets and profit and loss statements. They are also obliged to disclose major acquisitions and transfers of their shares. The other obligations include: notifying the NBP of cases in which the deposits, or procedures of deposit, of its clients are deemed suspicious, or where cash deposits exceed amounts suggested by the NBP; publishing the interest rate offered on deposits, interest on credits and loans, and fees for services offered. New stricter penalties and procedures for dealing with persons or entities carrying on deposit-taking activity and providing credit without a permit from the NBP were imposed. The NBP set up requirements concerning the statutes of a newly established bank, the procedures in granting a licence to a bank with participation of foreign capital, and the repatriation of profit by foreign persons contributing capital to the establishment of a new bank.

The stronger grip on the banks by the NBP develops along with broadening the scope of their activity. According to the amended Banking Law, banks gain the right to acquire securities abroad, and the companies under the aegis of the Polish Commercial Code are given the possibility to carry on selected banking activities. As for the latter element, the amended law defines the procedure for obtaining such permits.

In order to strengthen the regulatory and supervisory network for the financial sector, the NBP has, recently, developed a comprehensive ambitious programme which includes four main components: off-site analysis; on-site supervision; a training plan; and senior advice.

Development of the Capital Market

The most striking feature of the Polish capital market is its comparatively well-developed institutional structure and small, although rapidly growing, turnover.

The Warsaw Stock Exchange, based on the French stock exchange model from Lyon, was opened on 16 April 1991. Its equity market registered rapidly growing weekly turnovers in the second and third quarters of 1993 (up to about 30 million US$) due to a fairly improved privatisation performance and clear signs of economic recovery. The fully computerised trading system, completed in June 1992, makes it possible to carry a market of a much larger size.

Founded originally as a non-profit joint-stock company with the sole participation of the Treasury, the Warsaw Stock Exchange underwent privatisation and a majority of its shares have been sold to banks and brokerage houses.

Banks are allowed to undertake brokerage activities provided that their securities operations are financially and administratively separate from their banking activities. Banks and brokerage firms must fulfill the following conditions to be members of the Exchange: namely, to be an entity conducting a brokerage business; to be a shareholder in the Exchange; to be allowed to operate in the market and to complete transactions on the Exchange. Foreign brokerage firms are allowed to operate in Poland subject to their acquisition of a permit from the Securities Commission.

The following criteria are applied to securities to be listed by the Stock Exchange Board:

- the transferability of the securities is not limited;
- the value of the shares to be introduced to the market is at least 10 billion zloty and for other securities 2 billion zloty;
- at least 20 per cent of the issuer's shares were or are made available by public offering or their value exceeds 20 billion zloty;
- the distribution of the ownership of the shares ensures suitable liquidity and an orderly course of market transactions;
- information is made available allowing investors to assess the quality of acquired assets.

The Stock Exchange is open to foreign investors. They can simply open an account with a member of the Stock Exchange and place their orders. However, if they make an acquisition amounting to more than 10 per cent of a company's issued share capital, and if their acquisition is to lead to the ownership of 33 per cent or more of the listed company, a takeover bid must be announced.

IV THE OUTLOOK FOR FURTHER DEVELOPMENT OF THE FINANCIAL SECTOR

In the middle of 1993, Poland approached a threshold in the systemic transformation. The 'critical mass' for a definite change of the Polish economic system from a socialist to a market one was reached when the two essential programmes received parliamentary approval, namely:

– The Programme of Financial Restructuring of Enterprises and Banks (PFREB), and
– The Mass Privatisation Scheme.

As a result, about 1400 state-owned enterprises are expected to be privatised within one year. Another 500–600 enterprises can be privatised on different existing privatisation tracks (mainly through the liquidation of small or medium sized enterprises), so that by the end of 1994 nearly 50 per cent of the initial stock and about 40 per cent of industrial output may belong to the private sector. As a result, the share of the private sector in GDP (including agriculture and retail trade of which 80 per cent is already in private hands) may surpass 65 per cent.

The tide of privatisation implies a massive development of the capital market, which – as indicated earlier – is able to develop turnovers on a much bigger scale, and leads to a reduction of the monopolistic role of banks as financial intermediaries. Securitisation of debts and an expansion in share ownership offer new possibilities for also investing savings outside the banking sector. *The surge of competition in the Polish financial markets can contribute to lowering the costs of financial intermediation and the easing of cost-driven inflationary pressure.* Diversification of channels for borrowing and lending money normally has a positive impact on the general economic activity and there is no reason to deny this effect in Poland.

The growing competition in the money market in Poland, working in disfavour of an easy life for the banks, is also connected to a gradual expansion of forms of financial intermediation such as:

– low-cost financing by using commercial papers generally understood to be short-term and negotiable (securities, bonds, promissory notes, Treasury Bonds and other miscellaneous matters);

- development of cooperative deposit–credit societies, as recommended by the World Credit Union, which has started to be involved in corresponding activities in Poland;
- development of regional guarantee funds making loans accessible for small and medium size enterprises;
- development of pension funds and building societies.

The growing competition mentioned can result in the protection of producers against a spectra of inefficient financial intermediators and speculators deriving a perverse rent from a badly developed production capacity. Nothing else will have a more positive impact on the course of the hitherto pursued reforms, and make the system more producer-conducive than up to now.

On the other hand, banks, the nine commercial banks which seceded from the NBP in particular, are to play the role of an 'agent of change', inspired and backed up by the state. They are granted the right to conduct 'conciliation proceedings' under the PFREB, to foreclose on the assets of enterprises, as well as to acquire shares in privatised enterprises. Before it will happen on a large scale, some 25 billion zloty is put into banks' purses by the government. One can expect that in this way, along with reducing the 'old bad debts', the banks will expose themselves to risks connected with acquiring and possessing the various fixed assets of ailing enterprises. The probability that under the PFREB the banks may convert a part of their 'bad debts' into a burdensome equity or may not be able to sell their claims on bad debtors is not low, all the more so as the Ministry of Finance is to 'take a series of steps including mandatory actions to be imposed on the banks', in exchange for their ex ante capitalisation, and it admits that an outright liquidation of numerous loss-makers is politically impossible and economically undesirable. In other words, there is a danger of only changing the nature of the banks' difficult assets while leaving the causes of high credit costs and the banks' risk-averse attitudes.

A significant government intervention, not only in the PFREB, but also in the Mass Privatisation Scheme (under which the state enterprises to be privatised are assigned by the Ministry of Ownership Changes), is a matter of concern. Firstly, significant interference of state bureaucracy in processes such as large-scale privatisation and the restructuring of banks and enterprises almost automatically implies corruption scandals. Notwithstanding their economic consequences, slipping in the mud of scandals may worsen public confidence in the political economy of transformation and make national consensus on reforms difficult to be forged. Secondly, the nature of state intervention is such that the acts of intervention need to be repeated. When too many minority creditors of the restructured enter-prises under the PFREB are unsatisfied and banks are burdened by too many unsaleable fixed assets and securitised claims as a result of a half-compulsory action, the government may be compelled to assign new amounts of budgetary resources to prevent an undesirable collapse of banks and firms. This would be undesirable while the Polish financial sys-tem remains under the strain of fiscal imbalance and growing public debt.

As the implementation of the PFREB bears a risk of inducing additional costs for the state, more attention needs to be paid to the state budget. In this context, three questions are of vital importance, namely:

- the creation of Western-style pension funds,and in this way relaxing onerous budget expenditures on financing pensions
- an enhancement of the negotiations for a reduction in Poland's 12.1 bil-lion dollar debt to foreign commercial banks, with the aim of relieving budgetary expenditure of the burden of part of the foreign repayments and of paying a hefty credit risk premium;
- strengthening fiscal discipline along with a reconsideration of tax rate policy, in order to avoid a drop in total tax revenues because of the disincentive effect outweighing the high tax rates.

The other challenging issue for the Polish financial system to cope with constructively is the development of regional guarantee funds making accessible loans for enterprises, small and medium sized ones in particular. Since many business ventures have difficulty gaining access to bank credit without guarantees, especially at a time when bank managers have become increasingly risk-averse and cannot rely on state intervention under the PFREB as a potent medicine for their non-performing assets, the establish-ment of guarantee funds at central and local levels is a matter of high prior-ity. The lack of guarantee mechanism for loans to municipalities also has a negative impact on the absorption of external financing, which – is and will be – much needed to finance investments beyond those possible with only domestic savings.

Last but not least, the recent development of the Polish banking system is characterised by the growing independence of the NBP and the expan-sion of its regulatory and supervisory functions, as shown in Section III of this chapter. The former evolution needs no counter-argument since the independence of central banks seems to be an admitted ally of lower infla-tion and a better overall economic performance. As for the latter process, going beyond the duty of safeguarding the nation's currency carries the risk of making the NBP distracted and consequently inefficient in its numerous activities. The NBP may not be able to perform its extended supervision effectively, and in the case of a bank's failure it may face not only the risk of damage to its reputation, but also the danger of a financial recourse on the part of the banks. The NBP is also involved in the business of protecting depositors and intends to launch a special rescue package for ailing banks. Moreover, the NBP manages government funding and intervenes in disputes between leaders and borrowers. Such a range of activities for the NBP offers advantages of synergy within the Polish banking sector, but at the cost of the NBP assuming the widely criticised role of an overgrown central bank. The NBP's wide range of activities may also undermine its fledgling independence since a central bank that intervenes so widely is likely to find it difficult to resist political pressure.

References

Borys, G., 'Przeksztacenia mechanizmu refinansowania banków polskich', Bank i Kredyt N0, 7-8, Warsaw, 1992.

Clague, C. and Rausser, G. (eds), *The Emergence of Market Economies in Eastern Europe*, Cambridge and Oxford, 1992.

Consolidated Banking System 1989–1991, Warsaw: NBP, 1982.

Development of Polish Capital Market, Report of the Polish Securities Commission for the OECD, Warsaw, March 1992.

Draft Economic Review of Poland, Paris: OECD, 1992.

Gadomski, W., 'Prywatyzacja przez oddłużenie', *Gazeta Bankowa*, 21–27, June 1992.

Kalderan, L., *Poland – Debt Management, Findings and Recommendation to the Government*, Washington: World Bank, 1991.

Kołodko, G., *From Output Collapse to Sustainable Growth*, Washington: IMF, 1992.

Poland. Country Strategy and Implementation Review, Warsaw: World Bank Mission, 1991.

Poland – Financial Institutions Development Project, Warsaw: World Bank Mission, 1992.

Poland: Commercial Paper, *Central Europe Newsletter*, November 1992.

Ranking Bankow Polskich, *Gazeta Bankowa*, 23–29 August 1992, Warsaw.

Raport o systemie bankowym, Warsaw: NBP, 1993.

Rosati, D., *Teoria i Polityka Programów Stabilizacyjnych MFW*, Warsaw: Instytut Koniunktur i Cen, 1990.

Sjodal, L., *Poland – Debt Management, Budget and Cash-Flow Considerations, Expertise for the Government*, Warsaw: World Bank Mission, 1991.

Sprawozdanie roczne z działalnosci Zwiazku Banków Polskich, Warsaw: Zwiazek Banków Polskich, 1993.

The Banking System in Poland, Warsaw: Ministry of Finance, 1992.

Założenia polityki spoleczno-gospodarczej w 1993 roku, Warsaw: Centralny Urzad Planowania, 1992.

Założenia polityki pienieżnej na 1993 rok, Warsaw: NBP, 1992.

Part III

Lessons from Developing Countries

8 Financial Liberalisation, Growth and Adjustment: Some Lessons from Developing Countries
Rob Vos*

I INTRODUCTION

The experience of developing countries has shown that successful financial liberalisation is clearly not a simple matter of 'getting the prices right'. Attempts towards financial liberalisation in several Latin American countries have provoked major banking crises and related economic recessions, requiring subsequent government interventions at considerable economic cost. In various East Asian countries financial reforms are rated to have been more successful, but the common denominator to this success appears to lie in a very gradual and cautious approach towards financial liberalisation. Importantly, in these cases good economic performance preceded the liberalisation process and heavy government controls of the financial sector played a key role in successful industrial development.

These different experiences have to do with the timing and sequencing of financial liberalisation measures in relation to the overall macro-economic conditions, with the institutional structure of the financial sector and with the effectiveness of government interventions and adequacy of financial sector supervision. In this sense parallels can be drawn with the process of transition from central planning to a market system in Eastern Europe. The importance of defining appropriate and realistic timeframes for reform and creation of credible financial institutions and regulatory systems have been key elements in the discussions on reform. An important difference may be that most developing countries have been market economies for a long time, with many of the required market-regulating

* The author is grateful to Stephany Griffith-Jones, Valpy FitzGerald and participants at the ACE-EC Workshop on 'Financial Sector Developement and Macroeconomic Policies in Transition Economies' (Brighton, 21–22 September 1993) for helpful comments on a previous draft of this paper.

institutions in place, but have been or are facing large imbalances and distortions necessitating reforms. By contrast, market instruments have to be put in place in the formerly planned economies and agents have to gain experience in responding to market signals. Nevertheless, the parallels are important enough to yield important lessons from the developing country experience. In Eastern Europe policy makers face the problem of having to implement a great variety of reform measures at the same time and have to choose priorities in where to start. As argued in this chapter, developing country experience shows that certain reform measures, such as interest-rate liberalisation may fail and create severe macroeconomic problems when implemented in an unstable macroeconomic environment and where supervision and regulation of financial institutions is inadequate. It is argued at the same time that these reform failures stem from insufficient understanding of market imperfections, some of which are inherent to financial markets (such as asymmetric information and problems of moral hazard) and some of which are rooted in the historical development of financial institutions (such as bank concentration and interlocking interests between bank and non-bank firms). Country situations differ for these reasons and therefore it is of little help to advise the government of, say, the Czech Republic that it should follow the policy of Malaysia, South Korea or Hungary. It should look at its own macroeconomic environment and institutional structure. It is good policy advice, however, to have governments study other experiences to understand where things may go wrong and when things are more likely to work out well.

In this chapter an overview is given of the structural problems hampering financial sector development and reform in developing countries, with special reference to Latin America and East Asia. In Section II, it is argued that these relate to (i) weak, or sometimes perverse, responses of savings and investment to financial market price signals; (ii) heavy bank concentration and interlocking interests between banks and non-financial enterprises and related inefficiencies in credit allocations; (iii) ineffective bank supervision and prudential regulation; and (iv) ill-conceived macroeconomic policies. Bad loan problems have severely impinged upon financial sector development in many developing countries and the analysis suggests these are caused by a combination of the listed structural financial sector weaknesses and ill-conceived economic policies, including financial liberalisation in economies characterised by these weaknesses. Financial liberalisation has been more successful in cases where the macroeconomic environment was stable when implementing reforms and a long and good practice of financial sector supervision was in place. In these cases reform measures were gradual and spread over several years or longer. Developing countries have also built up some experience in resolving problems of non-performing assets and bank crises. These are reviewed in section III, where it is argued that these have tended to be excessively costly, for three reasons. Firstly, prudential regulations and bank supervision failed to provide appropriate guidelines and instruments at the time of the outbreak of the financial crises and, at least initially, rehabilitation and recapitalisation of ailing financial institutions were predominating solutions and a lot of good money was thrown after bad to many non-viable institutions. Secondly, the rescue operations saddled governments and central banks with a lot of the non-performing assets. To finance the related losses governments had to resort to either the issue of high-yield securities contributing to a domestic public debt crisis or to the money-printing press with undesired inflationary impact. Thirdly, measures to deal with the structural weaknesses, like strengthening of prudential regulations or improving bank competition, generally came too late and, even if effectively implemented, took time to materialise. The lessons that might be drawn from these experiences are enumerated in section IV. Clearly, no blueprint solutions emerge. At best, a list of factors (or, rather, warnings) is given to be taken into consideration when implementing financial reform policies.

II MACROECONOMIC PERFORMANCE, INSTITUTIONAL CONSTRAINTS AND FINANCIAL LIBERALISATION

Financial reform policies in developing countries usually focus on freeing interest rates, reducing or eliminating government control over credit allocation, easing restrictions on market entrance of new financial institutions and lifting controls on foreign exchange and capital inflows. Financial liberalisation programmes can usually count on strong support from the World Bank and the IMF. The need for reform originates from the belief that government interventions, such as ceilings on nominal interest rates, direct control of credit allocation and high reserve requirements, have limited economic growth in developing countries and that the ill-functioning of financial markets has become a source of macroeconomic instability. Much of the theoretical underpinning of financial reform policies in developing countries stems from the so-called 'financial repression' school of thought developed by McKinnon (1973) and Shaw (1973), which argues that lifting controls on interest rates and credit allocation will reduce the 'repression' of financial development and will increase the willingness to save in financial assets and improve investment efficiency under market-determined financial discipline. Financial liberalisation is thus believed to raise savings, investments and growth, as well as to bring about a more efficient use of resources. Usually a distinction is made between two types of efficiency in this context (see e.g. Tobin 1984, Fry 1988): allocative and productive or financial efficiency. Allocative efficiency is defined as the allocation of scarce savings to the most productive uses in terms of the highest (social) rate of return. A financial system guided by market principles is in this view believed to intermediate most efficiently between savers and investors. Productive efficiency relates to the ability of the financial system to supply finance to investors at the lowest possible costs. These costs involve not only the interest paid by the ultimate borrower (the lending rate), but also the cost of intermediation between lenders and borrowers (usually expressed in the spread between deposit and lending rates). By fixing nominal interest rates, regulating credit allocation, limiting market entrance and maintaining foreign-exchange controls, developing country governments have distorted financial markets and have hampered the optimal allocation of savings. The McKinnon–Shaw view that financial liberalisation will increase both the quantity of resources available for investment and the efficiency of their allocation is also strongly present in assessments of financial sector reforms in Eastern Europe.

This may sound good in theory, but practice tends to be quite different. Developing country experience with financial liberalisation indicates that increased savings, investment and financial efficiency are by no means necessary outcomes of the reform measures. Financial markets in developing countries are imperfect and financial institutions are usually not the textbook-type agents optimally allocating resources. What is more, a number of countries showing good economic performance, like South Korea and Taiwan, maintained heavy government controls over the financial sector over several decades. However, in other cases, like in Latin America, government interventions in the financial sector are rated to be less successful and have contributed to inefficiencies and market segmentation. The experience is thus mixed and the success or failure of financial reform measures appears to depend on a complex of factors relating to the domestic economic structure and the organisation of the financial system, external conditions and the timing and nature of government interventions. Lessons to be drawn from the developing country experience are therefore not straightforward and by no means deliver blueprints for successful financial policies elsewhere. What can be learned from these experiences is a better understanding of the workings of the ingredients that are considered as part of recipes for financial and economic reform under varying circumstances. After studying the experience with Latin American financial liberalisation, McKinnon himself (1988, p. 38) recognises the limitations of his own original approach and states that the order in which the monetary system is stabilised in comparison with the deregulation of banks and other financial institutions 'must be more carefully considered than had previously been thought'.

Reviewing the available evidence, the following elements merit consideration:

(a) structural determinants of savings and investment;
(b) the nature of financial institutions and determinants of credit allocation;
(c) the degree of competition in financial markets;
(d) the organisational structure of the banking system;
(e) effectiveness of bank supervision and prudential regulation and lender-of-last-resort function through monetary authorities;
(f) macroeconomic policies and timing of financial liberalisation.

Savings, Investment and Financial Reform

According to financial repression theory, freeing of interest rates will raise the availability of financial savings by both raising the savings rate and shifting portfolio choices towards financial assets. Greater credit availability and the shift out of unproductive assets such as commodity holdings will subsequently allow for a higher level of productive investment. However, there are no compelling theoretical reasons why higher real interest rates will necessarily lead to higher household savings or will be a sufficient condition for improved allocative efficiency. Even according to conventional theory (Gersovitz, 1989; Aghevli *et al.*, 1990), the response of real private savings to higher interest rates will be ambiguous: higher savings out of higher rentier incomes may be offset by substitution effects from expected higher future income from wealth earnings. Econometric studies have found little support for a significant and positive relationship between real interest rates and private savings (e.g. Gupta, 1984; Giovanni, 1985; Molho, 1986). Equally, there is no systematic pattern in the effects of liberalisation of interest rates and the level of savings in developing countries (see e.g. Cho and Khatkhate, 1989, on a sample of Asian countries; and Massad and Eyzaguirre, 1990, on Latin America). Stronger evidence exists that higher real interest rates stimulate *financial* savings (Gupta, 1984; Fry, 1988), implying a substitution from real assets (e.g. real estate, commodity stocks) or shares to interest-bearing financial assets.

Higher interest rates may even have a negative impact on private savings, particularly under unstable macroeconomic conditions. In situations of economic stagnation and high inflation, freeing of interest rates may lead to a situation where national savings fall, while financial savings, and thus financial deepening increase. With falling per capita incomes, high inflation, and high nominal interest rates, small savers may be inclined to liquidate real assets and invest in interest-yielding financial assets to contain the fall in their living standards by consuming (part of) the additional interest income (Akyüz, 1992). Also, higher interest rates will redistribute income from debtors to creditors. This may not only discourage investment in real assets, but also lower private savings, particularly corporate savings. In developing countries the equity basis of firms is often weak and the maturities on loans is short, such that they tend to have a high leverage and corporate debt carries variable interest rates.

Turkey, Chile, Argentina and the Philippines provide examples where financial liberalisation and macroeconomic instability led to a combination of lower household savings and higher financial savings. Brazil, Chile, Argentina, Uruguay, the Philippines, among others, are examples where in the 1980s corporate profits and savings were depressed drastically, when domestic interest rates were raised or liberalised in attempts to stabilise the economy.[1]

In South Korea and Taiwan, by contrast, low interest rates and high real estate prices have raised household savings during various instances in the 1970s and 1980s (Amsden and Euh, 1990; and Park and Park, 1993). Moreover, development in these countries form in general a marked contrast with the financial-repression hypotheses, as decades of controlled interest rates have not impeded savings rates from moving up to 30–40 per cent of GNP. It should be noted, however, that in South Korea and Taiwan interest rates were managed much more flexibly in the 1970s and 1980s than in other developing countries with controlled nominal interest-rate regimes, ensuring that *real* interest rates remained positive. Together with growing real savings positive real deposit rates stimulated growth of financial savings and thus financial intermediation. Interest rates are currently being deregulated in Korea and Taiwan, but only gradually. Interest-rate ceilings still exist, but in South Korea lending rates are to be fully liberalised by the end of 1993 and deposit rates by 1997. In these countries, good economic performance under far-reaching government intervention in financial sectors has been a reason for slow progress with financial liberalisation, rather than the latter being seen as a precondition for a better growth performance (Haggard and Maxfield, 1993).

This developing country evidence shows that freeing of interest rates is not a sufficient condition to boost savings, investment and economic growth. What is more, under conditions of macroeconomic instability and highly leveraged firms, financial liberalisation may have a negative impact of a sometimes devastating magnitude, as shown in section III. Another important lesson that can be derived from the above is that if the interest-rate elasticities of savings and investment are low, large interest-rate changes may be required to match supply and demand in certain financial market segments. Domestic public debt problems in many developing countries are related to this problem, as the domestic financing of public sector deficits under controlled monetary expansion and liberalised interest rates has required the issue of very high-yielding government securities in order to attract enough investment funds. As discussed further below, also costly solutions to bad loan problems have created Central Bank losses which have significantly contributed to the domestic public sector debt overhang and high real interest rates in countries like Argentina, Chile and the Philippines. Demand for bank deposits and private investment has been crowded out as a consequence.

These are not arguments to sustain financial repression in the form of negative real interest rates. The Korean and Taiwanese experiences suggests that provided macroeconomic conditions remain stable interest rates may be effectively controlled at positive real levels and without seriously impeding financial sector development. However, as argued below, interest-rate management should also be assessed in relation to financial market imperfections, bank behaviour and bank supervision.

Credit Rationing

Financial liberalisation is supposed to improve allocative and productive efficiency of investment finance, particularly through a market-based pricing of the cost of borrowing. To achieve this, markets should be sufficiently competitive and should provide complete information. Such market conditions generally do not apply to financial markets in developing countries (and elsewhere). Financial market systems tend to be incomplete (i.e. futures, secondary and securities markets are missing or poorly developed), thus providing less information than more developed market systems. Informational imperfections are also inherent in the 'product' itself. That is, investors have to face the risk of default by the borrower. This risk might be covered through a premium over the interest rate, but it has been convincingly shown that – in theory and practice – lenders are more likely to avert such risks by rationing credit supplies over different classes of borrowers, even in competitive markets.[2] Credit rationing thus serves as a rational device for lenders to avoid exposure to risky loans, which in practice implies that the poorer potential borrowers lack access to formal sources of finance. In developing countries it means that, typically, peasants, small manufacturing enterprises and urban informal services activities, which usually occupy two-thirds or more of the labour force, have no source of credit supply or have to resort to informal money lenders.

The above observations have important implications for assessing the role of interest-rate management in the process of financial reform. As shown by Stiglitz and Weiss (1981), imperfect information in the market for bank credits means that the interest charged on the loan will differ from the expected return to the bank, which is the interest rate *times* the repayment probability of the borrowers. This probability is always smaller than 100 per cent because banks do not have full information about the default risks of borrowers. The probability of payment is itself inversely related to the interest rate: that is, when a higher interest rate is charged, the probability of full repayment will decline. Above a certain interest rate level expected returns may actually decline, with further interest rate increases, and banks will close the credit window for some borrowers even if they are willing to pay a higher interest. This *inherent* feature of the market for bank loans shows the limits to which interest rates can be raised, and rational behaviour of banks, under perfect competition and proper prudential regulation (e.g. adequate provisions for bad loans), leads to credit rationing and interest rates below market-clearing levels.

Now what are the effects of macroeconomic instability, inadequate bank regulation and imperfect bank competition on the market for bank credits? Macroeconomic instability will affect the performance of investment projects and this will increase the risk of default on bank loans. In search of higher returns banks may be inclined to lend to borrowers with potentially high-yielding investment projects, but which are also more risky. This potential risk of moral hazard in the bank itself, induced by greater economic instability, may be contained if bank supervision and regulation commands that banks hold adequate reserves against loan losses and if explicit or implicit deposit insurance is either absent or adequately priced (Villanueva and Mirakhor, 1990). Such reserve requirements will lower expected profits at a given lending rate, and if bank behaviour is risk averse, they will lower interest rates and ration credit more severely. Cho and Khatkhate (1989) and Villanueva and Mirakhor (1990) provide evidence that low and stable bank lending rates can be observed where bank supervision and prudential regulation are strong and effective (such as in Malaysia).

Weak and inadequate bank supervision and regulation may be a critical source of financial instability and bank crises. If rules about provisioning against loan losses are inadequate or poorly enforced, unsound banking practices may go unpunished if authorities also provide implicit deposit insurance. Banks will be inclined to supply high-interest loans for risky projects as they will not have to pay for the full costs of large losses under bad economic conditions. As argued further below, this is part of what happened in Argentina, Chile and Uruguay in Latin America and the Philippines and Indonesia in Asia.

Bank Concentration and Interlocking Ownership

However, banks may also engage in other than marginal return calculations if bank competition is imperfect. Risks of moral hazard are often compounded by the fact that financial markets tend to be heavily concentrated. Bank concentration is very high in many developing countries and has usually remained high in countries undergoing financial sector reforms. Table 8.1 shows bank concentration ratios (defined as the share of assets of the four or five largest banks in total assets of the financial system) for a number of developing and industrialised countries. While banking in the latter group of countries is usually already characterised as oligopolistic (Weston, 1980; Born, 1983), banking in developing countries tends to be

Table 8.1   Bank concentration ratios for selected developing and industrial countries

	Year	Bank concentration ratio[1]
Argentina	1987	82[2]
Chile	1988	54[2]
Philippines	1990	47[3]
Thailand	1988	69[3]
Malaysia	1988	54[3]
Indonesia	1986	81[3]
South Korea		
Taiwan	1987	63[2]
France	1987	52[3]
Germany	1984	26[3]
Spain	1987	43[3]

[1]Percentage share of assets of largest banks in total assets of banking system.
[2]Four largest banks.
[3]Five largest banks.
Source: Lamberte (1990) for ASEAN countries, except Thailand; World Bank (1990) for Thailand; Fischer (1993) for Argentina, Taiwan and industrial countries.

significantly more concentrated. Heavy bank concentration has to do with a number of structural features usually present in developing countries. One aspect relates to the determinants of savings and investment performance, as discussed above. The scope for broadly based and competitive banking will be limited if savings and investment levels are low because of their structural determinants and cannot be simply raised through changes in financial policies. Further, government regulations often severely limit the entrance of new financial institutions, particularly of foreign banks and branches. Pressures to maintain such barriers to entry are usually strongly and effectively exercised by powerful economic interests behind the banking industry. Finally, bank concentration is rooted in the historical formation process of financial institutions. Banks in developing countries typically have been formed by rich family groups with a stake in trading, industry and agri-businesses. Consequently, besides a high degree of concentration, financial sectors are also characterised by the prevalence of interlocking ownership, where banks form part of a conglomerate of firms with operations in various economic activities (e.g. Leff, 1976; Drake, 1980; Galves and Tybout, 1985).

These market imperfections, i.e. incomplete markets, risk, credit rationing, oligopolistic banking structures and interlocking ownership patterns, strongly affect the productive and allocative efficiency of financial markets. Concentrated banking usually leads to large bank spreads, thus keeping the cost of financial intermediation high (see Table 8.2), while credit rationing practices may exclude whole classes of borrowers from credit market access and not necessarily allocate funds to investment projects with the highest (social) rates of return. Such factors have been primary reasons for government intervention. Governments in developing countries have intervened to reduce the cost of borrowing by imposing interest-rate ceilings and to enhance access to credits to specific borrowers through the creation of special credit schemes and banking institutions. Government-directed and preferential credit schemes have made an important contribution to successful industrialisation in a number of East Asian countries, such as South Korea and Taiwan. In the early 1960s, when both countries embarked on a course of export-led industrialisation, their financial systems were highly segmented, with highly fragmented informal credit or 'curb' markets coexisting with a highly concentrated commercial banking system. For policy-makers at that time it was clear that the financial system would not be able to allocate limited domestic resources to export industries. Governments in both countries moved to a system of tight interest ceilings, direct control over a number of large commercial banks and credit rationing (Vos, 1982; Amsden, 1989; Park, 1989; Cho and

Table 8.2   Real bank spreads in selected developing countries and industrial countries (annual averages, percent)

	1980	1981	1982	1983	1984	1985	1986	1987	1988	1989	1990
Argentina	11.4	16.1	14.6	20.8	15.0	20.5	24.8	36.3	-3.0	142.0	–
Chile	4.6	15.4	15.0	9.7	18.0	5.0	7.3	7.6	6.1	8.2	8.5
Colombia	0.9	1.4	0.6	3.3	0.6	0.2	9.4	10.3	9.2	9.3	8.8
Ecuador	4.5	5.1	4.4	4.3	0.8	2.4	3.4	5.9	11.0	10.2	6.1
Mexico	5.6	9.7	13.7	17.7	13.7	18.9	26.4	20.4	–	–	–
Uruguay	10.4	9.6	8.4	11.4	6.9	11.3	18.7	21.3	21.1	23.8	36.0
Philippines[1]	–	1.1	0.8	0.1	2.8	1.3	5.1	4.9	5.8	7.6	7.8
Thailand			6.0	4.6	5.8	6.0	7.3	5.5	5.5	5.5	–
Malaysia			-1.0	3.1	1.8	2.7	3.6	5.2	3.9	2.4	1.3
South Korea											4.5
Japan											1.2
US											2.4

[1]Bank spread for the Philippines calculated as difference between actual interest income on domestic assets (corrected for bank intermediation tax) and actual interest payments on deposits (see Lamberte, 1992).
Source: Morris *et al.* (1990); Lamberte (1992); Kang (1993); IMF, *International Financial Statistics* (CD-ROM, June 1993).

Khatkhate, 1989). Targeted industries received loans at preferential interest rates, but loans were made strictly conditional on good performance. Although strong economic conglomerates (in Korea these are called the *chaebol*) were strongly favoured under these policies, the conditionality was forcefully implemented. The success of this credit allocation policy has been further attributed to the fact that performance was subject to competitiveness in world markets, which provided relatively reliable indicators about whether the support was effectively used (Westphal, 1990). This success has not been replicated in Latin America, where subsidised credits mostly have lacked the conditionality and effective control of efficient use. It cannot be denied that preferential credit schemes have helped foster industrial and agricultural development in Latin America (García-Zamor and Sutin, 1979), but these schemes have been sustained for decades under highly protective import-substitution policies, and criteria of competitiveness and good performance have mostly been lacking. Cheap credits thus turned into simple hand-outs, often at considerable fiscal and monetary costs.

Interlocking ownership patterns also impinge upon the allocative efficiency of credit supplies. Financial intermediaries operating within a larger economic group tend to pursue the interests of the group rather than those of creditors and depositors. Owners, firms belonging to the conglomerate and related interest groups typically have priviliged access to the bank's credits, often with disregard of 'normal' risk considerations. Such 'in-house' lending practices are closely associated with important shares of non-performing loans in the portfolios of the banking sector provoking many banking crises in the 1970s and 1980s in developing countries, as discussed in some detail in section III. Prudential regulation and super-vision by the monetary authorities, such as restrictions on bank's exposure to single and allied borrowers, should prevent such malpractices, but these may be difficult to implement in practice (see below).

Universal versus Specialised Banking Systems

Which types of financial institutions and markets to promote is an import-ant issue in financial reform in both developing countries and Eastern Europe. Existing evidence from developing countries suggests, however, that the organisational form of the financial system by itself is not a factor that will prevent allocative inefficiencies of the type discussed above. Two types of financial arrangements are usually distinguished, according to whether banks and capital markets serve different functions or not.[3] One form of financial arrangement, usually labelled as the Anglo-American sys-tem, is to separate 'typical' banking activities (deposit-taking and extend-ing commercial credits) from 'typical' capital market operations (security issues, secondary markets, etc.). The latter should be operated via special-ised financial institutions, such as investment banks. Alternatively, in the German type of universal banking, banks also engage in underwriting and brokerage of securities issues and other capital market operations. Under the German system, banks may also hold control over corporate firms. Arguments in favour or against will not be assessed in full here. However, it is relevant to mention that it has been argued that a strong connection between banks and firms under a universal banking system will improve corporate performance, as it will help firms to take a long-term view on their portfolio structure and they will need to worry less about day-to-day variations in the market values of their assets than under an Anglo-Ameri-can construct implemented in a context of incomplete markets (see e.g. Corbett and Mayer, 1991; and Akyüz, 1992). Further, banks would be in a position, as shareholders and creditors, to monitor firm management through direct access to information and be able to interfere when needed in order to prevent failure (Akyüz, 1992). However, as indicated, close bank–firm ties already prevail in developing countries and interlocking interests may be a source of allocative inefficiency and excessive risk-taking. In this respect, the Anglo-American system is not necessarily better, since in practice also finance companies and other specialised non-banking financial institutions (NFBI) may be set up and owned by the large economic conglomerates and be used to primarily serve the interests of the economic group as a whole and with disregard of the financial soundness of the finance company.

In Latin America, financial systems resemble the Anglo-American system, and there is ample evidence that the investment houses (*financieras*) are linked to large economic groups engaged in excessive risk-taking. This has led to over-leveraging of corporate firms and a widespread bad-loan problem in the 1980s triggered by external shocks and domestic liberalisation measures (Galves and Tybout, 1985; Morris *et al.*, 1990; and below, section III).

The Philippines make an interesting case, as financial reforms of the early 1970s regulated an Anglo-American system, while those of the beginning of the 1980s moved towards a system of universal banking (Lamberte, 1989; Vos and Yap, 1984). Starting in 1972, authorities encouraged financial development through non-bank financial institutions (NFBIs) engaging in issuance of deposit substitutes and short-term money market instruments and underwriting corporate securities. Interest-rate controls and reserve requirements were much less tight in this separate market segment than in the market for bank deposits and loans. Less than a decade later, in 1980, a financial reform under the auspices of the World Bank and the IMF completely reversed the policy of financial specialisation and a system of universal banks was introduced and interest rates were freed. In the 1970s, bank–firm conglomerates used the largely unregulated finance companies they owned to serve their own financing requirements. These finance companies would underwrite commercial papers issued by allied companies and provide loans to managers, owners and officers associated with affiliated banks and firms. The NFBIs proved an effective mechanism to circumvent Central Bank regulations which were meant to restrict 'in-house' lending practices of commercial banks and their exposure to single borrowers.[4] The regulations did not apply to NFBI operations. The interest-rate liberalisation, in combination with a number of external shocks (oil price increase, increase in world interest rates), triggered a full-scale liquidity crisis. The default and flight from the country of a major entrepreneur, Dewey Dee, provoked a series of bankruptcies and exposed the weakness of the investment and broker houses, allied to the commercial banks, which carried large exposures to single borrowers. The Dewey Dee scandal exposed this as a widespread practice. The financial crisis precipitated the move towards a universal banking system and many commercial banks were forced to merge with their affiliated investment houses. Under the circumstances, the interest-rate liberalisation of the early 1980s was a key factor in triggering the financial crisis (though not the fundamental cause). The financial crisis and the move towards universal banking in fact enhanced the concentration of the banking sector and reduced competition in financial markets, instead of making it more competitive, which was the main objective of the 1980 financial reform.[5] The concentration of the Philippine bank industry and its interlocking interests with large conglomerates of firms formed the preconditions for a heavy concentration of lending with a limited number of borrowers. By the early 1990s, these conditions had not fundamentally changed, indicating that 'it could happen again'. Unregulated, off-balance trust fund operations of commercial banks now appear to form the new channel the circumvent restrictions on 'in-house' lending.

Bad-Loan Problems and Inadequate Bank Supervision and Regulation

Prudential regulation and supervision is a *conditio sine qua non* for maintaining a viable financial system. Strong regulatory and supervisory measures are required to minimise moral hazards (including corruption, fraud and excessive risk-taking) in the banking system and to ensure its financial viability and stability. Risks in the financial system tend to increase under greater competition and uncertainty after deregulation and liberalisation, requiring strengthening of bank supervision. The experience in most reforming Latin America and East Asian countries has been that inadequate prudential regulation prevailed when initiating liberalisation policies and that banking crises were needed to pursue reforms in the system of bank supervision.

A large array of factors should be considered in the setting-up of an adequate system of prudential regulation and bank supervision. The scope of this chapter does not allow us to go into all of these.[6] A few critical areas include the effectiveness of bank supervision; deposit insurance systems; and guidelines for resolving bank crises and bad-loan problems.

Firstly, most developing countries have some form of supervisory system, but even in cases where these seemed fairly adequate (e.g. in Thailand or even in the Philippines), banking crises could occur (cf. Sundararajan and Baliño, 1991). Existing regulations have often been poorly implemented. A variety of reasons may underlie poor implementation. One is that seemingly detailed regulations often prove vague and imprecise in practice. For instance, limits on loan concentration to single borrowers and allied firms may be specified in great quantitative detail, but difficulties usually arise over the definition and identification of what and who single borrowers and allied firms are. Another problem of effective implementation relates to the coverage of prudential regulations. Usually, regulations have been confined to the commercial banking system, leaving NBFIs and off-balance transactions of commercial banks (such as trust funds in the Philippine case, see above) largely unregulated and uncontrolled. As discussed above, the *financieras* and finance companies in Latin America and the Philippines were used precisely to circumvent regulations on loan concentration and were a major source of bad loan problems.

Also, supervision of government-owned development banks has been weak, as state bank managers often have more political weight than bank supervisors. Argentina, Brazil and the Philippines are typical examples of this situation. In the Philippines, this changed after the failure of two major state banks in the mid-1980s; the management was changed and bank operations are now closely monitored by the Central Bank. Inadequate auditing and loan classification systems have been other factors hampering effective bank supervision (e.g. Morris *et al.*, 1990; and Sundararajan and Baliño,1991). Finally, bank supervisors have lacked sufficient autonomy. In many cases bank supervision is done by the Central Bank. This may have advantages, given the Central Bank's role as lender of last resort, so it makes sense for it to be in charge of assessing the viability of financial institutions. However, it has also been argued (World Bank, 1989) that the objectives of bank supervision should not be mixed up with the tasks of monetary policies. Morris (1990) observes that the countries in Latin America that experienced the severest banking crises (i.e. Uruguay, Argentina and Bolivia) are the ones where the Central Bank exercised bank supervision. However, also in countries (Chile, Colombia, Ecuador) where an autonomous body was in charge, i.e. a Superintendency of Banks, serious banking crises emerged. As elsewhere, the Central Bank had to step in to resolve problems of non-performing assets and to prevent bank failures. In most industrial countries central banks are in charge of bank supervision. Thus, the crucial problem may not be the existence or not of an autonomous supervisory agency, but that any authority charged with the task should be able to carry it out with an operational set of rules and regulations in hand and a good information and auditing system, and be sufficiently free from political interference to apply these with an eye exclusively on the good management and viability of financial institutions.

Secondly, there is some controversy about the role of *deposit insurance systems* in safeguarding the stability of financial systems in developing countries.[7] Explicit deposit insurance helps to cover costs incurred in rehabilitating and liquidating distressed financial institutions, and may help to prevent bank runs and enhance depositors' confidence in the banking system and thereby increase levels of financial intermediation. An important reason for opposing deposit insurance is that it reduces the incentive to depositors to put money in well-managed institutions and thus encourages risky lending by banks, i.e. it can be a source of 'moral hazard'. While this argument may be valid, it is preferable to have a form of explicit deposit insurance, as both depositors and creditors may expect that monetary authorities will provide *de facto* insurance because of the fear that bank runs might undermine the stability of the financial system with unpredictable macroeconomic consequences. Developing country evidence indicates that *de facto* deposit insurance has indeed been provided by central banks in a majority of cases where bank crises emerged. This has been the case is most Latin American countries, including those with no deposit insurance system. In Argentina, abandonment of the full deposit insurance in 1979 helped to propagate the financial crisis (Baliño, 1991). Further, the degree of capitalisation of deposit insurance funds is important. Undercapitalised systems may be incapable of preventing bank runs. In the Philippines, for instance, insufficient resources of the deposit agency and the delays in settling depositors' claims contributed to the bank runs that took place in the 1980s and depositors incurred considerable losses from bank failures (Lamberte, 1989; Nascimiento, 1991).

Deposit insurance systems therefore should be set up cautiously, ensure adequate capitalisation and build in incentives to minimise moral hazard problems. For instance, the new insurance system established in Chile in 1987 distinguishes demand deposits from other deposits. The former have a state guarantee and banks must invest demand deposits in government or Central Bank securities. Other deposits have no guarantee and bear full market risk. This mechanism at least safeguards the integrity of the payments system. Farther-reaching proposals to reduce moral hazard problems, like differentiating insurance premiums according to the bank's riskiness (e.g. Benston *et al.*, 1986; Sundararajan and Baliño, 1991), tend to assume that there is enough information in the market to assess soundness of financial institutions. This is generally difficult in developing countries, although – as it is now regulated under the new Chilean banking legislation – supervisory authorities could reduce the information gap by publicising solvency indicators of individual financial institutions.

Finally, guidelines on how financial crises should be handled are important. Authorities in most Asian and Latin American countries lacked well-defined criteria on whether and which banks should be bailed out or liquidated. In some countries, e.g. Thailand, the Central Bank even lacked a mandate to intervene in ailing financial institutions. The lack of guidelines on how much assistance the Central Bank or Superintendency of Banks should give to each bank has led to unequal financial support to banks and/or unnecessary heavy exposure of the Central Bank to financial institutions with an irreversible, insolvent financial position. In many cases indiscriminate bailouts were organised which proved very costly to governments and the economy as a whole. The practice of solving bad loan problems and banking crises in East Asia and Latin America is discussed at some length in the next section. Many of the countries that experienced banking crises have recognised the need for clear guidelines on bank rehabilitation and liquidation and have started to change regulations to handle crises, including explicit deposit insurance schemes.[8]

Macroeconomic Policies and Financial Liberalisation

The failure of financial liberalisation policies conducted in the Southern Cone countries had led to a consensus on the general groundrule that one better not try to deregulate the domestic financial sector or move towards financial opening if the economy is facing major macroeconomic instabilities, reflected in high inflation and large fiscal deficits (Corbo and de Melo, 1985; McKinnon, 1988; Roe, 1988; Edwards, 1989). This is a conclusion in retrospect. At the time of implementing the reforms, liberal economists firmly believed these would help stabilise the economy. Financial repression theory provided the analytical support. The discussion in the preceding paragraphs suggest, however, that macroeconomic stability is but one condition to take into consideration when designing financial reform policies. Conventional bank errors and loan market failure originating from heavy bank concentration and interlocking ownership patterns may be more fundamental causes of crisis-bound deregulation policies. Equally, if, as argued, responses of savers and investors to market price signals is weak and/or slow, deregulated markets are likely to be highly volatile, e.g. reflected in large interest rate fluctuations. Such conditions, and in particular their combined occurrence, may endanger the effectiveness of fiscal and monetary policies. This is examplified by the widespread domestic debt problems that emerged in the developing world in the 1980s.

Domestic debt crises may take two forms: (i) widespread bad loan problems endangering the solvency of the banking system at large and (ii) a large domestic public debt overhang causing macroeconomic instability.

The first form is where a large build-up of bad and doubtful debts of the financial institutions of a country lead to a substantial excess of liabilities over assets, if the bad debts are to be properly reflected in the valuation of bank assets. If the problem affects large banks or a large number of institutions the whole financial system may be endangered and turn into a widespread banking crisis. This is most likely to occur when moral hazard is present, bank supervision is loose and corporations have high gearing ratios, e.g. as a consequence of financial repression policies (low interest rates) or 'in-house' lending practices. Macroeconomic instability will increase distress borrowing at higher interest rates from firms needing to roll over maturing debt and from (allied firms) nearing bankruptcy. In *Chile*, the rollover of bad loans and capitalisation of interest arrears were estimated to be about 72 per cent of outstanding peso loans in 1982 (Velasco, 1991). Much the same happened in Argentina, Uruguay and the Philippines following financial liberalisation.

Malaysia portrays a very different picture. Cho and Khatkhate (1989) observed only a modest impact on domestic interest rates after financial liberalisation. They explain this by three factors. Firstly, the freeing of interest rates, which was implemented rather quickly (3 years), was done after a long period of economic stability. Secondly, in the period prior to liberalisation, market forces already influenced interest rates and the government kept real interest rates positive. Thirdly, Malaysia has a long tradition of strong banking supervision, which kept bad-loan problems within limited boundaries (but see section III) and sound gearing ratios cushioned the corporate sector against interest-rate shocks. This last condition has led some analysts (Villanueva and Mirakhor 1990, p. 520) to argue that inadequate prudential regulation of the banking system in the presence of moral hazard and the presence of full and costless deposit insurance is the most crucial factor in explaining failure of financial liberalisation policies. As also pointed out by Cho and Khatkhate (1989), the *gradual* approach to financial liberalisation in *Sri Lanka* and *South Korea* gave priority to achieving macroeconomic stability first and to strengthening the system of monitoring and supervision of banks, ensuring that banks do not engage in excessive risk taking and that bankruptcy would be costly. Moreover, in the Korean case authorities showed great concern for the financial vulnerability of the corporate sector. This latter point may also be interpreted, however, as a result of the pressure of the *chaebol* on the government not to undermine the implicit contracts between the banks and allied corporate borrowers.[9]

The other form of domestic debt crisis is where the government and the public sector at large have build up a large domestic public debt such that it creates severe fiscal problems and loss of control over monetary variables. Interest payments on domestic debt may take a high share of public

expenditures and 'crowd out' other current expenditures and public investment. As explained in Appendix 8.A, the money supply and thereby monetary control may be endangered if the domestic debt overhang also affects
the Central Bank accounts, e.g. after taking over non-performing domestic
assets and foreign liabilities of ailing banks and firms. This may create
losses on the monetary authorities' income statement. Central Bank losses
lead to an expansion of the domestic money supply. This may create inflationary pressures if not sterilised. If the monetary expansion is sterilised
this may have other negative macroeconomic consequences. For example,
the Central Bank may issue securities which may be costly if financial markets are thin and savings interest-rate inelastic (see above). It could also
force commercial banks to purchase such bonds below market rates, but
this would work as an additional reserve requirement. In each case, proper
use of monetary instruments is endangered as they are operated to improve
the cash flow of the monetary authorities, possibly to the detriment of
macroeconomic stability and development objectives. As discussed in the
next section, central bank losses have caused macroeconomic problems in
various developing countries; for example, the Philippines and Argentina
have been faced with this problem since the early 1980s and fiscal adjustment and monetary control were still strongly conditioned by large central
bank deficits in the early 1990s.

III SOLVING BAD-LOAN PROBLEMS AND BANKING CRISES

The simultaneous occurrence of the structural characteristics leading to
allocative and productive financial efficiencies and exogenous shocks
underlie the widespread bank failures in Latin America and some Asian
countries, like the Philippines, in the 1980s. Smaller financial crises, but
with similar origins, have also taken place in developing countries which
showed relatively good economic performance in the 1980s, such as
Korea, Malaysia and Thailand. These crises could occur despite the strict
restrictions imposed by the government on the financial system due to the
inadequate design of such regulations and factors impeding their effective
implementation. We have seen that banks may be able to find various ways
to circumvent restrictions on lending to a single enterprise or to allied
firms, officials and owners. Further, legal provisions against bad assets are
often ignored or poorly monitored. By contrast, governments often hasten
to rescue ailing banks.

There are various ways of dealing with bad debt problems and banking
crises. The distribution of the costs between various options and over the

Table 8.3   Quality of bank assets in selected developing countries (non-performing loans to total loans; percent)

	1980	1981	1982	1983	1984	1985	1986	1987
Argentina	–	–	–	16.9	29.1	30.3	24.6	25.1
Chile[1]	1.2	2.3	8.2	18.4	19.6	30.0	35.4	33.3
of which:								
Bad loans of commercial banks	1.2	2.3	4.1	8.5	9.0	3.5	3.6	2.7
Colombia	1.4	3.0	5.1	5.7	8.5	18.5	5.4	11.3
Ecuador	9.9	13.5	16.2	17.4	13.9	11.9	10.8	–
Mexico	1.5	1.5	2.4	2.9	1.8	1.6	1.0	0.6
Uruguay	8.9	14.6	30.4	24.7	22.3	36.2	45.9	25.2
Philippines	11.5	13.2	13.0	8.9	12.7	16.7	19.3	–

[1]Includes past due loans as recorded in accounts of financial institutions plus risky loans sold to the Central Bank.
Source: Larraín (1989) for Chile; Morris *et al.* (1990) for other Latin American countries; Nascimiento (1991) for the Philippines.

different interested parties would form obvious criteria to establish an optimal solution. The difficulty is that the exact costs of resolving a bad-loan problem may be difficult to estimate, particularly if the size of it is large enough to be able to produce a full-scale banking crises. Table 8.3 provides some data on the bad-loan situation in a number of developing countries in the 1980s. Asset quality varies significantly across countries mainly because the definition of non-performing loans is not unified, accounting and prudential regulations differ, fraudulent behaviour of banks obscures actual portfolio quality and, obviously, there are differences in economic conditions and measures taken influencing the extent of the bad-loan problem. In the most extreme cases, Argentina and Uruguay, non-performing assets ranged between a third and half of total bank loans. The low estimates for Mexico, which was also confronted with a severe financial crisis in the 1980s, probably correspond to poor accounting practices.

A market-conform solution would be to let ailing banks go bankrupt (along with debtors in arrears) and the cost would have to be carried by depositors and by owners and shareholders. However, bank failure, even of one single bank, may have important externalities, particularly if the problem is (believed to be) systematic. It could trigger bank runs, widespread bank failure and the collapse of productive firms with liquidity problems. Fears of a widespread financial and economic crisis have led developing country governments more often to avert such a situation by providing funds to the banks and refinancing ailing portfolios, rather than letting the market do the job. Government-supported bailouts have been the predominant practice in most of the Latin American and East Asian countries with a distressed domestic financial system. This often went at considerable fiscal costs. Only in a few cases (like in Argentina after 1985 and the Philippines) were a large number of financial institutions closed down. Generally, the crisis triggered important financial reforms, particularly in the area of prudential regulation and bank supervision. In South Korea, the crisis helped to push more liberal financial policies.

Latin America

At the time of the emergence of the financial crisis, banking laws and supervisory regulations of many Latin American countries provided inadequate means for handling banks in distress (Morris *et al.*, 1990). Major indiscriminate bailouts were organised, the results of which were very costly to governments. In most cases depositors were paid in full, even in cases where no explicit deposit insurance systems were in place. Governments not only provided new finance, but usually took over much of the bad debts and 'dedollarised' external liabilities. If this was not enough, further assistance was given in the form of subsidies embedded in the refinancing of the bank debts.

In *Colombia*, the Superintendency of Banks had to intervene in about 20 major financial institutions (Superintendencía Bancaria, 1989) between 1982 and 1986. Financial distress was not directly related to financial liberalisation measures, but it was a result of banks' overexposure to allied firms within the industrial-financial conglomerates they belonged to (Morris *et al.*, 1990; Hommes, 1988). Deterioration of macroeconomic conditions following economic slowdown after the 1976–80 coffee boom, plus exchange rate overvaluation and the global shocks in world interest rates and oil prices, led to the failure of two of these conglomerates in 1982. Authorities were more or less taken by surprise. Until shortly before the solvency problems of the banking system became manifest, the Colombian banking system was believed to be sound with low leverage ratios and few loan portfolio problems (the share of registered bad loans in total was only 3.0 per cent (see Table 8.3). Banco Nacional and Banco del Estado (accounting for 5 per cent of the assets of the financial system) were intervened. The Banco Nacional was liquidated after a run on deposits, but small depositors were covered through Central Bank funds and despite the non-existence of an explicit deposit insurance scheme. The Banco del

Estado was not liquidated, but nationalised, penalizing former shareholders and managers. In subsequent years, several other major commercial banks and finance companies were nationalised (e.g. Banco de Colombia, Corporación Financiera Grancolombiana), while others (e.g. Banco de Bogotá) were given new credits using the banks' shares as collateral. Following these interventions, bank legislation was changed, authorising nationalisation of intervened banks and improving bank supervision. A deposit guarantee fund (FOGAFIN) was established which would not only insure depositors for a fee, but was also assigned a supervisory role and was allowed to take over, liquidate or recapitalise ailing banks. By the end of the 1980s, FOGAFIN owned several commercial banks which would be offered on sale to foreign banks.

In *Ecuador*, the Central Bank provided *de facto* deposit insurance, for lack of an explicit scheme, and bailed out ailing banks and non-bank financial institutions in the 1980s. Portfolio problems of the financial system were caused by factors similar to these in Colombia, i.e. 'in-house' lending practices of bank–firm conglomerates and, more so than in Colombia, heavy exposure of banks and firms to external debt accumulated during the 1970s. Foreign debt was 'sucretised' (i.e. 'dedollarised') by the Central Bank and subsidised credits were provided to the ailing institutions to recapitalise and restructure portfolios. Only one bank was liquidated and one was nationalised. To date no deposit insurance scheme exists, but the Central Bank has provided *de facto* insurance. Also in *Mexico*, nationalisation of ailing banks formed a key mechanism to resolve the banking crisis of the mid-1980s, but this was done before providing any assistance.

Banking crises in *Argentina*, *Chile* and *Uruguay* are often seen as the result of ill-conceived or badly timed liberalisation policies (e.g. Corbo and de Melo, 1985; Edwards, 1989; World Bank, 1989).[10] One of the lessons drawn from these experiences is that financial liberalisation measures carried out in a context of macroeconomic instability can lead to more instability and deep economic crisis. Clearly, as pointed out in section II, the failure of liberalisation policies should be viewed in the light of the structural weaknesses of the financial system. Also in these countries oligopolistic banking and 'in-house' lending practices had led to an overleveraged corporate firm sector, while existing systems of bank regulation and prudent supervision proved inadequate to stem inviable portfolio structuring.

In *Argentina*, a financial crisis emerged as early as 1980. The largest private commercial bank was liquidated and 42 other financial institutions over the next year. Financial distress remained and the crisis was deepened in 1982 under the influence of the Falklands War, the external debt crisis

Table 8.4   Argentina: initial wealth redistribution effects of 1982 interest rate regulation of commercial and savings banks, 1982–3 (percent of GDP)

	Borrower subsidy	Depositor cost
1982	16.8	–12.8
1983	7.4	– 8.8
Total for 1982–3	24.2	–21.6

Source: Baliño (1991, table 18).

cutting off new foreign credits, severe fiscal problems and expectations of large devaluations. Import restrictions severely hit economic activity and corporate bankruptcies spilled over into further liquidity and solvency problems for financial institutions. The Central Bank intervened in 93 financial intermediaries between 1980 and 1989, with refinancing and bank rehabilitation initially constituting the key form for resolving non-performing bank portfolios. In 1982, strongly negative real interest rates applied after reintroducing ceilings on short-term rates in order to erode the value of existing bank loans and deposits, a Central Bank rediscount facility (*Préstamo Básico*) was introduced allowing banks to refinance loans to the private sector and foreign liabilities were 'dedollarised' (Fanelli, Frenkel and Winograd, 1987; Casas, 1989). The measure succeeded in reducing the debt burden of the private corporate sector, but at the high costs of loss of confidence in the financial system due to heavy losses incurred by depositors, a tremendous income and wealth redistribution favouring debtors and owners of banks and firms (estimated at 24.2 of GDP over 1982–3; see Table 8.4) and huge subsidies provided by Central Bank through the rediscount facility and debt relief operations. Unstable macroeconomic conditions persisted along with the structural weaknesses of the financial sector. Only 7 out of 93 intervened financial institutions were successfully rehabilitated, such that since 1985 liquidation has become Argentina's main device to resolve bank failures (Casas, 1989). Bank runs are the public's response to Central Bank intervention as this is seen as a prelude to liquidation. Despite the fact that most ailing financial institutions were liquidated, the Central Bank incurred substantial costs through the use of the rediscount facility. The implicit subsidy on these Central Bank assets formed a major factor in the creation of Central Bank losses (Chisari *et al.*, 1992; Dornbusch, 1992). This quasi-fiscal deficit contributed significantly to the overall fiscal deficit in the 1980s and affected monetary policies (Table 8.5). Monetary instruments like reserve requirements, issuance of

Table 8.5   Argentina: Central Bank losses and total public sector deficits[1],
1980–91 (percent of GNP)

	Central Bank quasi-fiscal deficit	Total public sector deficit[2]
1980	−0.6	6.8
1981	1.0	13.1
1982	2.6	17.6
1983	3.4	18.9
1984	5.5	15.9
1985	2.8	7.9
1986	1.6	4.1
1987	0.9	6.5
1988	0.7	7.0
1989	5.9	21.8
1990	1.0	3.3
1991	0.6	1.8

[1]Negative figure indicates a surplus.
[2]Includes national government, non-financial public enterprises and Central Bank.
Source: Chisari *et al.* (1992) for 1980–84; Dornbusch (1992) for 1985–91.

government securities and money printing were all used in various stages primarily to meet Central Bank payment obligations and to the detriment of objectives of macroeconomic stability.

Rescheduling, refinancing and take-over of bad loans by Central Bank characterised *Uruguay*'s handling of the banking crisis in the early 1980s. The programme generally proved insufficient as macroeconomic conditions did not improve and because, in retrospect, it created expectations for future bailouts for banks and debtors (Cikato, 1989). Debt moratoria had to be announced to avoid massive bankruptcies and four large private banks had to be put under government control in 1986–7.

In *Chile*, 'in-house' lending practices of the heavily concentrated banking system, combined with macroeconomic factors affecting the payment capacity of the heavily indebted corporate sector led to a critical increase in non-performing loans. Bad loans (the sum of recorded past due loans and risky loans sold to the Central Bank) jumped from 2.3 per cent of the total loan portfolio in 1981 to 18.4 per cent in 1983 (Larraín, 1989; and Table 8.3). The total volume of non-performing loans was in reality much higher, but this was not reflected in the publicised data, because the large banks that were intervened in 1983 were not allowed to sell risky loans to the Central Bank until 1985. The full magnitude of the problem became visible in 1986 with bad loans representing 35.4 per cent of total bank loans. While Argentina followed a rather unplanned strategy of rehabilitation first and then liquidation, the Chilean authorities went for an intermediate strategy from the start: some institutions were liquidated, while others were bailed out and rehabilitated according to their degree of insolvency. Losses were primarily taken by the government, but also by shareholders of the liquidated banks and to a lesser degree by depositors. The government paid depositors 75 per cent of face value in the case of bank liquidation. The Chilean dealing with bank crises and bad-loan problems is rated to be successful (Larraín, 1989; Fischer, 1993). Improvements in the performance of the financial sector and the economy at large since 1984 may prove the point and contrast positively with the experiences in Argentina and Uruguay. Chile's way to rehabilitate domestic banks looked like a radical 'Brady-plan' for domestic bad debts. The Chilean government recapitalised banks by purchasing bad loans with long-term government bonds carrying a yield above the banks' cost of funds. Problem loans were gradually eliminated and the positive income flow from government securities bank capital could grow over time. Shareholders of the intervened banks were obliged to repurchase the bad loans from future profits (Arellano, Cortázar and Solimano, 1987; Larraín, 1989). Large intervened banks (i.e. Banco de Chile and Banco de Santiago) were directly recapitalised, however, as the Central Bank would not purchase risky loans from these banks until there was a considerable improvement in their debt-equity ratio. The capital increase was offered first to existing shareholders and subsequently to the public. The Central Bank would buy remaining shares not purchased by existing shareholders or other private investors, but this could not exceed 49 per cent of existing capital of the intervened banks to avoid government control. Small investors were offered generous credit facilities (at zero real interest rates) to purchase shares of intervened banks to stimulate wide ownership (labelled as *'capitalismo popular'*).[11] New shareholders were not obliged to repurchase the non-performing assets from the Central Bank. Further, the authorities took measures to improve borrowers' repayment capacity through across-the-board debt reschedulings and coverage against exchange losses on foreign liabilities of the banking system. The latter was important because banks had intermediated nearly half of Chile's external debt and by 1981 more than 40 per cent of debts owed by financial institutions was denominated in dollars.

Obviously, this way of resolving the bad-loan problem of the Chilean banking system was extremely costly to the taxpayers. The total costs are difficult to estimate as these have been spread over several years. An indication of these costs are the losses incurred by the Central Bank which

Table 8.6   Chile: Central Bank losses, public deficits and national savings (percent of nominal GDP)

	Public savings		Private savings	Total savings	Total investment
	Central Bank	NFPS[1]			
1980–89	−2.4	5.3	7.0	9.9	16.9
1990	−2.1	7.5	12.0	17.4	20.2
1991	−1.3	6.6	13.6	19.0	18.8

[1]NFPS = savings of non-financial public sector.
Source: Labán and Larraín (1992).

amounted on average to 2.4 per cent of GNP per year between 1980 and 1989 (Table 8.6). These losses directly relate to the rehabilitation of the banking system, but the effect on the Central Bank's accounts have been gradually declining since 1986 (Labán and Larraín, 1992). This quasi-fiscal deficit could be absorbed relatively easily by the public sector's own finances because of surpluses run by the non-financial public sector. Nevertheless, similar to the Philippines case, high-yielding Central Bank bonds[12] were issued to finance current losses thereby undermining attempts to improve the Central Bank's own financial structure. This complicated macroeconomic adjustment by the end of the 1980s, as short-term speculative capital flowed massively to Chile, attracted by the large difference between domestic and international interest rates. The Central Bank tried to contain the subsequent tendencies towards exchange rate appreciation. While the pressure on the Central Bank's accounts of the immediate costs of the bank rescue operations had been reduced substantially by the early 1990s, the aftermath (or 'hangover') in the form of high-cost CB bills and foreign-exchange losses to support the peso continues to produce negative net worth for the Central Bank. Nevertheless, this negative side-effect occurs in a much more favourable macroeconomic environment of growth and a sound fiscal situation. These factors also account for the fact that the potential timebomb under the rescue operations did not explode. The repurchase requirement attached to the domestic debt–bond swap operations did not saddle the banks anew with an unmanageable amount of bad loans, as both banks and firms benefited from growth and stability in the second half of the 1980s.

East Asia

While bank crises were severe and widespread in Latin America in the 1980s, crises also occurred in the dynamic East Asian region, but mostly –

with the notable exception of the Philippines – the solution found for dealing with bad-loan problems was much less costly and macroeconomically hardly devastating. However, there are also clear parallels. In Asia also bad-loan problems have been closely related to the concentrated nature of the banking system and ineffective regulatory and supervisory systems. In some cases, the financial crises motivated authorities to implement stronger regulatory measures which should help to detect bad lending practices at an earlier stage; in others, like in the heavily regulated Korean financial markets, to foster a move towards liberalisation.

In *South Korea* a small financial crisis emerged from a series of scandals of bad-loan practices of intermediaries operating in the informal (curb) market which had lent large sums of money to large corporations. When two large companies defaulted on debt in May 1982, confidence in non-bank financial institutions (NBFIs) was shocked and a number of them faced serious runs. Assistance first went to the borrowers. In order to restore confidence and assist ailing firms, bank interest rates were lowered (Haggard and Maxfield, 1993). This was accompanied, however, by the introduction of a more uniform interest-rate system, replacing the complex system of differential rates for different economic activities and classes of borrowers. Further, privatisation of government-owned commercial banks and deregulation of barriers to entry for foreign banks were set in motion, albeit cautiously and gradually. The most radical change was the deregulation of NBFIs. The big firm conglomerates, the *chaebol*, turned this into the most dynamic market segment, creating and taking over many finance companies. Being previously a main factor opposing financial liberalisation, the *chaebol* now lobbied for further deregulation of the NBFIs. Though treated as a state secret, available evidence indicates that the growth of NBFIs also led to growth of non-performing assets in the banking system (Woo, 1993) and this moved the Federation of Korean Industries (FKI), which represents the largest firms, to oppose the government's efforts to cut subsidied bank credits. Liberalisation efforts were further slowed down by the bankruptcy of the sixth largest business group in the country, Kukje, in 1984, and to avoid further failures the government used the Korean Exchange Bank to provide relief to ailing firms by granting loans at low interest rates. The crisis did not spread and resumption of high economic growth rates enhanced repayment capacity of indebted firms. Non-performing assets of the Korean banking system are nevertheless a persistent problem requiring continuing Central Bank support to commercial banks (Woo, 1992; Haggard and Maxfield, 1993). The Korean financial system is still highly segmented and prudential regulation requires further strengthening. These financial sector problems cannot be identified as immediate impediments to economic performance in Korea;

on the contrary, the prosperity in Korea and in the crisis-ridden liberalisation attempts in Latin America have given Korean authorities legitimate reasons to approach deregulation with caution and gradualism. The powerful and protected economic conglomerates also pressed for such an approach.

The financial system of *Thailand* also faced a crisis in the first half of the 1980s. Oligopolistic banking and 'in-house' lending practices, accompanied by inadequate regulations and supervision, led to a deterioration of the balance sheets of financial institutions (World Bank, 1990). A slowdown in economic activity related to a various external shocks revealed the poor portfolio positions. Early in 1983 the Bank of Thailand had to intervene in about 50 finance and security companies (NBFIs) and 5 commercial banks, holding about one-quarter of the total assets of the financial system (Johnston, 1991). The main approach of the Thai authorities was refinancing and remedial action. No commercial bank was allowed to fail and the intervened commercial banks received 'soft loans' through a variety of refinancing schemes. Some 24 finance companies were closed, however, while 9 others merged into 2 new companies and 13 were bailed out by the government. The cost of cleaning up the bad loan positions of the financial institutions in the form of interest subsidies have been estimated at 0.2 per cent of GDP per annum (Johnston, 1991). The monetary authorities analysed that subsidised refinancing would be less costly than paying back depositors over a ten-year period. Also Thailand lacked an explicit deposit insurance system and the government was expected to provide *de facto* insurance. It turned out that the cost of keeping the finance companies and commercial banks open was much higher than originally estimated, because the magnitude of bad debts was underestimated, the recovery of collateral proved difficult and the staff of the Bank of Thailand that took over management of the ailing finance companies showed a lack of experience. As a consequence, at least in the case of the rescued finance companies, new capital injections were wiped out by continued losses and failed to improve their solvency. It is uncertain, however, whether allowing for bank failures would have been a better strategy. Macroeconomic imbalances in Thailand remained fairly manageable – due, among other things, to a long-lived conservative fiscal stance – and strong economic recovery aided by large inflows of direct foreign investment in the second half of the 1980s prevented the spreading of the crisis (Akrasanee, Jansen and Jeerezak, 1993). The way in which the crisis was dealt with may have increased moral hazard in lending practices, as financial institutions will expect to be bailed out. Possibly, this risk was counteracted by the strengthening of the prudential supervision imposed in the years immediately after the crisis. Powers of the Bank of Thailand were expanded, permitting direct intervention in troubled financial institutions, e.g. through ordering reductions or increases in capital, replacement of directors and managers and arranging takeovers or mergers of ailing institutions. These powers were not effective when the crisis emerged in 1983, but only after 1985.

While the Thai dealing with its financial crises was not fully effective in restoring solvency of finance companies, the approach chosen by *Malaysia's* authorities is rated more successful (Sheng, 1989; Fischer, 1993). Bad-loan problems emerged in the mid-1980s. Financial practices of the concentrated banking system are similar to those found in Thailand, the Philippines and elsewhere, and highly leveraged firms allied to the banking system had to face liquidity problems as the deregulated interest rates went up and economic growth slowed down. The extent of the bad-loan problem was not as severe in Malaysia thanks to effective bank supervision (see section II). Nevertheless, the authorities responded to the crisis by reintroducing interest ceilings. Ailing banks were forced to recapitalise. The approach showed some resemblance to the Chilean case as shareholders were forced to inject as much capital as possible through a rights issue. The Central Bank supplemented the private capital injection where necessary to meet minimum requirements of capital adequacy. The Central Bank held its shares in a buy-back scheme, allowing shareholders who had participated in the provisioning of new capital to buy back unsubscribed shares. Ailing banks were liquidated if not enough private subscribers could be found. This way government involvement was more limited and less costly than in Chile's dealings with the financial crisis.

The *Philippine* case is another prototype example that shows that financial liberalisation and financial opening policies can be extremely hazardous when implemented at times when the economy is in a downswing. As indicated, freeing of interest rates in the early 1980s provoked a financial crisis as most industrial and commercial firms had highly indebted themselves under the low real interest-rate conditions and uncontrolled 'in-house' lending practices through allied finance companies. The Central Bank's reaction to practices that tend to circumvent its rules and regulations and endanger the viability of the financial system has been slow (Lamberte, 1989). Nevertheless, the Philippine monetary authorities did a good job in containing the effects of bank failures in the 1980s. Between 1983 and 1987, the Central Bank closed down a total of 131 banks. The bankruptcy affected among others a number of government-owned banks and the Royal Savings Bank, one of the leading thrift banks. However, the larger commercial banks and development banks that entered into solvency problems, including the government-owned Philippine National Bank (PNB) and Development Bank of the Philippines (DBP), were rehabilitated. The direct costs of the bankruptcies were shared by depositors, bank owners and the government, but losses to depositors have been most considerable (Lamberte, 1989; Nascimiento, 1991). Less than half of the deposits of the banks that went bankrupt were insured through the Philippine Deposit Insurance Corporation (PDIC) and the heavily under-capitalised PDIC was only capable of refunding two-thirds of the amount of insured deposits and could only do so by heavily borrowing from the Central Bank.

Prior to their rehabilitation, the government used PNB and DBP in bailing out financial institutions and large corporations that collapsed right after the second oil shock. The 1983–4 foreign-exchange crisis further aggravated their already tainted loan and investment portfolios. PNB and DBP assumed huge foreign liabilities contracted by private corporations which could no longer repay, but for which the state banks had provided the public guarantees. The losses incurred by PNB and DBP during the period 1984–6 amounted to 29.8 billion pesos (about 5 per cent of 1986 GNP). In 1986, both institutions underwent a rehabilitation programme which involved the transfer to the national government of their non-performing liabilities and related accounts, burdening the fiscal balance. As in the Southern Cone countries, the financial sector crisis saddled the Central Bank of the Philippines with an unsound portfolio structure producing huge losses. These losses became a major macro-economic burden towards the end of the 1980s. Central Bank losses stem from an excess of interest outlays over income on both domestic and foreign liabilities and assets and, further, from losses on foreign exchange operations due to exchange rate changes. Besides the losses due to excessive foreign liabilities resulting from taking over much of the external debt of other parts of the public sector, also interest income from *net* domestic assets turned negative starting in 1985. This is the result of interest subsidies provided by the CB to many government institutions, because many of the CB's loans went bad during the economic crisis and, further, because the interest obligations on foreign liabilities were increasingly financed through domestic borrowing in the form of high-yielding CB bills. Table 8.7 shows that CB losses reached a staggering 5.3 per cent of GNP in 1984 and remained around 2.0 per cent of GNP from 1986 onwards. Over the period as a whole the CB contributed one-third to one-half of the total public sector deficit. The Philippine case shows that, while financial institutions may be rehabilitated, the macro-economic costs may be felt over a prolonged period of time.

Table 8.7   The Philippines: Central Bank losses, public deficits and national savings (percent of nominal GNP)

	Central Bank losses[1]	Public sector deficit[1]	Total savings	Total investment
1980	−0.1	−4.7	23.3	29.1
1981	−0.4	−7.9	21.8	27.6
1982	−2.3	−6.0	19.5	28.2
1983	−3.8	−3.2	21.7	30.1
1984	−5.4	−3.7	18.8	22.5
1985	−2.8	−2.8	15.4	15.8
1986	−3.1	−3.6	19.6	16.3
1987	−1.6	−2.1	16.9	18.3
1988	−2.1	−2.3	17.5	18.6
1989	−2.3	−2.2	18.6	22.1
1990	−2.0	−5.4	18.6	24.7
1991	−1.7	−1.4	18.4	20.6
1992	−1.6	−1.4	20.2	22.1

[1]Negative figure refers to deficit.
Source: Vos and Yap (1994, forthcoming).

IV   CONCLUSIONS

The central focus of this chapter has been on structural factors that have hampered successful financial liberalisation in developing countries or, at least, which created major financial crises following deregulation measures. No blueprints emerge from the variety of experience. Financial policies supporting growth and stability have been successfully conducted in South Korea and Taiwan, but these clearly formed the opposite of a deregulation strategy. Governments of both countries heavily intervened through control over financial institutions, interest-rate management and steering of the allocation of credits. Credit allocation policies were coercive and access to directed credits was subject to strict market-oriented performance criteria. The movement towards more liberal financial systems in these countries has been gradual and cautious. In Korea, interest rates are still regulated and their gradual liberalisation announced in 1991 foresees full liberalisation of lending rates by the end of 1993, while deposit rates will not be fully deregulated until 1997. A similar approach is being followed in other areas of government control over the financial sector. The government intervention in the allocation of resources in early stages of development could be justified on the grounds of the inefficiency of the financial system itself. However, why did the Korean and Taiwanese governments insist on retaining their roles of prime financial sector agents while their economies became more developed and sophisticated? The longstanding government intervention in the industrilisation process and the related financial market interventions probably have made it difficult to abandon control, while, in addition, the big economic conglomerates have not pressed heavily for financial liberalisation. Further, the failure of premature liberalisation policies in Latin America, persisting financial market segmentation and a looming bad-loan problem of commercial banks have been additional arguments for the strategy of gradualism.

In Latin America and elsewhere, financial liberalisation failed to foster growth and stability because it inadequately coped with the structural problems hampering the development of financial markets. These problems include strong market segmentation, lack of banking competition, inadequate prudential regulations, severe (latent or manifest) bad loan problems and structural weaknesses in savings and investment performance. The analysis of this chapter tried to show, among other things, that these problems are largely interrelated and that financial deregulation may have strongly adverse effects if they are inadequately addressed. Further, it has usually been a combination of macroeconomic instability and several institutional weaknesses that made deregulation policies create banking crises. A proper ordering and coordination of financial reform policies is therefore required to avoid such upheavals. The main lessons to be drawn include:

(1) *Macroeconomic Balances*　From the literature on the sequencing of adjustment policies in developing countries it is clear that financial liberalisation, particularly freeing of interest rates, is hazardous under conditions of great macroeconomic imbalances and related unsound portfolio positions of private and public agents. Some of the microeconomic factors underlying this were discussed in section II. Savings may show little responsiveness to higher real interest rates, or may even respond negatively if the increase leads to a substantial redistribution of income from debtors to creditors. Company profits may decline and public finances come under stress, with severe macroeconomic consequences if both private corporations and the public sector have large financial liabilities. Lower savings availability and emerging bad loan problems may put financial markets under further stress and push up real interest rates. Under the circumstances, governments recurring to domestic financing of fiscal deficits will have to guarantee very high yields on securities to attract private savings, thereby probably exacerbating macroeconomic and bad loan problems. Governments resorting to the money-printing press will

have to face an acceleration of inflation and the loss of private sector confidence due to the erosion of financial asset values. The role of financial liberalisation in macroeconomic stabilisation thus seems very limited and it may well work in the wrong direction. Financial sector policies should be based on a cautious assessment of savings and investment behaviour and of the other structural features listed below. Deregulation of financial institutions are best conducted after macroeconomic stability has been achieved.

(2) *Lack of Bank Competition* Concentrated banking sectors and interlocking ownership patterns have been causes of allocative and productive financial inefficiencies throughout the developing world. Much of the bad loan problems found in a great variety of countries have roots in (i) unsound bank behaviour related to the colliding interests of proper bank management and easy loan provisioning to allied firms and (ii) ineffective bank supervision. But, of course, these institutional factors alone do not explain the emergence of bad loan problems; rather, their presence in combination with macroeconomic instabilities due to external shocks and ill-conceived liberalisation policies appear to underlie such financial crisis. Measures to stimulate bank competition include freeing of interest rates, privatisation of government-owned banks, establishment of direct securities markets and lifting barriers on new bank entry. When taken in isolation, such measures may fail to enhance competition. Freeing of interest rates may trigger a banking crisis under the conditions specified above. Bank consolidation and merging, and thus larger bank concentration, may be required as part of the solution of the crisis. Chile and the Philippines in the 1970s and 1980s exemplify the case. Stimulating securities markets and other NBFI activities may be an effective way to stimulate competition, but if financial markets are shallow – as is also the case in most economics in transition in Eastern Europe – because of a weak savings performance of the economy as a whole, it may mainly stimulate high interest rates and speculative behaviour. With wealth concentrated in the hands of a limited number of investors, expansion of NBFI activities may centre around agents with a stake in existing commercial banks and economic groups. Problems of interlocking interests do not disappear, but are reinforced, as happened in various Latin American countries and in the Philippines. Privatisation of state banks does not necessarily lead to enhanced competition, for the same reasons.

Allowing foreign bank entrance may become an important option if chances to enhance domestic competition are remote. To ensure competition on an equal footing and minimise the risk of massive take-overs of weaker domestic financial institutions, balance sheets of domestic banks may have to be cleaned first from non-performing loans, and high minimum reserve requirements may have to be reduced to give domestic banks more competitive edge to compete with foreign banks which can more easily raise funds abroad (see also Fischer, 1993).

(3) *Credit Rationing and Allocative Efficiency* Problems of risk, imperfect information and credit market segmentation inherently lead to credit rationing mechanisms. In financial markets which are not fully developed and which have only a reduced number of financial instruments on offer, it may imply that certain groups of borrowers are excluded from market access. Developing country experience is that small-scale farms and small- and medium-scale industries find difficulties in obtaining adequate amounts of credit. Specialised, government-owned financial institutions have usually been set up to fill the gap. Subsidised loans and poor management of such institutions have generated high costs to taxpayers in many cases. Nevertheless, if – because of imperfect risk assessment – markets fail to meet credit demands of important parts of the productive sector, the development of specialised financial institutions (e.g. savings and loan cooperatives) through government stimulus is justified, although the government need not take control, nor subsidise credits.

Allocative inefficiencies related to 'in-house' lending practices require adequate measures enhancing bank competition (see above) and improving prudential regulation and bank supervision (see below).

The choice between an Anglo-American or a German type financial system, or some intermediate form, is relevant for the development of market institutions and regulations, but neither form of financial arrangement is a guarantee to eliminate financial inefficiencies. The developing country experience suggests that under both forms, bank concentration, interlocking interests, and 'in-house' lending practices may persist.

(4) *Prudential Regulation and Bank Supervision* Bad loan problems and financial crises could emerge in developing countries because of inadequate supervisory regulations, but probably most of all because implementation of existing regulations was weak. Lack of sufficient autonomy of supervisors from political interference has been one issue of concern. One option is to establish an autonomous agency (as in many Latin American countries), but this is no guarantee for better bank supervision. It can be done by the Central Bank (as in most countries), but competent staff should be able to apply a set of sound rules, have authority to enforce decisions and to intervene in ailing institutions, and be able to

focus on the soundness of individual institutions and the financial system as a whole without interference of other policy objectives. Regulations on 'in-house' lending practices may have to be made enforceable by disclosing certain bank secrecy regulations (e.g. in the Philippines). Further, coverage of prudential regulations should extend to the whole financial system (banks and NBFIs) and 'off balance sheet' financial transactions of banks. In Latin America and the Philippines, 'in-house' lending practices have found effective channels through the largely unregulated finance companies and 'off balance sheet' transactions, undermining the effectiveness of existing prudential regulations limiting lending to single borrowers and allied firms.

The role of deposit insurance systems is controversial. Full explicit deposit insurance may form grounds for excessive risk-taking by bank managers, as does the expectation (usually based on experience) of *de facto* insurance by the monetary authorities. Some differentiated form, as introduced in Chile in the late 1980s, which penalises moral hazard and encourages depositors to assess the viability of financial institutions, may be recommendable in situations with underdeveloped financial markets. For the well-functioning of such a system minimum requirements will include the *publication of credit ratings and quality of asset structures* of financial institutions and the adequate capitalisation of the deposit insurance system to ensure confidence and full compensation of insured deposits held in failed banks.

(5) *Resolving Bad Loan Problems* The domestic debt overhang in the public sector and widespread non-performing assets of the banking system have formed an important barrier to successful financial liberalisation. Solving the bad-loan problem is essential for a proper functioning of the financial system. Across-the-board bailouts of banks and borrowers by the monetary authorities have been extremely costly and in some countries, e.g. in the Philippines and Argentina, have contributed to Central Bank losses, accelerated growth of domestic public debt and loss of monetary control. Proper guidelines of how to deal with bad-loan problems should form part of the system of prudential regulations. Clear loan performance criteria should be in place and should form the basis of the identification of the magnitude of the damage and the decision to liquidate or recapitalised ailing financial institutions. The cost of bailouts and bank rehabilitations will depend to a great extent on the importance of the structural problems listed above. Questions should be raised such as: Is the bad-loans problem widespread and a systemic cause of 'in-house' lending practices and ineffective bank supervision? Will the financing of bail-outs require the

issue of high-yielding CB bills and government securities because of the shallowness of domestic capital markets and thereby exacerbate the domestic debt crisis? In other words, the measures to be taken to resolve bad-loan problems should be well coordinated with macroeconomic stabilisation measures and should address the issue of moral hazard (i.e. avoid across-the-board bailouts) to reduce the risk that 'it happens again'.

Obviously, the above lessons provide no blueprint for financial reforms in developing countries or reforming economies in Eastern Europe. However, since bankers and financial markets have shown weak memories where it comes to recollect financial crises (cf. Kindleberger, 1978), tales from the distant and recent past and from different country situations cannot be told often enough.

APPENDIX 8.A   Relationship between Central Bank Losses and Money Supply[13]

Central Bank losses can be shown to lead to monetary expansion. The money supply may be defined as:

$$M = m \cdot RM \tag{1}$$

where: M = Money supply
m = Money multiplier
RM = Reserve money

For any value of m, the money supply expands with the level of reserve money.
Losses of the Central Bank may be derived from income and outlay statements of the Central Bank, which can be specified in simplified form as follows:

Income and Outlay Statement of the Central Bank

Income *(Y)*

$i_L L$ Interest income on loans (i_L is interest rate and *L is outstanding loans by Central Bank*)

ERG   Exchange rate gains on foreign assets and gains/losses on foreign exchange dealings (forward cover, swaps, etc.)
$[(e_t - e_{t-1}) \, FA]$

Expenditures *(E)*

$i_d Q_G$ *Interest payments on government deposits (Q_G)* held in Central Bank, where i_d is interest rate on government deposits)

ERL	Exchange rate losses on foreign liabilities $[(et - e_{t-1})\,FL]$
$i_d LB_0$	Interest payments on other liabilities (LB_0)

Surplus (S)

S	Surplus = Income − Expenditures

From the above the surplus (deficit) of the Central Bank for a given period is:

$$S = Y - E \tag{2}$$

The Central Bank's balance sheet may be specified as:

Balance Sheet of the Central Bank

Assets

L	Loans and discounts to banks
$e.\,FA$	Foreign assets converted to local currency value using exchange rate e.

Liabilities

RM	Reserve money (currency in circulation and reserves of commercial banks against deposits)
Q_G	Deposits of national government
$e.\,FL$	Foreign liabilities converted to local currency at exchange rate e
LB_0	Other liabilities (CB bills, reverse repurchase, etc.)
W_n	Net worth

Thus,

$$L + eFA = RM + Q_G + eFL + LB_0 + W_n \tag{3}$$

Rearranging (3):

$$RM + (L + eFA) - (Q_{G + e}FL + LB_0 + W) \tag{4}$$

where W_n is the net worth of the Central Bank. Equation(4) can be simplified to:

$$RM = NFA + NDA - W_n \tag{5}$$

where: $NFA = e\,(FA - FL)$ = net foreign assets
          $NDA = L - (Q_G + LB_0)$ = net domestic assets

Any surplus of the Central Bank will be added to its net worth, so that:

$$S = \Delta W_n \tag{6}$$

We can now link Central Bank losses to the conduct of monetary policy. Taking first differences of (5):

$$\Delta RM = \Delta NFA + \Delta NDA - \Delta W_n = \Delta NFA + \Delta NDA - S \qquad (7)$$

Equation (7) states that any surplus realised by the Central Bank will lead to a reduction in reserve money and hence in the money supply. Conversely, any deficit will lead to an increase in reserve money. The equation brings out the important point that the money supply may change even in the case that NFA and NDA remain unchanged.

Notes

1. See Akyüz (1990) on Turkey; Lim (1991) and Vos and Yap (1984) on the Philippines; Arellano, Cortázar and Solimano (1987) on Chile; Fanelli, Frenkel and Winograd (1987) on Argentina; Cardoso, Paes de Barros and Urani (1992) on Brazil.
2. See Stiglitz and Weiss (1981) for a solid theoretical elaboration of this point.
3. See e.g. Corbett and Mayer (1991) and Akyüz (1992) for more extensive descriptions of the various systems.
4. The Philippine Central Bank in the 1970s stipulated that bank lending to directors, officers, shareholders and related interests could not exceed the value of their outstanding deposits and the book-value of their paid-in capital. In addition, outstanding loans to a single borrower could not exceed 15 per cent of the net worth of the bank. These regulations were tightened after the 1980 reforms, including the rule that the 'in-house' loans could not exceed 30 per cent of total outstanding credit. As indicated in the text, the Central Bank had difficulty enforcing these regulations. See Lamberte (1989) for further details.
5. As shown in Vos and Yap (1994), the degree of bank concentration increased substantially during the 1980s and bank spreads were raised. During 1985–6 there was a steep increase in the bank spread, clearly reflecting attempts of banks to cover the costs of the financial crisis and provisioning for non-performing assets. Spreads were on the rise till the early 1990s, along with the increase in bank concentration, which more likely relates to oligopolistic pricing practices. A regression of the bank concentration index on bank spread showed that:

$$\text{SPREAD} = -0.08 + 2.046 \text{ H} - 0.03 \text{ DUM85} \qquad R^2 \text{ adj} = 0.88, DW = 1.69,$$
$$\qquad (-4.01) \quad (6.46) \quad (-8.81) \qquad F = 35.1$$

where H is the Herfindahl concentration index of deposits liabilities of the five largest banks. DUM85 is an intercept dummy for 1985.
6. See e.g. World Bank (1989) and Morris *et al.* (1990) for more elaborate discussions.
7. See Talley and Mas (1991) for a good overview of arguments in favour and against deposit insurance systems in developing countries.

8. See Morris *et al* (1990) and Sundararajan and Baliño (1991) for country details of such regulatory changes.
9. See e.g. Haggard and Maxfield (1993) on the political economy of financial reform in Korea.
10. Morris *et al.* (1990) expose the same view, but add the importance of a lack of an appropriate supervisory framework. Oligopolistic banking and interlocking ownership related 'soft budget constraints' applied on lending to allied borrowers are labelled euphemistically as 'bank mismanagement'.
11. This policy appears to have been successful: Banco de Chile and Banco de Santiago had 39 000 and 16 000 shareholders respectively by the end of the 1980s.
12. For most of 1980s real interest rates on government securities were well over 10 per cent.
13. Taken from Vos and Yap (1994, forthcoming) and adapted from Lamberte (1992).

References

Aghevli, B. *et al.*, 'The Role of National Savings in the World Economy', *IMF Occasional Paper* No. 67, Washington D.C: IMF, 1990.

Akrasanee, N., K. Jansen and P. Jeerezak, *International Capital Flows and Economic Adjustment in Developing Countries*, Bangkok: TDRI and ISS, 1993.

Akyüz, Y., 'Financial System and Policies in Turkey in the 1980s', in T. Arincali and D. Rodrik (eds), *The Political Economy of Turkey. Debt, Adjustment and Sustainability*, London: Macmillan, 1990.

Akyüz, Y., 'On Financial Deepening and Efficiency', UNCTAD Discussion Paper No. 43, Geneva: UNCTAD, 1992.

Amsden, A., *Asia's Next Giant. South Korea and Late Industrialization*, New York: Oxford University Press, 1989.

Amsden, A. and Y-D. Euh, 'Republic of Korea's Financial Reform: What are the Lessons?', UNCTAD Discussion Paper No. 40, Geneva: UNCTAD, 1990.

Arellano, J.P., R. Cortázar and A. Solimano, *Chile*, WIDER Country Studies on Stabilization and Adjustment Policies and Programmes No. 10, Helsinki: WIDER, 1987.

Baliño, T., 'The Argentine Banking Crisis of 1980', in Sundararajan and Baliño (eds) (1991) pp. 58–112.

Benston, G. *et al.*, *Perspectives on Safe and Sound Banking. Past, Present and Future*, Cambridge, Mass.: MIT Press, 1986.

Blejer, M. and S. Sagari, 'The Structure of the Banking System and the Sequence of Financial Liberalization', in M.C. Gonzalez Vega and C. Gonzalez Vega (eds), *Economic Reform and Stabilization in Latin America*, New York: Praeger, 1987, pp. 93–107.

Born, K., *International Banking in the 19th and 20th Centuries*, New York: St. Martin's Press, 1983.

Cardoso, E., R. Paes de Barros and A. Urani, 'Inflation and Unemployment as Determinants of Inequality in Brazil: The 1980s', paper presented at IDB/NBER Conference on 'Stabilization, Economic Reform and Growth', Washington D.C., 17–18 December 1992.

Casas, J.C. (ed.), *Saneamiento de Bancos*, Buenos Aires: Ediciones El Cronista Comercial, 1989.

Chisari, O., J. Fanelli, R. Frenkel and G. Rozenwurcel, 'Ahorro público y recuperación del crecimiento en la Argentina', BID Documentos de Trabajo No. 110, Washington D. C.: Inter-American Development Bank, 1992.

Cho, Y.J. and D. Khatkhate, *Lessons from Financial Liberalization in Asia: A Comparative Study*, World Bank Discussion Paper No. 50, Washington D. C.: The World Bank, 1989.

Cikato, M., 'La crisis bancaria en el Uruguay', in J.C. Casas (ed.), *Saneamiento de Bancos*, Buenos Aires: Ediciones El Cronista Comercial, 1989.

Corbett, J. and C.P. Mayer, 'Financial Reform in Eastern Europe: Progress with the Wrong Model', CEPR Discussion Paper No. 603, London: Centre for Economic Policy Research, 1991.

Corbo, V. and J. de Melo, 'Liberalization with Stabilization in the Southern Cone: Overview and Summary', *World Development*, 13, 8 (1985) pp. 863–66.

Dornbusch, R., 'Progress Report on Argentina', paper presented at IDB/NBER Conference on 'Stabilization, Economic Reform and Growth', Washington D.C., 17–18 December 1992.

Drake, P., *Money, Finance and Development*, Oxford: Martin Robinson, 1980.

Edwards, S., 'On the Sequencing of Structural Reforms', OECD Working Paper No. 70, Paris: OECD, 1989.

Fanelli, J., R. Frenkel and C. Winograd, *Argentina*, WIDER Country Studies on Stabilization and Adjustment Policies and Programmes No. 12, Helsinki: WIDER, 1987.

Fischer, B., 'Impediments in the Domestic Financial Sector to Financial Opening', in H. Reisen and B. Fischer (eds), *Financial Opening. Policy Issues and Experience in Developing Countries*, Paris: OECD Development Centre, 1993, pp. 119–32.

Fry, M., *Money, Interest and Banking in Economic Development*, Baltimore: Johns Hopkins University Press, 1988.

Fry, M., 'Nine Financial Sector Issues in Eleven Asian Developing Countries', University of Birmingham, International Finance Working Papers No. 90–09, Birmingham, 1990.

García-Zamor, J.-C. and S. Sutin (eds), *Financing Economic Development in Latin America*, New York: Praeger, 1979.

Galves, J. and J. Tybout, 'Microgroup Adjustments in Chile during 1977–81: The Importance of Being a Group', *World Development*, 13, 8 (1985) pp. 969–94.

Gersovitz, M., 'Savings and Development', in H. Chenery and T.N. Srinivasan (eds), *Handbook of Development Economics. Volume I*, Amsterdam: North-Holland, 1989, pp. 381–424.

Giovanni, A., 'Saving and the Real Interest Rate in LDCs', *Journal of Development Economics*, 18 (1985) pp. 197–217.

Gupta, K., *Finance and Economic Growth in Developing Countries*, London: Croom Helm, 1984.

Haggard, S. and S. Maxfield, 'The Political Economy of Liberalizing the Capital Account', in H. Reisen and B. Fischer (eds), *Financial Opening. Policy Issues and Experience in Developing Countries*, Paris: OECD Development Centre, 1993, pp. 65–84.

Hommes, R., *Colombia's Financial System*, World Bank, Washington D.C., 1988 (mímeo).

Johnston, R.B., 'Distressed Financial Institutions in Thailand: Structural Weaknesses, Support Operations and Economic Consequences', in Sundararajan and Baliño (eds) (1991) pp. 234–75.

Kang, M.S., 'Monetary Policy Implementation under Financial Liberalization: The Case of Korea', in H. Reisen and B. Fischer (eds), *Financial Opening. Policy Issues and Experience in Developing Countries*, Paris: OECD Development Centre, 1993, pp. 201–26.

Kindleberger, C., *Manias, Panics and Crashes. A History of Financial Crises*, New York: Basic Books, 1978.

Labán, R. and M. Larraín, 'Continuity and Change in the Chilean Economy', paper presented at IDB/NBER Conference on 'Stabilization, Economic Reform and Growth', Washington D.C., 17–18 December 1992.

Lamberte, M., 'Assessment of the Problems of the Financial System: The Philippine Case', PIDS Working Paper Series, No. 89-18, Manila: Philippine Institute for Development Studies, 1989.

Lamberte, M., 'Trade in Banking Services in ASEAN Countries', PIDS Working Paper Series, No. 90-22, Manila: Philippine Institute for Development Studies, 1990.

Lamberte, M., 'Assessment of the Financial Market Reforms in the Philippines, 1980, 1992', paper presented at Third Convention of the East Asian Economic Association, Seoul, 20–21 August 1992.

Larraín, M., 'How the 1981–83 Chilean Banking Crisis was Handled', World Bank Working Paper No. 300, Washington D.C.: The World Bank, 1989.

Leff, N., 'Capital Markets in Less Developed Countries: The Group Principle', in R.I. McKinnon (ed.), *Money and Finance in Economic Development*, New York: Marcel Dekker Inc., 1976, pp. 97–126.

Lim, J., 'The Philippine Financial Sector in the 1980s, UNCTAD Discussion Paper No. 35, Geneva: UNCTAD, 1991.

McKinnon, R.I., *Money and Capital in Economic Development*, Washington D.C.: The Brookings Institution, 1973.

McKinnon, R.I. (ed.), 'Financial Liberalization in Retrospect: Interest Rate Policies in LDCs', in G. Ranis and T.P. Schultz (eds), *The State of Development Economics. Progress and Perspectives*, Oxford: Basil Blackwell, 1988, pp. 386–415.

Massad, C. and N. Eyzaguirre, *Ahorro y formación de capital. Experiencias latinoamericanas*, CEPAL Santiago, 1990.

Molho, L., 'Interest Rates, Savings, and Investment in Developing Countries', *IMF Staff Papers*, 33(1), 1986.

Morris, F., with M. Dorfman, J.P. Ortiz and M.C. Franco, *Latin America's Banking Systems in the 1980s. A Cross-Country Comparison*, World Bank Discussion Papers No. 81, Washington D.C.: The World Bank, 1990.

Nam, S.W., 'Korea's Financial Reform Since the Early 1980s', KDI Working Paper No. 9207, Seoul: Korean Development Institute, 1992.

Nascimiento, J.C., 'Crisis in the Financial Sector and Authorities' Reaction: The Philippines', in Sundararajan and Baliño (eds) 1991 pp. 175–233.

Park, Y.C., 'Comparing Liberalization in South Korea and Taiwan', paper presented at conference on 'Attempts at Liberalization', Budapest, 16–18 November 1989.

Park, Y.C. and W.A. Park, 'Capital Movement, Real Asset Speculation and Macro-economic Adjustment in Korea', in H. Reisen and B. Fischer (eds), *Financial Opening. Policy Issues and Experience in Developing Countries*, Paris: OECD Development Centre, 1993, pp. 93–114.

Roe, A., 'The Financial Sector in Stabilisation Programmes', Discussion Paper 77, University of Warwick, Warwick, 1988.

Shaw, E., *Financial Deepening in Economic Development*, Oxford: Oxford University Press, 1973.

Sheng, A., 'Bank Restructuring in Malaysia, 1985–88', World Bank Working Paper No. 54, Washington D.C.: The World Bank, 1989.

Stiglitz, J. and A. Weiss, 'Credit Rationing in Markets with Imperfect Information', *American Economic Review*, 71, 2 (1981) pp. 393–410.

Sundararajan, V. and T. Baliño, 'Issues in Recent Banking Crises', in Sundararajan and Baliño (eds) (1991) pp. 1–57.

Sundararajan, V. and T. Baliño (eds), *Banking Crises: Cases and Issues*, Washington D.C.: IMF, 1991.

Superintendencia de Bancos, 'Intervención, liquidación y rehabilitación de bancos en Colombia', in J.C. Casas (ed.) *Saneamiento de Bancos*, Buenos Aires: Ediciones El Cronista Comercial, 1989.

Talley, S. and I. Mas, 'Deposit Insurance in Developing Countries', World Bank Working Paper Series No. 663, Washington D.C.: The World Bank, 1991.

Tobin, J., 'On the Efficiency of the Financial System', Lloyds Bank Review, 153, 1–15, (July 1984).

Velasco, A., 'Liberalization, Crisis, Intervention: The Chilean Financial System, 1975–85', in Sundararajan and Baliño (eds) (1991) pp. 113–74.

Villanueva, D. and A. Mirakhor, 'Strategies for Financial Reforms', *IMF Staff Papers*, 37(3) 1990, pp. 509–36.

Vos, R., 'External Dependence, Capital Accumulation and the Role of the State: South Korea, 1960–77', *Development and Change*, 13, (1982).

Vos, R. and J. Yap, *East Asia's Straycat. Finance, Adjustment and Growth in the Philippines, 1970–92*, London: Macmillan (forthcoming, 1994).

Weston, R., *Domestic and Multinational Banking*, New York: Columbia University Press, 1980.

Westphal, L., 'Industrial Policy in an Export-Propelled Economy: Lesson's from South Korea's Experience', *Economic Perspectives* (Summer 1990).

Woo, Jung-en, *Race to the Swift. State and Finance in Korean Industrialization*, New York: Columbia University Press, 1992.

World Bank, *World Development Report 1989*, New York: Oxford University Press, 1989.

World Bank, 'Thailand: Financial Sector Study', Report No. 8403-TH, Washington: The World Bank, 1990.

Part IV

Conclusions and Policy Implications

9 Financial Sector Development in Central and Eastern Europe: Conclusions

Stephany Griffith-Jones and E.V.K. FitzGerald*

1 THE ISSUE OF BAD DEBTS

The development of the financial sector in the reforming economies of Central and Eastern Europe face important short-term and long-term challenges.

Amongst the short-term challenges, it seems that the key one is the manner in which bad debts (both old and new) are dealt with, the fiscal implications of this, and the implications for the future structure of the financial sector and governance of enterprises.

Many analysts have stressed the crucial importance of solving this problem as a key precondition for channelling savings to productive investment in the transition economies. For example, Dittus[1] argues that 'the most important of the unresolved problems which undermine growth prospects is the restructuring of state-owned enterprises and the breaking of their mutual life support relationship with the banking system'. Dittus and others argue that if no measures are taken, savings will continue to flow into the black hole of enterprise losses and will therefore not lay the basis for a return to growth. Less emphasised in the literature, but also extremely important, is the need to preserve the stability of the banking system, crucial at any time, but particularly important in a transition economy.

Our case studies confirm that the scale of the problem, though difficult to quantify with precision, is a very important one (for data of estimates of magnitude of bad debts, see Table 9.1).

*The authors would like to thank their project colleagues for valuable comments made during a workshop in Sussex University on a first draft. Insightful comments are also acknowledged from David Begg, Henrik Kierzkowski, John Roberts and Tad Rybczynski.

Table 9.1   Estimates of bad bank loans as percentage of total bank loans

Czechoslovakia

1991 (1)	(2)	December 1992 (3), (4)	1993 (5)
c.29%	c.66%	c.16%	11%

(1) *Source*: World Bank C.S.F.R., *Financial Sector Review*, 31 March 1991.
(2) Working paper of Czechoslovakia Central Bank and estimates by M. Kerouš.
(3) Refers to classified assets (non-standard, doubtful and loss).
(4) Includes all non-performing loans, not just 'old ones', as 1991 figure does; excludes, however, loan portfolio of the Consolidation Bank (which reach 92 b CSK). If these were included, total bad debts would reach around 25% of total bank debts.
(5) Only for Czech Republic.
Source: M. Kerouš, 'Key Issues in Czechoslovak Banking' (Chapter 3 in present volume), plus author's estimates.

Hungary

1987(1)	1988(1)	1990(1)	1991(1)	1992(2)
0.3%	0.6%	2.6%	4.7%	12.9%

(1) 1987–91 data based on regulations in force at the time.
(2) 1992 figures reflect new standards, in conformity with international norms.
Source: R. Nyers and G. Rosta Lutz, 'Development of the Financial Sector in Hungary' (Chapter 6 in present volume).

Poland

	June 1991	Dec. 1991	July 1992	Sept. 1992	June 1993
Total commercial banks	24	20	20	–	30
Specialised bank 1 (1)	–	56	–	75	72
Specialised bank 2 (1)	–	14	–	26	27

(1) % share in total portfolio of that bank.
Source: T. Łamacz, 'Financial Sector Development and Macroeconomic Policy in Poland' (Chapter 7 in present volume).

However, it is interesting that at least in one of the three countries analysed in the case studies (Czech Republic) the scale of the problem has been contained, if not actually reduced. Thus, according to the data presented in Table 9.1, the problem seems to have diminished in the Czech Republic in 1993, partly because some of the companies that owed large debts to banks (registered as 'bad' or 'high risk') have seen their financial performance improve significantly; an example of such an apparently favourable evolution relates to the debts of Skoda-Plzeň, after the change of management and other changes improved prospects. However, the fact that the 1993 data only includes bad debts for the Czech Republic, whereas the previous statistics included also debts for Slovakia, which on average may have a higher percentage of bad debts, could imply that this improvement is partly an effect of the change in the statistical base linked to the country's division.

In Poland there had been some improvement in the ratio of 'bad' to total debts owed to banks, particularly until mid-1992; however, during the first part of 1993, the ratio deteriorated quite significantly. Nevertheless in Poland there is the expectation that the bad debt overhang will be reduced, once and if the programme for recapitalisation of the banks (described below) defined by the government and agreed with the World Bank is implemented. In the Polish case, it is also important to highlight that one of the specialised banks faces an extremely high – though recently slightly declining – proportion of bad debts in their total debt portfolio.

In all three countries, but especially in the Czech Republic, there seems to be a further distinction between banks, as new banks – which are more aggressive in their lending practices, and often have lower initial levels of provisions – seem to be becoming more exposed to bad debts than the larger, more established banks.

Also in contrast to the somewhat encouraging trend of some improvement in this very serious problem in the Czech Republic, is Hungary, where there has been a steady deterioration of the share of bank loans that are defined as bad, though this is to some extent explained by revised auditing standards and new definitions (and reportedly, in this field, Hungary has gone further than the other countries); it reflects also a deterioration of the quality of loans, linked both to the deep – and deeper than expected – recession in Hungary over the last few years and the tighter bankruptcy regime in 1992.[2] Increasingly, as in the other countries, the problems of bad debt for the Hungarian banks relates not just to those owed by the state-owned enterprises, either still in the state sector or recently privatised (problem of 'old bad debts'), which has been largely dealt with, but with bad debts from the emerging private sector, the so-called 'new bad debts'.

Some doubts, however, emerge from the case studies on the extent to which 'bad debts' are the exclusive or even the main factor that distort credit policy in Central and Eastern Europe (CEE), in the sense that, as many analysts have argued, continued credits to loss-making state-owned enterprises implies crowding out or increased costs for the new private enterprises. Indeed, it would seem that other factors are as, or possibly more, important in constraining access to credit by the emerging private sector, especially the small and medium enterprises. For example, as Dědek shows in Chapter 5 of this volume, their lack of track record, high administrative costs and the lack of physical collateral are important factors constraining access to bank credit for the new emerging private SME sector in the Czech Republic. Kerouš in Chapter 3 confirms that banks attach great importance to physical collateral or guarantees as a precondition for lending to the emerging private sector in that country.

However, it should be emphasised that there is of course an important link between the bad debt overhang of state-owned enterprises and restricted lending to the emerging private sector, as well as high costs of such lending, and particularly high spreads between deposit and loan rates. As regards the former, the Czechoslovak case shows a rapid increase in the share of credit going to the private sector (from 0.6 per cent of total credit in 1990 to 26.3 per cent of total credit in 1992); however, interviews carried out in late 1992 show that only one in five applications for credit from the private sector were approved by private domestic banks and only one in ten applications from the private sector were approved by foreign banks (see Kerous, in Chapter 3). As regards costs of lending, these are particularly high in the case of the new banks in Czechoslovakia (as they need to pay higher costs for obtaining resources); this is again especially serious for the emerging private sector as reportedly these new banks tend to lend proportionally more to private enterprises.[3] The fact that spreads between deposit and loan rates are very high, implies higher costs than would otherwise be available to borrowers and/or lower deposit interest rates, which discourage savings.

It can therefore be concluded that overcoming the problem of bad debt overhang is an important necessary, but not sufficient, condition for assuring appropriate access to the private sector to bank credit. This is crucial for supporting private sector growth. As pointed out, it is also essential to overcome this problem for ensuring the stability of the banking system. Any major threat to the stability of the banking system would be very negative for the introduction of a market economy, as well as for political support for it.

For analytical purposes, and at the risk of some simplification, we will attempt a typology for the possible range of solutions to the bad debt and relate it to the problem of corporate governance and finance. The typology therefore examines two dimensions: first, whether banks are being recapitalised or not, and second, whether banks are involved in the restructuring of enterprises in a major way, as a result of the recapitalisation exercise. Indeed, increasingly the question is being asked whether dealing with the bad debt problem on its own is sufficient for improving efficiency in the non-financial enterprise sector. Therefore, the key issues now are clearly not purely financial, but include also: (a) the need to improve long-term efficiency in the non-financial enterprise sector, (b) the need to define the role which banks (as well as possibly government agencies) will play in restructuring such enterprises, and later monitoring their financial performance, and (c) the need to work out specifically how banks (and possibly government agencies) will play such a role.

As Table 9.2 indicates, the adopted solutions – and possibly also the best solutions – may vary from country to country, depending for example on different institutional realities and on how the process of privatisation had been carried out. Thus, for example, the issue of companies' 'governance' will be different in the Czech Republic, where privatisation was carried out rapidly and prior to any restructuring – either financial or technological; in Hungary, where privatisation has been more gradual and has often followed companies' restructuring; and in Poland, where restructuring is planned to be carried out at the same time as companies are privatised.

The first solution (I), which implies doing nothing, is what characterised the initial stages of reforms in CEE (Central and Eastern Europe) and is also what has characterised the Chinese reforms. Though this method has

Table 9.2   Recapitalisation of banks

		NO	YES
Banks have major role in restructuring of enterprises	NO	I China Initial stages in CEE	II Hungary To an extent, Czech and Slovak Republic
	YES	Not relevant	III Poland

Sources: Dittus (1994) case studies.

been reportedly successful in China, this is for specific reasons, such as the existence of informal capital markets in China, based especially on savings accumulated during the sharp increase in agricultural output that followed market reforms in that sector. Clearly such conditions do not exist in CEE and therefore such a strategy would yield undesirable results.

The second approach (II) implies recapitalising banks, thus breaking their link with state enterprises; an independent solution would need to be found for restructuring enterprises and creating mechanisms for appropriate management control. This seems to be to some extent represented by the Czechoslovak (now Czech and Slovak) experiences where enterprises were privatised rapidly and prior to restructuring, and where partial recapitalisation of banks took place (mainly via the creation of the Consolidation Bank and debt write-offs financed by privatisation proceeds) independently of enterprise restructuring. It is also represented to an important extent by Hungary, at least till recently. As Nyers and Rosta Lutz explain in Chapter 6, in Hungary the government has introduced a bank consolidation scheme, which in 1992 implied that some bad debts were 'bought' at a discount by the state, which handed these claims over to a special institution. In 1993, a different scheme was implemented whereby banks sell their 'doubtful' or 'bad' debts directly to special market organisations, which will either collect debts, reschedule them or transfer ownership. Both in 1992 and 1993, banks were given interest-bearing negotiable government bonds in exchange for their debts. The 1993 scheme seems also to contain some elements of option III, as banks will play some roles in enterprise restructuring, though not as clear and large as is planned for the Polish case.

The third option (III) is the Polish one, which as Lamacz (Chapter 7) points out, combines capitalising banks (in the form of allotment of bonds), 'conciliation procedures' (which are a streamlined version of a chapter XI type of procedure already existing under the Polish bankruptcy law), debt to equity conversions and commercialisation of debts owed.[4] This Polish approach thus combines the restructuring and control of enterprises simultaneously with the recapitalisation of banks. The Polish programme would seem therefore to have the advantage of contributing to the achievement of the two main objectives of a well-functioning banking system, that is, improving efficiency in allocation of financial resources and imposing financial discipline on enterprises via a system of 'insider control' more akin to the German or Japanese system. This would imply avoiding disruptions to companies' long-term plans due to lack of short-term cash. The main problem of such an approach is that that banks may not be tough enough on enterprises in which it has equity, and may be tempted to renew credit lines or roll over debt, to maintain the value of companies which it owns. The most serious risk here would be that of decapitalisation of banks. Another risk is that banks may be reluctant to carry out debt equity transactions; indeed, this has reportedly been the case in the former Czechoslovakia, where banks were unwilling to use their creditors' status.[5]

Though the approaches described differ significantly, they also seem to have some common features. A striking one is that in all three countries analysed in our case studies, there has been discussion or implementation of trading of debts, either to be carried out by banks themselves, by specialised institutions such as the Czech Consolidation Bank or by special market institutions. This would lead to the creation of a sort of secondary market of debt, which implies in some ways a parallel with one of the market mechanisms used to help solve the LDC external debt crisis in the 1980s.

However, these and other measures have become more complex because the ownership of both banks and companies has changed significantly, with many of them now in private hands. As a result, those who, like the World Bank representatives, argued for clearing the balance as early as possible, and while property was mainly state-owned, seem to have been correct. With diversified ownership, the process becomes administratively complex and – more important – the use of public money more controversial.

Accepting that some mistakes have been made on the issue of timing of bank capitalisation, what criteria should be followed for future recapitalisation in other countries in transition to the market and in the three CEE countries studied, should the need for further recapitalisation arise?

(1) Firstly, the size of the recapitalisation should be large enough to break the link between banks and enterprises. Indeed, it has even been argued that half-hearted recapitalisation may be worse than none, as it increases banks' margin to lend but does not reduce the forces pushing new lending to their traditional state enterprise customers. Recapitalisation via a prolonged period of high spreads between lending and borrowing (as is occurring in the three countries studied) is inefficient, because it takes too long and because it penalises successful firms to fund losses of unsuccessful ones.

Also, insufficient bank recapitalisation contributes to increased involuntary inter-enterprise debt. Though a certain level of inter-enterprise debt is normal in a market economy, its involuntary nature may distort credit allocation by banks.[6]

Furthermore, as discussed, recapitalisation of banks must contribute to making the economy more efficient, either directly through banks taking stakes in companies, or indirectly via tighter financial constraints on existing debtors and redirection of the flow of savings towards the dynamic private sector. Such objectives of bank recapitalisation can only be achieved if the incentives banks and companies face are changed, at the same time as banks are recapitalised.

Appropriate incentives for bank behaviour relates not only to relations between banks and enterprises linked by 'bad debts' inherited from the past. It also relates to the need for the *new* credits granted by the banking system to satisfy criteria for allocative efficiency and prudential risk management, as well as attempting to ensure long-term solvency of the banks.

(2) Secondly, the recapitalisation programme must try to minimise the direct and indirect negative fiscal impact of such a programme. It has been argued that the creation of government debt to replace non-performing loans or augment banks' own capital is purely an accounting operation. This is strictly only true to the extent that banks and companies are state-owned; as pointed out above, this is no longer the case in CEE. Furthermore, even if banks and companies are state-owned, the creation of government debt to replace non-performing loans implies interest costs, which increase budget expenditure. This means either increasing budget deficits and/or in curtailing other government expenditures, and/or increasing taxation, all of which are undesirable options, if they occur on a very large scale.

The extent to which any additional fiscal burden arising from bank recapitalisation is problematic also naturally depends on the scale of existing and projected fiscal imbalances. Thus, it could be argued that the then Czechoslovakia could have probably 'afforded' a larger debt write-off and recapitalisation of banks than was carried out, because its fiscal situation was, and continues overall to be, fairly balanced. The cases of Poland and Hungary are somewhat different and more complex in this respect, as those countries have fairly significant fiscal imbalances. Contributions from foreign donors or lenders (as is occurring in the case of World Bank lending to Poland for this purpose) are therefore particularly appropriate for cases where fiscal imbalances limit the government's potential for sufficient action. In cases like the Czechoslovak one, where there have been fewer fiscal constraints, a more flexible attitude by international financial institutions, to allow and/or even encourage use of fiscal resources for necessary bank recapitilisation may be desirable.

The potential magnitude of the cost of such bank recapitalisation is not only shown by the scale of the problem in CEE (see Table 9.1 again), and by estimates (for example, by Dittus, 1994) that additional interest costs could increase budget deficits by as much as 2 per cent of GDP in the three countries analysed, but also by the LDC experience of solving the bad loan problem, as discussed in detail by Vos in Chapter 8. For example, in Chile the losses incurred by the Central Bank as a result of it dealing with a major internal bad debt problem, have been estimated to average 2.4 per cent of GNP per year between 1982 and 1989; countries like Argentina and the Philippines have seen a similar scale of losses, according to estimates presented by Vos. Naturally, if no explicit recapitalisation is done by a government, the losses of banks may be financed by the Central Bank anyway in a less explicit way. As van Wijnbergen[7] correctly argues, at least when debts are recognised and interest costs are brought into the budget, there is greater likelihood that an efficient tax structure can be set up to cover the costs. Furthermore, losses in the case of inaction could in fact be potentially higher because of the continuing allocative inefficiencies that inaction would imply.[8]

To minimise the fiscal impact of banks' recapitalisation programmes in economies in transition, several mechanisms can be used: (a) Limit the magnitude of the operation to what is the minimum acceptable, consistent with the first objective – that is, break the negative links between banks and loss-making state enterprises. (b) Attempt to find other sources of funding, besides the purely budgetary ones. These can include, for example, external funding preferably in the form of grants, possibly from the EEC PHARE programme. External loans (e.g. from the World Bank) are less attractive in this context in the long term; though they will alleviate the fiscal problem in the short term, external loans will need to be serviced in future and in foreign currency. Should the overall level of external debt be low, in relation to exports, and should exports grow rapidly, this would not be problematic. However, if those conditions are not met, the transformation of domestic debt into foreign debt could have negative implications in future.

Other sources can include, for example, privatisation proceeds; this is illustrated by the use in 1991 by the three National Property Funds (Czech, Slovak, and then Federal) in Czechoslovakia to finance both write-offs of old non-performing loans (35 billion Csk) and to recapitalise banks (15 billion Csk). Another source, used in the Hungarian case (see Nyers and Rosta Lutz, in Chapter 6) to fund a necessary increase in reserves against losses – and thus providing against bad debts – is to require that banks reduce their payment of dividends to their shareholders to a certain limit. It is interesting that a similar mechanism was successfully used in Chile, where after the domestic banking crises of the early 1980s, the government recapitalised banks by purchasing bad loans with long term government bonds, and shareholders of these banks were forbidden to receive any dividends until they could repurchase bad loans from their banks' profit (see Chapter 8 by Vos).[9] An additional, relatively untested source in CEE, is to use market mechanisms, and sell debts at a discount. This is attractive, but its scope may be limited by available savings (see Klacek in Chapter 4) and by lack of appropriate mechanisms. There are also other potential sources for bank recapitalisation, such as joint ventures with foreign banks, which would inject new capital into CEE banks; such joint ventures have of course other important advantages.

The method of dealing with enterprises' bad debts and bank recapitalisation also influences the magnitude of the fiscal contribution. In this respect, a debt equity type of solution to bad debts may reduce the fiscal cost of bank recapitalisation, as a creditor is either better off or equally off with a debt equity conversion than if he writes the loan off. As van Wijnbergen (1993) points out, equity cannot fall below zero, but if the firm's fortunes improve, the creditor will share in this improvement.

Though other mechanisms can and should be found to share the cost of bank recapitalisation, it is doubtless the case that there will need to be a budgetary contribution towards solving this important problem.

(3) The programme of recapitalisation of banks should ideally be perceived as a once-for-all operation, or – if previous operations have already occurred – as a final operation. It is important that the government makes a commitment to abstain from future support, and that this commitment is credible. This commitment can be signalled by making a sufficiently large bank capitalisation to deal with existing problems. It can be reinforced by plans and timetables for bank privatisations; the improvement of bankruptcy proceedings may also play an important role. The promotion of more competitive banking, managerial improvements and the opening of banking to foreign participants can also help.

However, one of the essential preconditions for assuring (or making more likely) that any major bank recapitalisation is not to be repeated is to strengthen bank supervision. Therefore, the improvement of bank supervision and regulation in CEE deserves the highest priority, both in terms of domestic effort and in terms of technical assistance, particularly as the new supervisory agencies lack the experience, manpower and training required.

Finally, the improvement of regulation and supervision should not be restricted to the banking sector. As Drábek, Chapter 2, shows, in CEE, the development of capital markets is important to provide long-term capital (especially as banks tend to be very risk averse and have also tended to shorten significantly the term for which they lend: see, for example, Kerouš, Chapter 3, for Czechoslovakia, as well as Nyers and Rosta Lutz, Chapter 6, for Hungary); capital markets are also important, to make other foreign inflows, as a mechanism to benefit foreign direct investment, feasible. The latter point is shown not just by the recent Latin American experience, but also by the experience of Hungary, which is the country in CEE with the relatively most developed capital markets and with the highest relative inflow of portfolio flows.

To make the development of capital markets sustainable in CEE, it is crucial to develop appropriate regulation from the start. Again technical assistance is essential here. However, it should be pointed out that even in developed market economies, some regulatory imperfections and gaps exist, for example in the regulation of securities' markets. This refers in particular to coordination of regulation of international securities markets, to regulation of off-balance sheet risks by banks (on which important work is currently being done by the BIS) and on the regulation of financial conglomerates, that is institutions which simultaneously provide banking, securities and other financial services.[10] Therefore, though very important lessons on capital market regulation can be learned from the experience of developed market economies, as well as from the experience and problems of less developed economies (for example, the 1992 serious problems in the Indian Stock Exchange, related at least partly to regulatory failure), it is important to understand that in these fields, not just CEE regulators but also those in market economies travel, at least in certain specific aspects, in uncharted waters.

Drábek's chapter reviews the development of capital markets in Central Europe and the major impediments for these markets to become an attractive venue for foreign investments. The chapter covers four countries – the Czech Republic, Slovakia, Hungary and Poland. The impediments of capital markets to foreign investments are analysed in four areas – the institutional features of capital markets, their liquidity, privatisation and macroeconomic performance.

As Drábek discusses, liquidity of capital markets in these countries has been greatly limited, with the possible exception of Poland where the capital market has been recently very buoyant. The shortage of liquidity reflects a number of factors. The markets are still very small and the trading is infrequent. But perhaps the most serious problem is the relatively limited amount of domestic savings. These are considerably smaller than the demand for long-term capital which arises from privatisation, restructuring and from the newly emerging private sectors. In Hungary this has created a specific problem of confidence for foreign investors who are expecting a much greater participation of domestic investors before expanding their holdings further. The liquidity of the markets is also affected by restrictions imposed on banks to participate more actively in capital markets which affect their risk exposure and the duration of equity ownership which is time-bound. The liquidity is also adversely affected by unclear regulations for investment funds and households to borrow in order to finance the acquisitions of shares and securities. In the Czech Republic and Slovakia some investment funds are not financially strong and in Poland and Hungary investment funds are still virtually non-existent. All countries also have selective restrictions for foreign investors to acquire shares in certain sectors. Taxation can also be a powerful instrument to encourage greater interest in stock markets as in Poland. In particular, better tax treatment of households' acquisitions of shares should be encouraged as has recently been done in Hungary.

Market liquidity will also increase if the countries concerned remove those remaining impediments to the expansion of capital markets that originate in the institutional framework of capital markets and in privatisation. On the institutional side of capital markets the main issue is the current dispute about the extent to which the markets should be regulated. According to Drábek in Chapter 2, the authorities have a tendency to regulate the markets as much as possible, perhaps to 'over-regulate' in order to avoid market manipulation and corruption. Nevertheless, investors still lack sufficient information about companies. The quality of auditing reports remains below the standards common in the West, and the role of market analysts and dealers tends to be muted by the authorities again for fear of corruption and market manipulation. The different regulatory treatment in the Czech Republic and Slovakia of investment funds as compared to that of other financial entities is also a potential source of problems. All countries suffer from the lack of effective enforcements of the whole spectrum of rules. In other words, the problem of the regulatory framework does not seem to be the regulations themselves but rather their enforcement. This is partly due to unresolved questions of responsibilities for supervision, as it is in the case of banks and their activities in the stock markets, which are subject to supervision of two institutions – the Central Bank for banking operations and the Securities Exchange Commission for stock market operations. Finally, the clearing and settlement mechanisms in these countries are fairly well established but the incorporation of their national systems into the European networks would be very helpful.

Privatisation is a vital element of capital markets and it will, therefore, play an important role in the development of capital markets in the countries concerned. Privatisation can take place through stock exchanges, and privatised companies can also raise long-term capital through these markets. At present, however, privatisation is not providing a sufficiently strong stimulus for the development of capital markets. The fundamental problem is, of course, that the mass privatisation schemes in Hungary and Poland have been unduly delayed. But there are also other reasons. One is that the number of companies which can satisfy strict conditions for listing on the stock exchanges is limited. This means that the trading in the stock markets in countries like the Czech Republic or Slovakia where privatisation has proceeded fast has been limited to shares of companies whose financial status is not questionable. Another reason is the need for restructuring of many companies, a process which has been slowed down by delays in the bankruptcy proceedings and by unresolved questions of restriction, old debts, environmental liabilities and some other impediments which can all be resolved by policy changes.

Though the development of capital markets is a very important challenge for CEE, it should be mentioned that in Western Europe, the US and in the successful East Asian countries (including Japan), bond and equity markets have played a relatively small role in financing enterprises; furthermore, their development has tended to follow rather than lead the take-off of South Asian economies.[11] Indeed, in East Asia, banks have played an increasingly important role in capital allocation. Therefore, care should be taken that excessive expectations are not placed on capital markets, and – particularly if there are constraints on skilled personnel – that sufficient efforts is put into the proper functioning and supervision of the crucial banking sector.

II OTHER ACHIEVEMENTS AND PROBLEMS IN BANKING DEVELOPMENT

Though the problem of bad debts and the form of their solution lies at the heart of banks' and enterprises' short-term problems, other issues also are important to evaluate.

Indeed, the banking systems in the former Czechoslovakia, Hungary and Poland have both had significant achievements during the period of transition to the market, and still face important challenges.

For example, in the case of the former Czechoslovakia, two clear achievements can be noted (see, for more detail, Kerous, in Chapter 3). The first is that there have – at least as yet – been no bank failures, in spite of the magnitude of the economic changes and the different pressures brought to bear on banks. The second is the very rapid improvement in the speed of clearing transactions via the banking system. It has to be stressed that when banking reforms began, in early 1990, there was no multilateral clearing and settlement system for all banks. This posed serious difficulties, as for example during 1991 the amount of clients and transactions – especially with foreign countries – increased for the large banks by about fifty or sixty times. At that time, payments to and from abroad needed several weeks or months to be settled. This was a major constraint for the efficient functioning of a market economy.[12] However, by 1992 the payment and clearing procedures had improved dramatically. Reportedly, several big banks can provide domestic payments in their own branch network in one day; if the transaction involves another domestic bank it will take in total around five days; payments in foreign currency are reportedly provided by the better banks within eight to twelve days. Their figures not only reflect a dramatic improvement in a very short period of time, but also a performance which is rather good by Western standards. Similarly in Hungary (see Nyers and Rosta Lutz, Chapter 6) important progress has been made in this field, though further development is required. These types of achievements, which are very crucial for the practical operation of a market economy, are not sufficiently stressed in the available literature on Central and Eastern Europe.

Another important achievement of banks in Central and Eastern Europe is the extent to which they have reoriented their lending to the private sector. Thus, in the case of Czechoslovakia, the share of bank credit going to the private sector by 1992 (26 per cent) exceeded the share of GDP generated in the private sector (around 20 per cent at that time). This gives some indication that banks were reflecting and supporting the aims of economic policy, by giving significant support to the private sector, whose growth is an important policy objective.

A number of problematic aspects were, however, also detected in the analysis of the banking sector. Several of these will require actions to be taken by policy-makers. One was the trend (particularly clear in the Hungarian and Czechoslovak case, but also reportedly taking place in Poland) for a fairly sharp change in bank credit structure towards a higher proportion of loans being short-term (less than one year) and medium-term (less than four years).

Secondly, banks seem to have been over-prudent in the three countries studied, and have often lent at levels below the ceilings allowed by the monetary programme. This has probably been a contributory factor in explaining declines of output.[13]

Thirdly, there are some worrying trends in the emerging new banks, partly explained by insufficient supervision and regulation. This seemed to be a particularly serious problem in Poland during the initial years of market reform (see Lamacz, Chapter 7). However, also in the former Czechoslovakia, specific problems can be detected in the new banks. Perhaps most problematic is the fact that their credit policy is under pressure from a limited number of shareholders (who represent a large proportion of their capital) to provide credits in their favour. As a result, in several new banks, loan portfolios have too high a proportion of credit going to companies tightly linked to banks' shareholders. Similar trends are reported by Lankes and Sommariva (1993) for most new banks in Russia and Ukraine. As Vos, Chapter 8, describes, interlocking ownership patterns and their related effect on distorting credit allocation is a well-known feature in many developing countries, which in countries like Chile has contributed in a significant way towards a high proportion of bank loans becoming non-performing; a further negative effect has been a distortion to the allocation of resources. If such risks are to be avoided, regulation must play a crucial role. In this sense it is encouraging that recent regulation (for example, the amended Banking Law in Poland in April 1992 and the new prudential rules introduced in Czechoslovakia in late 1992) limit banks' exposure to individual debtors, and especially to those where there exists interlinked ownership. These measures are encouraging. However, some doubts remain on two aspects. Are these regulations stringent enough? Perhaps more importantly, are these regulations being genuinely enforced? This is a particular area where further strengthening of bank regulation – and any required technical assistance from foreign experts – would be particularly valuable.

Fourthly, there are some important gaps and/or imperfections in the credit activities of banks and related financial intermediaries in Central and Eastern Europe. As Dědek discusses in Chapter 5, this is well illustrated by the provision of insufficient – and more expensive – credit from the banking sector to the newly emerging small and medium enterprises (SMEs). The factors that determine such limitations are both those common to other market economies (e.g. higher administrative costs in lending to a large number of small entrepreneurs, and low quality of projects submitted by SMEs), and those which are also common to other market economies, but are particularly acute in transition economies (e.g. lack of enterprises' track record, and lack of physical collateral).

There is therefore a similar, *though temporarily stronger*, case for economies in transition to the market to use specific government interventions to overcome market limitations, using similar mechanisms to those used in many mature market economies and in the successful South East Asian NICs. Reportedly, some of the most successful government-led interventions in credit markets are those which are rigorously linked to performance criteria, such as success in exports.

One such mechanism is the use of limited government guarantees. It is interesting in this context that in Czechoslovakia, the Czech-Moravian Guarantee and Development Bank (CMGDB) was created, which offers both guarantees and subsidies for interest rates for bank lending to SMEs. Though the CMGDB has several desirable features, such as risk-sharing between the borrower, the commercial bank extending the credit and the guarantee agency, it has one important constraint, the limited scale of its operation. This scale reportedly lags behind the efficient absorptive capacity of the SME sector, particularly if the needs of privatisation demands of small entrepreneurs and new private farmers are included. This justifies Dědek's proposal for a larger scale of government support for SMEs in the Czech Republic via existing mechanisms and via support for development banking and venture capital for SMEs; however, Dědek suggests that – as now – government support is channelled via the banking sector, and not via a special government agency that provides financial services, because the latter could undervalue risk in project assessment and because the lack of skilled professionals (particularly acute in government agencies) would limit a government agency's effectiveness. Furthermore, the channelling of government resources and guarantees to SMEs to the extent possible, via private financial institutions, is a growing trend both in Western Europe and many developing countries, as is the use of mechanisms such as government guarantees to encourage private lending to sectors such as SMEs, where private banks and financial markets do not on their own provide sufficient funding.

Other important gaps remain in the financial sector in Central and Eastern Europe. A major one, particularly in the case of the Czech and Slovak Republics, relates to the financing of housing construction. The development of a market for financing construction of housing and of mortgages is urgent, so as to complete the financial institutions essential for a market economy, to provide financial support for a sector (the building industry) which can boost economic recovery and to increase significantly labour mobility, the latter being particularly important in economies – such as those of Central and Eastern Europe – undergoing major structural transformations, including those with strong regional implications.

The balance of achievements and shortcomings of banking reform has by definition to be somewhat preliminary. In particular, one crucial issue can only be fully answered in a few years' time. To what extent will the new banking sector – and the rest of the financial system – contribute to the economic recovery which is expected to occur, and, in particular, support the emerging private sector?

Indeed as all the studies in this volume clearly indicate, despite remaining macroeconomic instability and serious problems of bad bank debt in Eastern Europe, some progress has been made towards their solution and – even more significant – there is growing consensus on the institutional rules required to avoid such systemic situations occurring again. In consequence, attention is now beginning to shift towards longer-term financial issues: particularly the overall savings–investment balance and the way this is handled by capital markets, on the one hand, and the establishment of efficient mechanisms for the provision of finance for capital investment and technological modernisation on the other. In retrospect, moreover, it would seem that the somewhat simplistic 'lessons' sometimes transmitted to Eastern European economies regarding the short-term benefits of rapid financial liberalisation were not only misleading as to the macroeconomic consequences but also ignored the implications for industrial reconstruction.

The development of the financial system in Eastern Europe over the coming decade is necessarily constrained by the broader macroeconomic framework. Despite commitments to IMF monetary targets and considerable progress towards fiscal balance, governments are likely to find it difficult in the medium term to reduce real interest rates and overall public sector borrowing requirements because of shortfalls in tax revenues and the need to fund infrastructure and other key sectors. Access to long-term international finance is somewhat limited by the reluctance of international commercial banks to increase their exposure, and by competition from other regions for foreign direct investment flows. In consequence, the stimulation of domestic private savings will inevitably becomes a major policy priority. This in turn requires not only the provision of suitable assets (in terms of security, liquidity, inflation-proofing etc.) for household savings and complementary tax provisions, but also a policy decision on the extent to which incentives should be designed so that those resources tend to be channelled towards 'social' investment requirements – particularly private sector housing and the underpinning of an autonomous social security system – as opposed to, for example, capital formation by enterprises. Moreover, in view of the need to keep real lending (and thus deposit) rates within reasonable bounds in order to stimulate private sector investment and households' aspirations to higher consumption levels (particularly imported durables), very high levels of net financial savings by this sector cannot reasonably be expected.

From the point of view of industrial reconstruction, moreover, there are obvious dangers implicit in financial intermediaries forcing firms into bankruptcy for short-term reasons, because liquidation proceeds tend to be much less than present value of a going concern, particularly where banks are not willing to give long-term support to firms with excess capacity or technological potential. This problem of asset deflation becomes particularly difficult to solve when inflation rates fall, as the recent OECD experience demonstrates. In the case of Eastern Europe, moreover, it would appear that excessively restrictive monetary policies have aggravated output decline, due to unexpected price shifts and underdeveloped financial markets which channelled the impact of budget cuts and trade liberalisation in an unbalanced manner (Calvo, 1993). However, the fear that even after banks' balance sheets are cleared of bad debts, 'soft budgeting' will re-emerge and that the required degree of inter-firm competition may not occur if excessive ownership concentration emerges after privatisation, seems to overlook the fact that close links between banks and corporations are an integral part of all industrial economies.

As Jan Klacek demonstrates in Chapter 4, the capital accumulation required for economic reconstruction is not only very large in itself but it also means that the financial sector must generate sufficient domestic savings and channel them to these investments, and that state institutions must adopt a more active role in initiating and shaping the recontruction process. His argument focuses on the Czech Republic but is applicable also to other countries in the region (see Rollo and Stern, 1992). The target of catching up with the poorer EU economies over two decades, even under optimistic foreign financing assumptions, requires a very high domestic investment rate (due to the scrapping of a large part of the existing capital stock which is obsolescent) and rapid technological advance based on enhanced human capital and a strong industrial policy. Klacek argues, however, that domestic savings will best be stimulated by a recovery in aggregrate demand (and thus household incomes) while private investment on the scale projected will require low real interest rates, and a somewhat more expansionary demand policy than currently pursued in the Czech Republic.

A central feature of a modern market-based industrial policy of this type will naturally be concerned with encouraging direct foreign investment in order to transfer these intangible assets and modern equipment, on the one hand, and with the enhancement of the existing stock of human capital through vocational skilling on the other. However, experience in some industrialising countries and in Japan suggests that in addition the directed finance of competitive industrial firms can form an essential part of such a strategy, especially if linked to particular performance criteria, and if these are related to exports.[14]

Inevitably, industrial modernisation involves technological advance and thus large-scale shedding of labour, while new investments in this sector cannot be expected to restore previous levels of employment in the forseeable future. In consequence, small business is widely regarded in Eastern Europe as the major generator of new jobs at reasonable levels of remuneration and thus a vital underpinning to social welfare provision – as Dědek, Chapter 5, points out with considerable clarity. However, as Dědek also shows, there is a marked tendency for banks to avoid lending to small business in Eastern Europe, particularly when monetary conditions are tight.

This situation, of course, is common to industrialising countries (Stiglitz, 1989) – as indeed it is within the OECD itself – and is caused by problems of asymmetric information combined with the lack of appropriate collateral. None the less, to the extent that employment creation by this means is a strategic objective, and commercial banks are free to make their own asset decisions, an alternative form of finance should be found. Equity markets in Eastern Europe are still very thin, as Zdenek Drábek argues in Chapter 2, and cannot be expected to provide capital to small firms – indeed, they do not really fulfil this role even in the UK or the US. In consequence, as discussed above, it may be desirable to introduce or expand directed credit schemes. Experience suggests that the operational emphasis should be on the provision of long-term support (combined with technical assistance and financial monitoring) rather than on subsidised interest rates, and that subsidies should be on a small scale. This emphasis would also reduce the fiscal cost and facilitate adequate performance criteria for such lending.

Larger firms, in the presence of narrow equity markets, are often denied longer-term lending even though they continue to have access to short-term liquidity on demand – as Nyers and Rosta Lutz demonstrate for the case of Hungary in Chapter 6. A common response to this problem in late-industrialising countries is for larger firms to coalesce in ownership groups which include an investment bank fulfilling the function of 'group treasury' in a conglomerate. In this sense, it has been argued (see Kerous, Chapter 3) that the creation of a relatively small number of large banks in the former Czechoslovakia in 1990-92 which were well regulated but independent of government, though leading to excessive concentration of loans has allowed a positive relationship to be built up with industrial corporations.

The existing tendency for privatisation issues to be bought up by investment funds, and proposals for social security funds to be endowed with ex-state assets, would lead to closer links between institutional funds and large corporations which could play a similar agglomerative role. It remains to be seen whether this relationship can replace the supportive role traditionally exercised by commercial banks, and thus avoid the 'disintermediation' implicit in the Anglo-American bank model which is probably unsuitable for Eastern Europe (see Corbett and Mayer, 1991).

In any case, the access of both large and small firms to capital markets and to banks in Eastern Europe is likely to be limited in the medium term for at least four reasons. First, continued uncertainty concerning the financial condition of enterprises and banks may limit equity trading to relatively low levels with a preference for less risky forms of investment, particularly indexed government stock. Second, depending on the way in which the bad loans issue is addressed, the combination of shrinkage in bank balance sheets, extensive enterprise bankruptcies and the fiscal cost of bankruptcies will take a long time to work their way through markets. Third, even when realistic asset prices are established banks are still likely to impose high interest charges, short repayment periods and strict rationing rules on industrial borrowers. Fourth, capital markets are likely to be dominated by government securities for the coming decade; although this may help to broaden the market in the long run it is very difficult for corporate securities to compete in terms of either return or risk.

In consequence it is logical to expect that most firms will have to rely on a high degree of self-financing from retained profits. Of course, as mentioned above, internal finance is the major source of funding for net investment expenditure in all OECD countries (Calvo, 1993; IMF, 1993) but this poses particular difficulties if a whole sector is expected to grow and invest rapidly. Effective corporate finance in Eastern Europe may thus require specific tax legislation favouring profit retention, as well as actions in other fields. Further research seems required on policy actions to increase the profitability of companies and their channelling of profits into investment in CEE.

The nature of corporate finance and the complex relationships between banks and their clients mean that wrongly timed financial deregulation can have effects quite different from those intended by policy-makers. As Vos, in Chapter 8, demonstrates from the recent experience of Latin America and East Asia, this is particularly likely when strong macroeconomic imbalances are reflected in capital markets (forcing up interest rates, stimulating capital flight, etc.) and there is a lack of effective bank competition or prudential supervision – as in the case of Latin America. In East Asia, in constrast, financial liberalisation has been very cautious due to the success of interventionist policies; the high levels of long-term household savings meant that capital shortage was not a serious problem, and in any case the national corporate conglomerates have not pressed strongly for deregulation.

Vos draws a number of important lessons from his analysis of four cases in Latin America (Colombia, Ecuador, Argentina, Chile) and three in East Asia (South Korea, Thailand and the Philippines). Bad loan problems are endemic to both these regions, due not so much to inadequate supervisory regulations as to the failure to implement them. Implementation, in turn, can be made more effective by expanding regulatory coverage to all finance companies and 'off-balance sheet' transactions on the one hand, and the publication of credit ratings and adequate capitalisation of deposit insurance systems on the other, both of which should also increase investor confidence. The resolution of accumulated bad loan overhangs has been extremely costly in a number of the countries discussed, leading to fiscal problems and loss of monetary control or the overloading of narrow domestic capital markets with government securities. Systems of prudential regulation in Eastern Europe should thus contain clear rules on bailouts, bankruptcies and recapitalisations.

From a longer-term perspective, Vos argues that credit rationing is an inherent part of Latin American and East Asian capital markets due to problems of risk and information. As in Eastern Europe, certain groups of firms (such as farms or small business) tend to be denied credit by private banks and have no real access to equity finance, so that specialised financial mechanisms may still be necessary. In all three regions premature complete financial liberalisation – particularly the freeing of interest rates – under conditions of major macroeconomic imbalance and related unsound portfolio positions of public and private agents have put financial systems under intolerable stress. It follows that close attention must be paid to the underlying private sector savings and debt position, on the one hand, and the fiscal implications, on the other, before real interest rates are raised. The lack of bank competition in both Latin America and South East Asia has tended to lead to unsound loan practices – particularly with allied firms – and to unrealistic demands on bank regulators. In consequence, lower barriers to entry (particularly for foreign banks) may be more effective in stimulating orderly competition than freeing interest rates or deregulating non-bank financial intermediation, although complementary prudential measures are also essential.

The widespread and persistent occurrence of these problems is probably better seen as a systemic characteristic of semi-industrialised open economies rather than as arising from mistaken policies or even exclusively from the transition period as such. Indeed, many of these issues are the subject of policy debate in Southern Europe, where since the mid-1980s integration with the rest of the EU has accelerated financial liberalisation, which allowed deeper equity markets and more efficient money markets but also led to new problems of monetary instability, corporate finance and bank regulation (Gibson, 1992). In general, the question of access to international capital markets is clearly closely related to the resolution of the domestic debt problem. The causal relationship is complex, however. On the one hand, foreign direct investment would clearly be directly attracted by the resolution of asset valuation problems and indirectly by the positive effect on business confidence, while the capital inflows would deepen capital markets and ease corporate funding constraints without monetary relaxation (World Bank, 1993). On the other hand, less desirable short-term capital inflows to emerging markets can lead to overvaluation of assets and increase instability, while unregulated access to foreign credit at overvalued exchange rates can easily lead to overborrowing by domestic corporations and thus excessive external exposure (IMF, 1993).

None the less, it is now becoming clear that positive lessons can be drawn for Eastern Europe from the case of the more advanced Asian industrialisers, regarding the potential role of regulated capital markets and government intervention in corporate finance in a strategy aimed at achieving international industrial competitiveness (Fry and Nuti, 1992). State-owned or state-controlled banking sectors in Taiwan and Korea allowed the government to subsidise targeted export activities, preferential loans (in combination with tax exemptions and export incentives), helped stimulate high levels of investment, and directed credit ensured corporate compliance with other policies (such as export market penetration) due to high debt-equity ratios (Lee and Lee, 1992).

A number of agenda items for future policy research in the field of financial development in transition economies seem to emerge quite logically from the implications of the present study for economic reconstruction. These include issues of longer-term finance for industrial reconstruction and the financing of welfare systems (Calvo, 1993).

In the longer run, for banking and capital markets to be able to perform their role in the transition to the market, internal efficiency is not sufficient. The next decade in Central and Eastern Europe will, it is hoped, see the resolution of, amongst others, the following two issues:

(a) the development of the investment and savings capacity of the major institutional sectors (government, firms and households), and in particular the channelling of high levels of personal savings into sound long-term assets which can support industrial investment;

(b) the establishment of effective corporate access to West European and even global capital markets (both bank credit and security flotations). An important element in encouraging this will be the further development of domestic capital markets. This will be a supplement not just to foreign direct investment, but crucially, to domestic savings mobilisation.

Comparative policy studies on these topics could well build on the groundwork provided by the research reported in the present volume. As the novelty of economic reform fades, it will be particularly important to distinguish between problems of financial development that can reasonably be attributed to the transition process as such – or even to national circumstances – on the one hand, and those that are common to other economies at a similar stage of industrialisation, on the other. In relation to the former issue, further case studies of institutional structures and policy regimes will probably require further development of the analytical framework applied in the present volume, complemented by the more reliable and comparable statistical data that is now becoming available. Considerable light could be thrown on the latter issue by systematic comparison with the experience of Southern Europe – for example Spain and Greece – in changing the balance between market-based and institution-based financial systems.

Such scholarly research may yield both immediate operational recommendations for decision-makers, and broader policy insights, as we hope this volume shows. These policy implications, we believe, are an essential part of the search for financial structures and policies conducive to the sustainable industrial growth and smooth integration to the international economy that will be necessary for the future of a wider Europe.

Notes

1. P. Dittus, 'Finance and Corporate Governance', forthcoming in B. Fischer (ed.), *Investment and Financing in Developing Countries*, Nomos Verlags gesellchaft, Baden Baden, 1994.
2. See 'Hungary' in *EBRD Economic Review Current Economic Issues*, London July 1993.
3. Interview material.
4. For more details, see also World Bank, *Proposed Enterprise and Financial Sector Adjustment Loan to Poland*, April 1993, Report no. P-5940-POL.
5. We thank M. Kerouš for this point.
6. We thank David Begg for this point.
7. S. van Wijnbergen, *Enterprise Reform in Eastern Europe*, World Bank mimeo, Sept. 1993.

8. H.P. Lankes and A. Sommariva, 'Banking Reform in Central and Eastern Europe', EBRD *Economic Review*, July 1993.
9. For more details see M. Larraín, 'How the 1981–83 Chilean Banking Crisis was Handled', World Bank Working Paper 300, Washington D.C. 1989.
10. For more detailed discussion, see S. Griffith-Jones, *'The Globalization of Financial Flows and the Need for their Regulation'* paper presented at FONDAD Conference, June 1993, Mimeo.
11. For a good analysis, see World Bank, *The East Asian Miracle,* World Bank Policy Research Report, Washington D.C., 1993.
12. We thank Barbara Insel for stressing this point.
13. For an interesting discussion of the links between declining real credit and declining output in the initial stages of stabilisation in CEE, see G.A. Calvo and F. Coricelli, 'Eastern Europe in Transition: From Recession to Growth?', *World Bank Discussion Paper 196*, Washington D.C. 1992.
14. See, again, for example, World Bank, *The East Asian Miracle.*

References

Amsden, A.H., *Asia's Next Giant: South Korea and Late Industrialization*, New York: Oxford University Press, 1989.

Begg, D. and R. Portes, 'Enterprise Debt and Financial Restructuring in Central and Eastern Europe, *European Economic Review*, 37, 1993.

Calvo, G.A. *et al.*, 'Financial Sector Reforms and Exchange Arrangements in Eastern Europe', *Occasional Paper 102,* Washington DC: International Monetary Fund, 1993.

Corbett, J. and C. Mayer, 'Financial Reform in Eastern Europe: Progress with the Wrong Model', *Oxford Review of Economic Policy*, 7, 4, 1991.

Dittus, P., 'Finance and Corporate Gorvernance', in B. Fischer (ed.), *Investment and Financing in Developing Countries,* Baden Baden: Nomos Verlagsgesellschaft, 1994.

Fry, M.J. and D.M. Nuti, 'Monetary and Exchange-Rate Policies during Eastern Europe's Transition: Some Lessons from Further East', *Oxford Review of Economic Policy*, 8, 1, 1992.

Gibson, H.D. and E. Tsakalotos, *Economic Integration and Financial Liberalization: Prospects for Southern Europe*, London: Macmillan, 1992.

IMF, *International Capital Markets, Part II: Systemic Issues in International Finance*, Washington DC: International Monetary Fund, 1993.

Lee, K. and H.Y. Lee, 'States, Markets and Economic Development in East Asian Capitalism and Socialism', *Development Policy Review*, 10, 2, 1992.

McKinnon, R.I., *The Order of Economic Liberalization: Financial Control in the Transition to a Market Economy*, Baltimore MA: Johns Hopkins University Press, 1991.

Rollo, J.M. and J. Stern, *Growth and Trade Prospects for Central and Eastern Europe*, London: National Institute for Economic Research, 1992.

Stiglitz, J.E. 'Financial Markets and Development', *Oxford Review of Economic Policy*, 5, 4, 1989.

World Bank, *Global Economic Prospects and the Developing Countries*, Washington DC: World Bank, 1993.

Index